NATURAL
HEALTH
HANDBOOK

NATURAL HEALTH HANDBOOK

CONSULTANT EDITOR:
A.H. Campbell MD, MRCP, FFHom

CHARTWELL
BOOKS, INC.

Contributors

R.S. MacDonald MD, MB, BS MRCP(UK), MLCOM
(Osteopathic physician)

A. Campbell MD, MRCP, FFHom
(Consultant Physician, Royal London Homoeopathic Hospital)

A QED BOOK

Published by Chartwell Books Inc A Division of
Book Sales Inc 110 Enterprise Avenue, Secaucus,
New Jersey 07094

Copyright © 1984 QED Publishing Limited
First published in the USA in 1984

ISBN 0-89009-791-7

Editorial Director: Christopher Fagg
Art Director: Alastair Campbell
Senior Editor: Jim Miles
Copy Editor: Jenny Mulherrin
Designer: Peter Laws
Picture Research: Keith Bernstein, Kate Parish
Paste-up: Leaper and Gard
Photography: Sarah King, Brian Nash, Jon Wyand
Grateful thanks to Jo Lawrence and Arnold Desser

Typeset in Great Britain by
QV Typesetting Limited
Printed in Hong Kong by Lee Fung Asco Limited
Origination by Rainbow Graphics, Hong Kong

All statements in this book giving information
or advice are believed to be true and accurate at
the time of going to press but neither the author
nor the publishers can accept any legal liability
for errors or omissions.

Photographs
Heather Angel: 157, 158, 168
Camera Press: 46
Mary Evans: 9, 47, 59, 78, 153, 154, 213
John Frost Historical Newspapers Services: 9
Richard and Sally Greenhill: 14, 15, 19, 20, 21,
    35, 39, 42, 48, 95, 96, 110, 111, 120, 121, 136,
    137, 140, 144, 148, 149, 159, 172, 184, 195,
    203, 204, 205, 209
Illustrated London News: 10
Keystone Press: 33, 99, 102, 118, 212
Mansell: 92
Pineapple: 18
Paul Popper: 33
Rex Features: 141, 200
Anne Ronan Picture Library: 10, 17, 94
Science Photo Library: 14, 15, 207
Frank Spooner: 114, 119
Tony Stone: 104, 108, 141
Sunday Times: 42
Daily Telegraph: 49
John Watney: 37, 67, 88, 89, 162, 163, 194, 195

Illustrations
Craig Austin
Charlotte Kennedy

Contents

SECTION ONE

❦

INTRODUCTION

LTERNATIVE medicine comprises all those kinds of treatment that are not taught in recognized medical schools. They are of many kinds, ranging from the near-orthodox to the frankly bizarre, and about the only feature they have in common is their lack of official recognition. And even here, the boundary is not clear-cut, for what is 'alternative' at one time may become accepted later. Hypnosis, for example, was once considered completely beyond the pale, but today has all but completed the transition to orthodox acceptance, while acupuncture is beginning the same migration.

None of the names that have been used to refer to these unorthodox forms of treatment is wholly satisfactory. 'Fringe' seems excessively journalistic. 'Complementary' has been favored by some, but it implies a closer and more amicable relationship between the orthodox and unorthodox than is always found in practice. 'Alternative', on the other hand, implies acceptance of the claim that unorthodox treatment can achieve the same results as orthodox treatment, although it suggests that there is often a connection between preference for unconventional medicine and an interest in other forms of 'alternative' lifestyle.

Whatever name one chooses for unorthodox medicine, however, there seems little doubt that it is here to stay. And it is a worldwide phenomenon. In 1978, the Threshold Foundation was set up in Switzerland to study this question among others. The Foundaton is a non-profit making organization which has been recognized by the Swiss Federal Authority as a charity. Among the projects recently supported by the Foundation have been studies of the development of solar energy — and the protection of tropical rain forests.

Between July 1980 and September 1981, the Foundation made a detailed study of the extent and significance of the trend towards unorthodox medicine throughout the world. It found that, in general, Third World and Asian countries are preserving and expanding their systems of traditional medicine, with the encouragement of the World Health Organization (WHO), but in many European Economic Community (EEC) countries (though not in Britain) the practice of unorthodox medicine by lay practioners is illegal. A poll in the Netherlands, however, showed 80 percent of the population to be in favor of freedom of choice in medicine and, as a result, the Dutch Ministry of Health set up a committee to investigate the position. It recommended legal changes and immediate government funding for training and, research, although so far these proposals have not yet been fully adopted.

In Britain, the most popular form of alternative medicine was found to be osteopathy, with 1.8 million consultations annually. Massage (1.3 million) and acupuncture (1.1 million) were almost as popular. These figures do not fully reflect the true position (for example, they refer only to therapists who belong to professional bodies) but they do give some idea of the present position.

It is not only patients who are turning towards alternative medicine; so too are some doctors. In 1983, a survey of attitudes was conducted at a general practitioner trainee conference held in Scotland. A hundred doctors were asked about their knowledge of and attitude to alternative treatments. The results were disturbing for the more conservative-minded in the medical profession. Of 86 doctors who filled in the questionnaire, 76 thought acupuncture useful, 74 hypnosis, 45 homoeopathy, and 39 osteopathy. Eighteen were themselves already treating patients using one or more of the alternative therapies, and more than a third had referred patients for such treatment. About 80 percent wished to train in at least one method. Twenty-two of the doctors had themselves been treated by an alternative therapy, and only two of these thought that they had not benefited. Eight of the 22 had had treatment from a lay practitioner.

These figures give the lie to the picture, often painted by lay enthusiasts for alternative medicine, of the medical profession as hopelessly narrow-minded and prejudiced against unorthodox ideas. Admittedly, this particular group is unlikely to be representative of the profession as a whole. Most were young, 69 being aged under 30, and they were general practitioner trainees; attitudes among a comparable group of hospital doctors would probably be less favorable towards unorthodox treatment. Even so, these findings do indicate a considerable change in the way that many doctors are thinking.

WHY THE CHANGE IN ATTITUDE?

At first glance, it may seem rather surprising that there should be so much interest in alternative medicine today, given the extraordinary achievements of orthodox medicine. Almost every week, our television screens and newspapers provide us with enthusiastic accounts of new medical techniques or discoveries — transplantation of all kinds of organs, 'test tube babies', incredibly complicated machinery that enables doctors (and viewers peering over their shoulders) to see into every nook and cranny of the body and even to spy on that most mysterious of all events, the moment of conception itself. And yet, it seems, an increasing number of people feel that all this is rather beside the point. No doubt it is wonderful that surgeons can now transplant a heart, but this is not much consolation to anyone waiting for months or even years in considerable discomfort for a new hip. Nor is it just a question of the unequal distribution of resources; for many people there is a feeling that the new technology is not merely ir-

Hypnosis was pioneeered by Mesmer in the eighteenth century. Patients held on to handles which projected from a circular tube filled with magnetized iron filings (*above*). Today patients are led into a state of deep relaxation and receptivity. The therapist can then explore repressed areas of consciousness to treat conditions that range from insomnia to overeating and alcoholism.

One of the most tragic examples of drug side-effects was thalidomide (*left*). It was originally developed as a non-barbiturate sedative for pregnant women.

relevant but even, somehow, hostile or malign.

If we look into what underlies these attitudes, we can identify a number of causes.

The dangers of modern treatment

The occurrence of 'side-effects' from drugs is nothing new, but the first time that the potential risks of modern treatment really were brought home to the general population was as a result of the thalidomide tragedy. Since then the media have continued to report new examples of 'iatrogenic' (doctor-produced) disease. In 1983, several antirheumatic drugs were withdrawn from the market on the grounds of severe (sometimes fatal) side-effects. Nor is it only drugs that carry a risk: surgery and X rays, for example, are also potentially dangerous.

It is fashionable these days to blame the pharmaceutical industry for putting drugs on the market that have been insufficiently tested, and it is true that commercial pressures often lead companies to produce new drugs which differ in only tiny details from those of their rivals; the new drugs offer little or no improvement over existing ones, and may have unforeseen, unwanted effects. It is an unfortunate fact, however, that no matter how much preliminary testing of a new drug is carried out, it is never possible to be sure that some unpredictable side-effect will not be found once its use becomes widespread. Moreover, the more therapeutically effective a drug is, the greater, very often, are its potential dangers. The perfectly effective, yet perfectly safe, drug is as elusive an ideal as the Philosopher's Stone of the alchemists. (Penicillin, perhaps, is the nearest we have yet come to it.)

Even when treatment is reasonably safe and effective, it may entail a disturbingly large number of unwanted consequences. A recent leading article in the *British Medical Journal*, for instance, dealt with the effects on patients' wellbeing of treating mildly raised blood pressure. There is now fairly convincing evidence that reducing even slightly raised blood pressure does reduce the risk of strokes and heart attacks. Unfortunately, the available treatments may also reduce the patients' sense of well-being: in one study, only half the patients said they felt better for treatment and eight per cent said they felt worse, while almost all their relatives thought the patients had deteriorated after receiving treatment. The authors of the article therefore question whether treatment of slightly raised blood pressure is justifiable, pointing out that a study in Australia showed that a total of 1,721 patients had to be treated for four years to prevent only 10 deaths. And they conclude drily that the honest answer to someone who asks whether treatment of his blood pressure will make him live longer is, 'Yes, maybe, but it will certainly seem longer.'

Emotional rejection of technology

There is no doubt that for some patients seeking alternative treatment, this is an important motive. Alternative medicine, in other words, is for them part of a wider revolution in lifestyle that goes back to the hippie movement of the 1960s (and beyond that to earlier attempts to 'return to Nature', especially in America). From this standpoint, orthodox medicine is seen as belonging to a technology-based society that is already destroying the earth by pollution and degradation of the environment and will, if unchecked, soon exterminate us all in a nuclear catastrophe. The alternative systems, in contrast, are seen as 'natural' and, therefore, good and desirable.

Orthodox medicine is not 'holistic'

If you go to an orthodox doctor, so the complaint runs, he will not be interested in you as a person, but will concentrate on looking for a diagnosis. If he can find an identifiable disease, he will treat it (probably with a potentially dangerous drug), otherwise he will fob you off with a prescription for sleeping pills or tranquilizers. What he will not do is to assess your lifestyle as a whole, and indicate ways in which you can prevent illness from occurring in the future. Orthodox medicine is almost exclusively concerned with an attempt to discover physical causes for disease, and is uninterested in the psychological, environmental, and social factors that contribute towards health.

Orthodox doctors are authoritarian

Doctors simple tell you what is wrong with you, without entering into a real dialogue with you. They regard themselves as the pro-

This woodcut from Jacob Rueff's *De conceptu et generatione hominis* ('Of man's conception and generation') shows a woman in labor while astrologers project the child's horoscope. Medieval medicine was dominated by the teaching of Galen, who formulated the theory of the four 'humours'.

Robert Koch
(1843-1910) — *above*
— demonstrated that
bacteria from outside
the body cause
disease, and he was
the first to isolate the
bacilli of cholera and
tuberculosis.

fessionals, and you as the lucky recipient of their knowledge and skill. They fail to realize that it is *you* who are ill, and who ought to have the last word about what treatment you need.

WHAT ARE THE ORIGINS OF MODERN MEDICINE?

In the Middle Ages, Europe relied on a set of medical precepts that derived from the ancient world, and ultimately from the Greek philosopher, Aristotle. The chief authority in medieval European medicine, however, was not Aristotle but Galen, a Roman physician of the second century AD. From Galen derived the theory that the human 'constitution' is a blend of four 'humors' - blood, bile, phlegm, and choler. Disease was held to result from a disturbance in the correct balance of these substances. Relics of this theory can be found in expressions still in common use today – as, for instance, when we speak of a person as being good-humored or phlegmatic. The task of the physician – as portrayed in Chaucer's description in *The Canterbury Tales* – was to restore the balance by the judicious use of drugs, taking into account astrological considerations, which were regarded as vitally important.

New ideas began to penetrate European medical thinking in the Renaissance, and by the seventeenth century a number of supposedly scientific theories of disease were in vogue. There is no need to examine these in detail but their practical consequences were important, for they lead to the widespread use of two main forms of treatment: bleeding and large doses of drugs. Bleeding was often carried to extraordinary lengths, and not infrequently it actually killed the patient – the death of George Washington is a notorious example. Drugs were given not only in large doses but also in complex mixtures, which made the effects almost impossible to assess. A favorite component of many prescriptions was calomel (mercurous chloride), which is highly poisonous and, like bleeding, often disabled or killed the patients. It is easy to blame the doctors for these excesses, but we must remember that it was often the patients who demanded these treatments, just as modern patients often demand antibiotics for colds and other

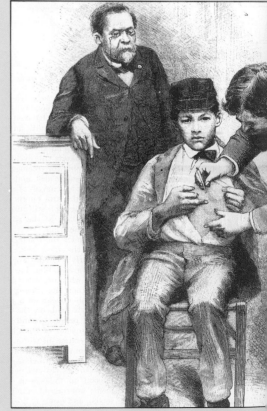

Besides his pioneering work in treating rabies and anthrax by vaccination with weakened forms of that virus, Louis Pasteur (1822-1895) — *left* and *right* also proved that the atmosphere was impregnated with micro-organisms. In one successful experiment he innoculated a shepherd bitten by a rabid dog (*below*).

Modern orthodox medicine relies heavily on machines of great sophistication, both in diagnosis and in reproducing certain activities of the body.

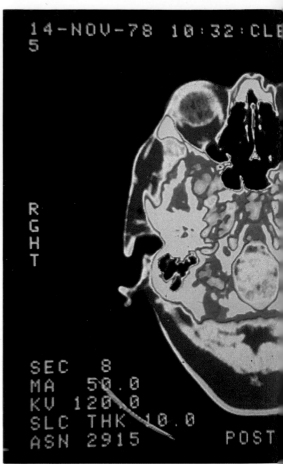

viral infections in which they can do no good.

These theories and practices persisted into the nineteenth century, but from about 1850 onwards a change came over the scene. The eighteenth-century medical theories had been founded almost entirely on speculation and had hardly any basis in scientific experimentation. Now, however, genuine scientists of the first rank — men like Pasteur, Koch, Virchow, and Bernard – began to introduce ideas that were to transform medicine. Koch, for example, identified the organisms responsible for cholera and tuberculosis.

Three ideas in particular were of central importance. The first was that chemistry – which had made enormous progress in the eighteenth and early nineteenth centuries – was fully applicable to the way the body works. It was now understood that the various fluids that composed the body were complex mixtures of chemicals, and so also were the solid structures. At first, the chemical processes of the body were thought to be special and unique to living things, hence the expression 'organic chemistry', but, as time went by, it became apparent that there was nothing special about these processes, and organic chemistry was seen to be simply the chemistry of carbon.

The second key idea was that the body is built up of a commonwealth of cells. The name of Virchow is most closely associated with this development. In previous cen-

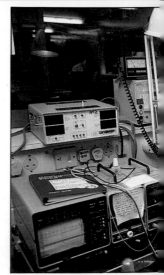

A premature baby (*above left* and *right*) is usually placed in an intensive care unit, where its respiration, heart beat and temperature can be carefully monitored. A CAT (Computer Axial Tomographic) scan of the skull (*top*). This technique enables cross sections of the body to be examined from any angle.

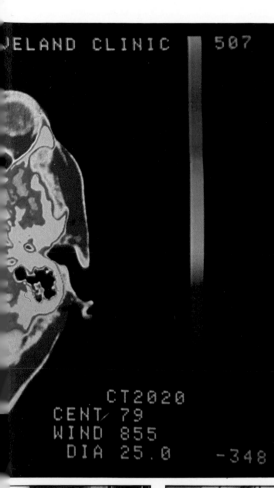

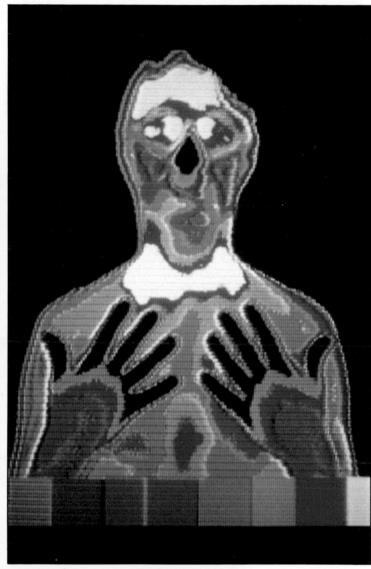

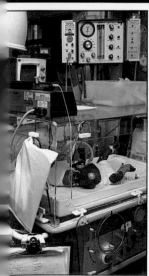

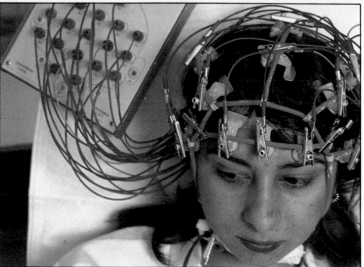

A thermograph of a man's hands (*above*); white is hot, black is cold. Thermography is a technique that registers temperature visually.

A portable electrocardiogram (*left*) traces the electrical activity of the heart. It can show the damage caused by a heart attack, or whether one is imminent.

turies, the changes that occurred in the tissues in disease had been studied, but not clearly understood. Now it was recognized that these changes could only be understood by considering what happened to the individual cells that composed the tissues; and scientists labored to devise methods of staining the cells with various dyes to show up these changes more clearly.

The third idea, and perhaps the most important of all, was the microbial theory of disease. The idea itself was not new but hitherto it had been mere speculation. Now, however, it was demonstrated (in the case of tuberculosis) by Koch, who went on to formulate a set of criteria for demonstrating that a given germ was the cause of a particular disease. These ideas were not accepted all at once; some people continued to regard germs as mere incidentals, and some even believed that they could be formed in the body without any infection from outside. Gradually, however, these beliefs were discarded, a trend encouraged by the researches of the French scientist, Louis Pasteur, and the dramatic success of his rabies vaccine. For young doctors, this was an exciting time, for if some diseases were demonstrably caused by germs, why not all? And if microbes did cause disease, would it not be possible to devise a 'magic bullet' to destroy them selectively?

The first such magic bullet was Salvarsan, used for the treatment of syphilis by Paul Ehrlich. For a long time, however, this success was not repeated, and not until the discovery of sulphonamides and penicillin in the twentieth century did more general antimicrobial drugs appear.

Long before this, however, the recognition of the role played by bacteria in causing disease had produced beneficial effects in another area – the prevention of infection during childbirth and surgery. Hitherto, patients had usually regarded admission to hospital as virtually a sentence of death – usually with justification, for infection, often fatal, was almost inevitable. The recognition that bacteria were the cause of infection brought about a radical transformation. At first, surgeons used to swab surgical wounds liberally with antiseptic, but later this practice gave way to precautions to prevent germs getting into the wound in the first place; hence arose the elaborate washing ritual and the masks, caps and gowns with which we are familiar today.

At about this time, too, surgery was duction of anesthetics. This development of its terrors were eliminated by the introduction of anesthetics. This development in turn arose from the discoveries of chemists and physicists who had identified and studied various gases from the late eighteenth century onwards; one of these was nitrous oxide ('laughing gas'), the first anesthetic to be used successfully.

The twentieth century has built on the foundations provided by the progress made in the nineteenth. The most dramatic medical advance was the discovery of the sulphonamides and penicillin, followed by a number of other antibiotics, but there have been several other major developments. These include an understanding of the action of various hormones – insulin and thyroid hormone, the sex hormones, and cortisone, to name just a few. When cortisone was first isolated, it was thought to be the answer to arthritis and other inflammatory diseases, but unfortunely it soon proved to have many serious side effects. Nevertheless, it continues to be a most useful drug for controlling, if not curing, a number of serious diseases, and it has given rise to various synthetic derivatives many of which are more powerful and selective in their action than the parent substance. The story of the sex hormones has been similar; from them derive the various oral contraceptives.

It would be possible to go on with this catalogue indefinitely; a modern formulary contains dozens of drugs acting on every system in the body: skin, lungs, heart, digestive system, nervous system, and so on. Instead of going into too much detail, however, it is better to draw some very general (and inevitably rather sweeping) conclusions.

SCIENTIFIC MEDICINE

It would be hard to exaggerate the benefits that we have obtained by applying scientific principles to medicine. Most bacterial infections, including that most notorious terror of Victorian times, tuberculosis, are curable today. Viral infections, it is true, are mostly still inaccessible to treatment but many of

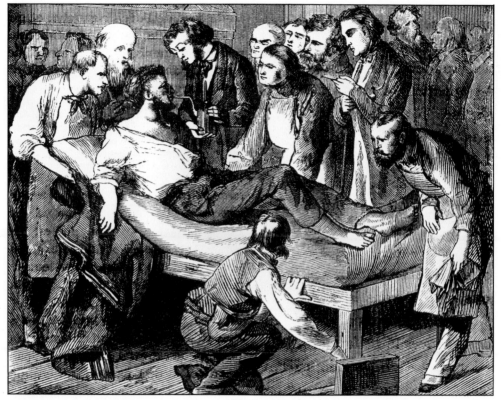

William Morton (1819-1868) demonstrating the use of ether as an anesthetic. Before this loss of blood, shock and the high risk of infection severely diminished the success of major surgery.

them can be prevented: smallpox has been virtually wiped out world-wide – an achievement that would have seemed almost miraculous to our grandparents – and poliomyelitis has ceased to be a major problem, at least in the Western countries.

Among the non-infective diseases, a number of the more serious can now be controlled or alleviated though not cured. These include pernicious anemia, glandular failures of various kinds including sugar diabetes, and metabolic disorders such as gout. Many other rarer diseases also come into this category.

It is, of course, true that some important areas of ignorance remain. In spite of decades of research in many countries, we still do not understand the cause or causes of coronary heart disease, cancer, or rheumatoid arthritis, three of the major killing or crippling diseases of modern societies. While we can often alleviate the effects of these diseases once they have occurred, we still do not know how to prevent them in the first place. However, there is no reason to suppose that this ignorance will continue; it seems quite possible that answers to some, or even all, of these mysteries may be found in the next few decades. There are also prospects for the radical cure, by 'genetic engineering', of diseases such as diabetes and hereditary disorders that can at present only be alleviated.

Many doctors believe that advances of these kinds will progressively squeeze out alternative medicine, as more of the problems it claims to deal with become amenable to orthodox medicine. Others, however, are certain that there will always be a place for alternative methods.

THE PROSPECTS FOR ALTERNATIVE MEDICINE

There are several reasons for thinking that the outlook for alternative medicine is good. For one thing, although the future may well bring dramatic improvements in the treatment of common disabling diseases like rheumatoid arthritis and asthma, that is not much consolation to anyone who is suffering

Dance studios are having a new lease of life as part of the growing mass consciousness of the value of physical exercise. The enjoyment of exercising to music under the guidance of an instructor is increased by sharing the experience within the group.

from these disorders now. Such patients will continue to gravitate towards alternative medicine in increasing numbers.

Secondly, it seems probable that for some disorders, including very common ones such as backache, certain forms of alternative treatment may actually give the best results. This will ensure that there are always practitioners of acupuncture and osteopathy, for example, and indeed an increasing number of orthodox doctors are taking up these techniques for this reason.

Thirdly, many patients suffer from symptoms that are not due to disease in the ordinary sense but are expressions of underlying unhappiness. They do not usually suffer from an identifiable psychological disorder and are not much helped by antidepressants or tranquilizers, though they may well be given these. What they require is time and opportunity to talk about their problems to a sympathetic listener. Overworked general practitioners seldom have enough time for this, whereas alternative practitioners do, because they make the time. Moreover, most alternative techniques involve paying close attention to the symptoms of

individual patients, which is exactly what people whose suffering is primarily psychological in origin want. We all like to talk about ourselves, but for patients of this kind it is a therapeutic necessity. Alternative medicine provides a valuable opportunity for this.

In fact, many alternative practitioners would probably not accept that it is justifiable to divide disorders into organic and functional, in the way that many orthodox doctors do. Instead they prefer to consider *all* disease as stemming from disordered functioning, or loss of 'balance', affecting the *individual as a whole*. Organic or structural change, on this view, is a late consequence of the initial functional disturbance, and could be prevented if tackled at an early enough stage.

Alternative medicine, in other words, is part of a wider revolution that has been going on for some time on the fringes of science. It belongs to a dispute between 'reductionists' and defenders of a 'holistic' view: 'splitters' and 'lumpers', as they have been called. The splitters believe that the right way to try to understand ourselves and the world is by breaking down problems into manageable bits and tackling those. This has been the guiding principle of science in the West since the seventeenth century. The motto of the reductionists might be 'divide and conquer'. The lumpers, on the other hand, maintain that the whole is greater than the sum of its parts. While conceding that the reductionist method has produced impressive practical results, they maintain that it leads to a one-sided and fragmentary view of the world. It is specially inappropriate to the study of psychology and medicine, in which, they claim, it is vital to see human beings as wholes, rather than as collections of interacting mechanisms.

Closely connected with this, is the insistence that medicine should move away from the idea that there are identifiable disease entities with causes that can be removed. During his medical training, a doctor is taught the principles of diagnosis, which depend in large measure on filtering out those symptoms that are 'incidental' (and therefore irrelevant) from those that really matter. For example, one patient with arthritis may prefer to warm his aching joints, while another may prefer cold. For a doctor

Ten years ago, an event like the London Marathon would have been unthinkable. However, the obsession with health that swept the USA in the 1970s is now firmly established in Europe, as more people realize the benefits of regular exercise and sensible diet.

making an orthodox diagnosis, this difference is irrelevant, but to a practitioner of alternative medicine it may be very important. Practitioners of alternative medicine usually reject the notion of disease categories almost completely, at least in theory – in practice, they often use them because they are convenient. This means that for alternative medicine there are really no such labels as eczema, arthritis, asthma, and so on, but only individual patients and their symptoms.

Alternative practitioners criticize doctors for concentrating on isolated aspects of their patients' problems and ignoring the overall picture. Doctors often feel nettled by such criticism, pointing out – with justification – that it is essential to good medical practice to take the wide-angle view. If pressed, however, many of them would admit that this principle is often lost sight of, owing to the enormous advances in sophisticated medical technology that have occurred. And partly as a result of the popular interest in alternative medicine, many doctors are now taking another look at the basis of their own practice and at the traditional way it is taught. The fundamental questions that need to be answered are, to what extent is medicine scientific, and should it become more scientific in future, or does the balance need to be redressed?

MEDICINE AND SCIENCE

Medicine today is becoming ever more technological. This simply reflects the changes that are occurring in every aspects of our lives – work, leisure, military planning. It is possible to rejoice at this trend or to deplore it, but not to reverse it.

These developments do not, in themselves, make medicine scientific; they mean only that modern medicine depends on the results of science. Many a physician who makes good use of the information provided by a CT scanner, say, would be hard put to it to explain how the machine works. There is, however, a deeper sense in which modern medicine is scientific. In order to be accepted as valid today, treatments have to demonstrate their worth in some kind of controlled trial; and a controlled trial is essentially a scientific experiment. If you open a modern medical journal, you will find it full of

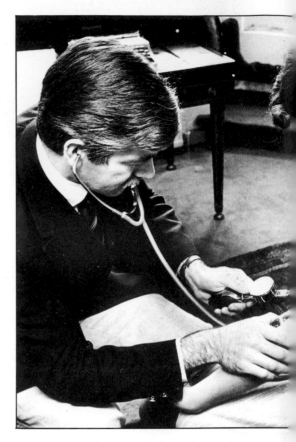

papers in which scientific hypotheses about the effects of treatment and other matters are put to the test; and the correspondence columns contain numerous letters challenging the conclusions that have been drawn. This is similar to the kind of discussion that you might find in a general science journal such as *Nature*, and it is quite different from what would have been found in a medical journal 50 or more years ago.

There is no doubt that to anyone with a scientific mind and imagination, this makes modern medicine profoundly exciting. Whether its ultimate effects are good or bad, the development of science is one of the greatest intellectual undertakings of the human mind – some would say it is the supreme human achievement. It would be unthinkable for medicine to be outside this great current of thought.

And yet there is an important sense in which medicine is not, and can never be, scientific. A scientist, such as a physicist

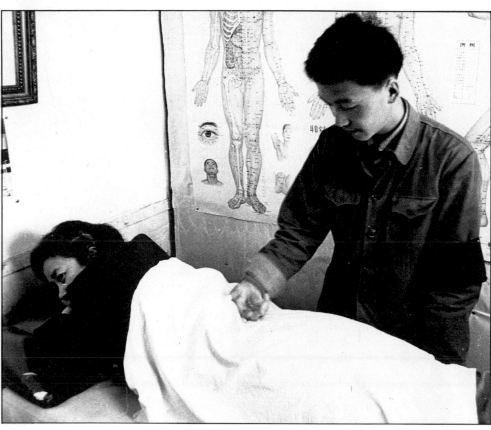

frames hypotheses which he then tests by experiment. A physician making a diagnosis, on the other hand, has to proceed for much of the time on a balance of probabilities. He has fewer facts than the physicist at his disposal, and usually he is working against the clock; he cannot take months or years to come to a conclusion.

Perhaps even more important than this is that doctors deal not with inanimate objects, but with people. This at once introduces a basic element of uncertainty into the situation, for human actions and reactions are unpredictable. What all this amounts to is that, although doctors do make use of technology and apply scientific standards to the evaluation of their treatments, the actual process of practising medicine will always remain partly a matter of intuition.

The contemporary philosopher, Professor Michael Polanyi, has drawn a valuable distinction between two kinds of knowledge. There is theoretical knowledge and there is practical knowledge – 'knowing how'. For example, learning to ride a bicycle is something that can be easily learned by a small child or even a chimpanzee. To specify how to ride a bicycle in terms of mathematical mechanics, on the other hand, is formidably difficult. And a mathematical description of this kind would not help anyone who wanted to learn to ride a bicycle; this is one of those skills that can only be learned on the job, so to speak.

Much of medical practice even today is similar to learning to ride a bicycle. It depends on skills that cannot be fully specified in descriptions, but can only be learned by watching other people performing them. Then one tries them out in practice oneself. This applies both to manual tasks, such as feeling an abdomen or removing an appendix, and also to psychological skills, such as taking a medical history. In other words, there is still an element of apprenticeship in the process of learning medicine.

In order to cope with a heavy workload of public patients, the British GP (*above left*) is trained to treat illness as specifically and objectively as possible — very often there is insufficient time for an in-depth consultation. An alternative practitioner (*above*), however, tries to base his diagnosis on a more wide-ranging, general consultation before beginning a physical examination.

The criticism of many alternative practitioners is that these intuitive, interpersonal aspects of medicine receive insufficient attention during medical education. They maintain that medical students are selected, not because of their ability to understand people and form good relations with them, but on their examination results in scientific subjects.

Probably quite a number of deans of medical schools would partly agree with this criticism, but would point out that doctors do need to be scientists, as well as humanists, if they are to make use of the new methods of diagnosis and treatment that technology makes available.

We can only guess at what will happen in the future, but it does seem likely that the present enthusiasm for alternative medicine will have an effect on the way orthodox medicine is taught and practised. This has already happened once: although homoeopathy was rejected by orthodox medicine in the nineteenth century, some of its ideas took hold and helped to change orthodox practice. For example, the idea of testing medicines on healthy volunteers, which is still done today, was pioneered by Samuel Hahnemann, the founder of homoeopathy, and the move away from using dangerously large doses of drugs in complex mixtures was probably also influenced by the example of homoeopaths. It seems likely that the popular demand for holistic medicine will lead to changes of emphasis in the ways in which medical students are selected and taught in the future. In addition, changes in the attitudes of society will inevitably be reflected in the ideas and aims of young people who come to medical schools.

THE CLAIMS OF ALTERNATIVE MEDICINE

There are many different kinds of alternative medicine but the claims made on their behalf – or on behalf of alternative medicine in general – are usually similar. These are that alternative systems are *safe*, *holistic*, and *effective*. Each of these claims needs to be looked at in more detail to see how far it is justified.

SAFETY

Orthodox medicine certainly has its dangers, but this does not mean that there are no dangers associated with alternative medicine. The risks here are of two main kinds.

The first risk is of missed diagnosis. Naturally, any practitioner, medical or lay, can make a mistake in diagnosis, but the danger of this occurring is far greater if the therapist is not medically trained. Many doctors know of patients who attended lay practitioners complaining of symptoms which, to anyone with a medical training, would at once suggest a serious underlying problem. Yet these patients were treated symptomatically by the lay practitioner until it was too late for orthodox medicine or surgery to cure the disease. Admittedly, the better lay practitioners are fully aware of this risk, and always refer patients with suspicious symptoms for medical investigation. But the problem is that they may not always be aware of the possibly serious significance of an apparently trivial complaint. It may not be obvious, for example, that a sudden change in bowel habit in a middle-aged man or woman is a symptom demanding urgent investigation.

Another and even more serious version of the same danger is that some lay practitioners are so convinced of the efficacy of their treatment that they continue to treat patients long after they ought to have been referred for an orthodox approach. Again, this is not a mistake committed by the better lay practitioners, but the problem is that anyone can set up as a therapist, without any training at all.

The second type of risk derives from the treatment itself. It is sometimes claimed that alternative treatment is 'natural' and therefore 'safe', but this idea will not stand up to criticism. There is nothing particularly 'natural' about sticking needles into people or giving them medicines, even if the medicines are derived from herbs rather than a pharmaceutical laboratory; all such practices do carry risks. Many herbal extracts are poisonous and, indeed, their toxicity is the other face of their ability to heal. Inserting a needle into the body is an inherently dangerous practice, which can cause infection, bleeding, and other complications. Manipulation also has its dangers; permanent paralysis has at times followed its ill-advised use.

Every form of treatment, alternative as well as orthodox, has its dangers, and anyone contemplating submitting to one of them ought to use his common sense to weigh the possible risks as well as benefits.

HOLISTIC

This is a loaded word. It is often used today to sanctify all kinds of unorthodox treatment and as a stick with which to beat orthodoxy. It is usually connected etymologically (probably incorrectly) with 'whole', and is supposed to signify 'treating the whole patient' – that is, all those physical, mental and spiritual aspects which alternative practitioners usually claim to take into account.

Now, it seems fair to treat this claim with a certain amount of scepticism for the following reasons:

Firstly, it is not only alternative practitioners who treat their patients 'as whole people'; good doctors also do this. Orthodox practitioners very often do try to take into account the effects of a patient's diet and lifestyle on his or her symptoms, and try to modify these, if necessary, whenever possible. However, it is not always possible; how many patients, for example, are willing to make even such elementary changes as stopping smoking and taking more exercise? Yet these two steps would by themselves make a considerable difference to the incidence of many diseases, as well as to physical and psychological wellbeing. The unfortunate fact is that most people are very resistant to any form of health education. Secondly, many alternative practitioners are not truly 'holistic' at all, but cling with obstinate belief to a particular form of treatment as the answer to nearly all ills. This is just as bad as believing that the answer will always be found in an orthodox drug. Thirdly, there are some problems for which a 'holistic' approach has little or no relevance; this is especially true of acute diseases. In addition, there are some important diseases, such as coronary heart disease, which we still do not know how to prevent by dietary or other measures; authoritative pronouncements about such things are quite unjustified.

EFFECTIVE

This is probably the area that excites most argument between practitioners of orthodox and alternative medicine. Naturally, the alternative practitioners insist that their treatments work. 'But', ask the orthodox, 'where is your evidence?' The alternative practitioners usually reply that the evidence is their own experience and that of their patients, but this seldom convinces the orthodox doctors, who continue to ask for 'controlled trials'.

What underlies this attitude is a major change that came over orthodox medicine just after World War II. At that time, doctors began to question seriously the value of many of the treatments they had inherited from their forebears, and they tried to devise methods of testing them objectively. When they did so, they found that many of these traditional treatments were quite ineffective. Similar tests were then applied to new treatments as well, and the procedure was established that treatments must be tested before being accepted. The unsubstantiated opinion of individual doctors or groups of doctors, no matter how eminent, was no longer enough.

Experience has shown that a number of things can lead to an unwarranted belief in the efficacy of treatments. Firstly there is the fallacy that because improvement *follows* a given treatment it must be *due to* that treatment. In fact, many diseases do get better by themselves, and even chronic disease often has its ups and downs, quite independently of any treatment. In the past, treatments have often been credited with curing patients who would have got better anyway.

Secondly, there is the placebo effect. It is now well known that some patients will show at least a temporary response to *any* form of treatment. The more impressive the 'treatment', the greater the placebo effect; thus, colored tablets are more effective than plain ones and certain colors are better than others, while injections are more effective than tablets. The fact that so many

A vast and bewildering range of drugs, cold cures, pick-me-ups and vitamin supplements is now available to the public without prescription. Part of their value is due, undoubtedly, to the placebo effect. A true placebo has no medicinal content, but the act of swallowing a pill may well have a powerful effect on a patient's symptoms. Ironically, their use by orthodox doctors is a step towards agreeing with the philosophy of alternative medicine.

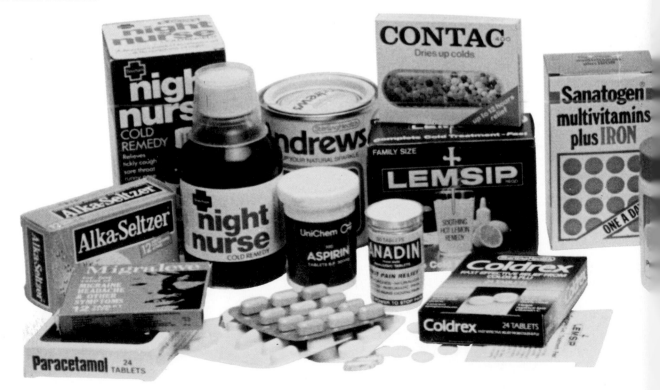

Controlled trials aim to overcome subjective responses to drug treatment. The left hand column indicates group A's positive response to treatment, the middle column group B's response to a placebo, and in the right hand column group C is given no treatment.

GROUP A	GROUP B	GROUP C
TREATMENT A	TREATMENT B	TREATMENT C
RESULT A	RESULT B	RESULT C

people spend vast sums each year on unnecessary vitamin supplements is a good illustration of the power of the placebo effect.

Thirdly, there is a natural human tendency to remember successes and forget failures. This leads to an unconscious bias in reporting the results of treatment, unless strict precautions are taken to eliminate it.

The 'controlled trial' is intended to overcome these difficulties. There are many varieties of controlled trial, but the general principle is to have one group of patients who are given the treatment to be investigated, and another (the 'controls') who receive either a placebo or a different treatment. The results in the two groups are compared by statistical analysis. The idea is simple in principle, but in practice all kinds of difficulties develop. The patients must be carefully matched with the controls for age, sex, type and severity of disease, and many other things. Considerable statistical expertise is required, both to design the trial properly and to evaluate the results. There can also be ethical objections on various grounds: for example, if the treatment to be tested is thought to be beneficial, is it ethical to withhold it from the controls? All kinds of objections can be, and have been, raised against the design of individual clinical trials. These days, attempts are being made to get away from the classic controlled trial, and to devise some other form of trial more applicable to the kinds of problems that occur when studying alternative therapies. However, the fundamental principle that subjective assessment of treatment is not good enough continues to be generally accepted by doctors.

Some practitioners of alternative therapies reject this principle, usually on the grounds that, because they treat individuals not groups, statistical assessment is impossible. However, although this is a valid objection up to a point, there are ways of getting round it, and the suspicion is hard to avoid that some of the reluctance to submit to objective assessment is due to uncertainty about the outcome. But not all practitioners of alternative medicine are hostile to the idea of clinical trials. Indeed, a limited number of such trials has been carried out, mainly in osteopathy and acupuncture and, to a lesser extent, in homeopathy.

However, it will be many years before enough firm evidence has accumulated to allow scientific assessment of the claims of alternative medicine.

The question of efficacy also arises in another way. For an orthodox doctor, it is not enough that a given alternative treatment *appears* to work; there also has to be some kind of explanation for *how* it works. Lay practitioners of alternative therapies often think this is unfair, and may counter by saying that no one knows how some orthodox treatments work either – aspirin is usually quoted as an example. Unfortunately for this line of argument, recent research has revealed quite a lot about how aspirin works, and, in any case, there is a world of difference between not knowing the details about a given form of orthodox treatment, and not having the faintest idea how a seemingly strange alternative treatment could possibly work. Unfair it may be, but doctors will continue to be led by their scientific training to demand at least half-way plausible explanations for any form of alternative medicine that they are asked to take seriously. One reason why acupuncture has recently gained a certain amount of acceptance in Western medicine is that there are at least some suggestions, based on experiment, about how it might work.

HOW DO THEY WORK?

When all is said, the fact that the alternative systems survive, in the face of competition and hostility from orthodox scientific medicine, must mean that they do 'work' in some way. Many thousands of people consult practitioners of alternative medicine annually and pay to do so, and many of them claim to be satisfied with the results. This calls for an explanation. What happens when a patient goes to a practitioner of alternative medicine – or, for that matter, to an orthodox doctor?

There are always three elements in such a situation: the patient, the therapy, and the therapist. Each contributes to the outcome in some degree, the relative importance of the respective contributions varying from case to case.

THE THERAPY

It is natural to think that this is the most important item in the equation, yet in many cases it may not be so at all. This applies not only to alternative medicine; it is true of orthodox medicine as well. The placebo effect and spontaneous recovery play an often unsuspectedly large part in the outcome of *all* kinds of treatment, and frequently this is not realized, because no one has thought it necessary to conduct a controlled trial. For example, doctors nearly always give antibiotics to children with middle-ear infections. This seems logical because many such infections are caused by bacteria which are sensitive to antibiotics. It is, therefore, 'obvious' that antibiotics must work in such cases. Yet a recent study has shown that, in the majority of cases, it makes no difference to the duration of the illness whether antibiotics are given or not.

Another illustration of the power of suggestion concerns electroconvulsive therapy (ECT), which is a somewhat contentious method of treating depression by passing an electric current briefly through the brain. A few years ago, the ECT machine at one British hospital was not working, but this went undetected for a couple of years. Eventually, the fact that the machine was out of order was spotted; it then emerged that all the patients who had supposedly received ECT during the preceding two years had not, in fact, been treated at all, yet the results had been as good as normal!

THE THERAPIST

Throughout the history of medicine, the vital role of the therapist or healer has always been recognized. A 'good bedside manner' has long been said to be a vital, if largely unteachable, prerequisite for success as a doctor. With modern emphasis on technology, the importance of the therapist has been played down somewhat, but it continues to be central in alternative medicine. Often, there develops between therapist and patient something similar to the 'transference' in psychoanalysis – that is, an emotional dependence of the patient on the therapist. This dependence can be valuable, provided it remains temporary and a means to an end. There is no doubt that the opportunity to talk to another human being about oneself is one of the most effective forms of therapy that exist. It is one of the principal strengths of alternative medicine that it provides a setting in which this interaction can occur.

The establishment of a good therapist-patient relationship requires time and the absence of a sense of hurry, and this again is an alternative great advantage of alternative medicine over much conventional treatment. In Great Britain most doctors work within the National Health Service (NHS), and the numbers of patients to be seen are usually so large that relatively little time can be spared for each. Alternative medicine, on the other hand, is nearly always private medicine, and there is no doubt that this difference accounts for a considerable part of the success of alternative treatments.

Another difference between the two forms of medicine is probably also important, although it does not seem to have received much emphasis. Psychological studies have shown that in human inter-actions generally – not only in the case of treatment – physical contact makes a great deal of difference. Many alternative treatments do involve the therapist touching the patient. It seems plausible to believe that the physical contact, in these cases, is a significant factor in promoting recovery.

THE PATIENT

The role of the patient is the hardest element in the equation to quantify, yet it is probably by far the most important. Indeed, a con-sideration of medical history prompts the thought that many, perhaps most, instances of healing are really self-healing. This should induce a considerable measure of humility in all therapists, orthodox or unorthodox. And it suggests the possibly heretical idea that, in many instances, the therapist's function is less to contribute anything of his own, than to reflect back to the patient his or her own thoughts and feelings.

Support for this notion comes from a recent anecdotal report. A researcher set up a computer program intended to mimic a psychiatric consultation. It did this by returning the patient's statements in the form of a question, which produced a dialogue of the following kind:

Computer: How do you feel today?
Patient: I feel sad today.
Computer: Why do you feel sad?
Patient: I don't know. Perhaps it's because of my brother.
Computer: Your brother?
Patient: Yes, his marriage is breaking up.
Computer: His marriage is breaking up. How does that make you feel?
Patient: Perhaps I feel a bit guilty. It may be partly my fault.
Computer: Your fault?

And so on. The researcher who set up the program was somewhat taken aback to find that patients found their conversations with the computer helpful. He was even more taken aback when he arrived one morning at the laboratory to find his assistant, who had helped to construct the program, seated at the keyboard. 'Would you please leave us alone?' she said. 'I have a personal problem I want to discuss with the computer.'

It is perhaps not surprising that some con-trolled trials have shown psychotherapy to be no more effective than placebo.

Even in the case of apparently 'objective' treatments, such as surgery, the response of the patient is absolutely vital. No matter how brilliant a surgeon's technical skill, it would be worse than useless without the patient's ability to heal the wound after-wards. Similarly, an antibiotic kills the infecting bacteria, which is fine, but still the patient's natural recuperative powers are needed to eliminate the dead bacteria and the poisons they have produced, and to restore to normal the tissues damaged by the infection.

It is not easy to summarize in a few words the processes that underly healing, but many of them can be characterized by the term *homoeostasis*. This means, literally, 'staying the same', and it refers to the complex processes by which the body main-tains its dynamic physical and chemical equilibrium. There are innumerable ex-amples. For instance, the levels of various substances in the blood (calcium, potas-sium, sodium, chloride, sugar and so on) are kept constant within fairly narrow ranges in spite of all kinds of influences (intake of food and water, excretion of water and salts, changes brought about by exercise) that tend to alter them. The acid-alkaline balance is closely controlled. A fairly constant body temperature is maintained in spite of wide fluctuations in the environment. The number of red cells in the blood is kept at a constant level and, if blood is lost, normality is quickly restored by a temporary increase in production.

In disease, homoeostasis is impaired, sometimes temporarily, sometimes permanently. When a patient is seriously ill in hospital, an important part of the treatment consists in tiding him over by replacing chemicals and water, usually intravenously, until the natural homoeostatic mechanisms can regain control. Often this is the most crucial part of the treatment; supplying simple kits for restoring fluid and salt balance in children with diarrhoea would do more for the infant death rate in Third World countries than all the campaigns of inoculation that could be undertaken.

The concept of homoeostasis can be applied to the mind, as well as the body. Thus, depression or anxiety can be due to loss of mental homeostasis. The great psychologist, C G Jung, believed that our conscious thought is compensated by unconscious processes which often act in a contrary direction — a kind of psychological homoeostasis.

Stress, on this view, can be regarded as something that threatens homoeostasis. Physical stress, such as excessive heat or cold, may overwhelm the homoeostatic regulatory mechanisms, particularly in the newborn and the very old. Psychological stress may cause anxiety or depression, and these in turn may act, via the nervous and hormonal systems, to disrupt and the physiological homoeostatic mechanisms, and so bring about physical disease.

This way of looking at health and disease provides a framework for thinking about how many kinds of treatment, both orthodox and unorthodox, may work. It is not so much that they *do* something to the patient; rather they provide a favorable setting in which the patient's own homoeostatic mechanisms, mental and physical, can restore normality.

The mental aspect of treatment is usually very important in such cases. This, of course, provides a lever for critics who often say that alternative treatment work purely by suggestion. This inevitably brings the argument round to the question of the placebo response.

THE PROBLEM OF THE PLACEBO RESPONSE

All the cures achieved by alternative practitioners which are not due to spontaneous recovery are attributable to the placebo response. This is the central point of debate in the controversy about alternative medicine, and it is easy to understand why. The placebo effect poses difficult and potentially embarrassing questions to anyone involved in treating patients by whatever means. As a recent leading article in a British medical journal remarked, 'Open discussion of the art of placebo is anathema'; and, in 1947, an eminent physician wrote that, 'The frequency with which placebos are used varies inversely with the combined intelligence of the doctor and his patient.' Today, hospital doctors and nurses still tend to believe that pain relief after placebo proves that the pain was not 'real' in the first place.

In other words, there is something not quite respectable about the placebo response. Yet one has only to look back to the past to see that nearly all traditional treatments were quite ineffective, and the fact that they often succeeded — as they did — was undoubtedly due to the placebo response, when not to spontaneous recovery. But not all patients and doctors in past times were unintelligent. And how many of our own cherished treatments will be seen to be placebos in the future?

So how do placebos work? Quite recently, it appeared as if we might have the answer. Some researchers suggested that the effect was due to the release of endorphins — natural opium-like painkillers found in the brain and elsewhere. This would have provided a physiological explanation for the action of placebos. Unfortunately, still more recent studies have cast considerable doubt on this idea and, in fact, it may not be possible to account for placebo action in pharmacological terms at all. Placebos, it seems, can imitate the effect of *any* drug, not just pain killers. For example, people given ordinary sugar, but told it was LSD, have ex-

The brain is split into four main areas:
1 The brain stem, rising from the spinal cord.
2 The right and left sections of the cerebellum.
3, 4 The right and left hemispheres of the main part of the brain. As a general guide, the right hemisphere controls the left side of the body and vice versa.

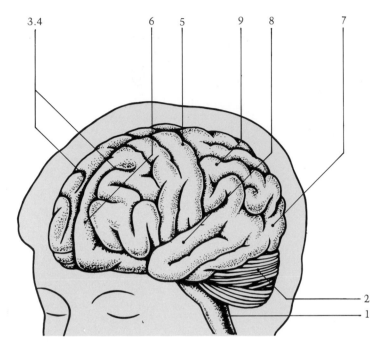

Deep grooves divide each hemisphere into four lobes, each area controlling a specific function:
5 Touch (parietal lobe — near the bones forming the walls of the skull).
6 Intelligence, emotion, higher mental functions (frontal lobe).
7 Vision (occipital lobe — back of the head).
8 Hearing and smell (temporal lobe).

Messages to and from the brain are relayed through:
9 The thalami, which receive sense impulses (except smell).
10 The cerebellum, which does not initiate actions,

perienced hallucinations. Perhaps even more surprising is the fact that suggestion can actually reverse the effects of a drug. Syrup of ipecac normally causes nausea and vomiting; one subject duly felt sick when given ipecac, but when given a further dose and told that it would stop the nausea, the nausea disappeared. The one conclusion that does emerge from a review of all the research into placebos — is that no one explanation can cover all the effects that have been found.

It is not only scientific questions that are raised by placebos; there are ethical problems as well. Is it legitimate for a doctor to give a patient a placebo, knowing that he is deceiving the patient, even for his or her own good? Again, is it better for a doctor to be sceptical, or to deceive himself as well as his patient, since the doctor's faith in his treatment will most likely communicate itself to his patient and assist recovery? There are no easy answers to such questions. However, to a greater or lesser extent, they confront every doctor who has received a modern scientific training for, in spite of all the clinical trials that have been done, the efficacy of a good deal of modern treatment is still uncertain.

Practitioners of alternative therapies mostly lack a scientific training, and usually do not experience these doubts to the same extent. Indeed, it is probable that their relatively unquestioning faith in their treatments plays a part in their success.

MIND AND BODY

The answer to the problem of the placebo response must be found, if it ever is, in a resolution of the mind-body enigma. Are mind and body two different things, united in some mysterious way? Or are they different aspects of the same thing? Western philosophy has still not resolved this question after thousands of years, and although most modern scientists would probably favor the view that mind and body are one, neurology itself continues to throw up facts that only deepen the mystery. One of the most startling discoveries of recent years is that it is apparently possible to be perfectly normal, mentally and intellectually, with virtually no brain at all!

Modern techniques of CT scanning allow clear visualization of internal organs, including the brain. When some adults who had been treated in childhood for hydrocephalus (water on the brain) were studied in this way, it was found that the cortex — the part of the brain regarded as

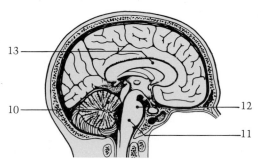

13 —

10 —

— 12

— 11

although it controls balance and coordination.

11 The medulla, a relay station for nerve impulses, which controls automatic activities, like heart beat, breathing, saliva glands etc.

12 The pons, another relay station, linking spinal cord, cerebellum and the cortex (the thin layer of grey matter, covering the two hemispheres, which makes up 40 percent of the brain).

13 The corpus callosum, the brain's white matter, relays information between both hemispheres of the brain.

responsible for the higher functions of memory and intelligence — had been squeezed so hard that it was almost obliterated. In some cases, it had been reduced to a layer only a few millimeters thick. We would expect such people to be idiots, if they survived at all; yet they were living perfectly normal lives, and one had even taken a degree in mathematics!

Such findings challenge all received wisdom about how the brain functions, and leave plenty of scope for those who still believe that mind and body are two separate though intimately interwoven entities. On the other hand, we do know that the brain controls all kinds of bodily functions — glandular, defensive, digestive, respiratory, and so on — via certain key areas at the base (the brain stem and hypothalamus). There is, therefore, nothing surprising in the fact that a patient's fears, hopes, ideas, memories, and so on could have all kinds of profound effects on the way the body functions in health and disease. Indeed, it has been known for many years that they do have such effects.

In one classic series of experiments, a Canadian laboratory worker called Tom was the subject. As a result of an injury, Tom had an opening into his stomach which allowed its lining to be inspected directly from out-

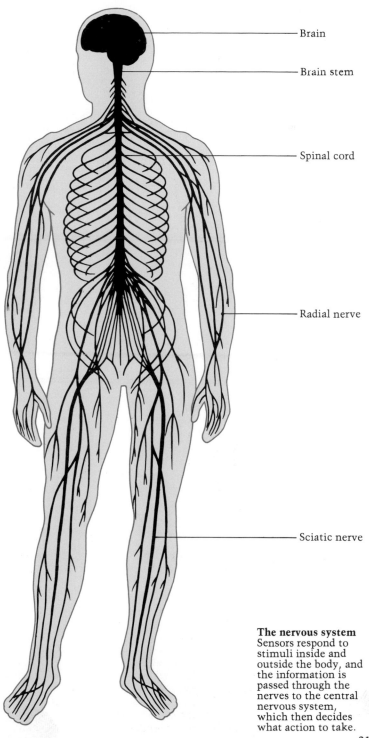

Brain

Brain stem

Spinal cord

Radial nerve

Sciatic nerve

The nervous system
Sensors respond to stimuli inside and outside the body, and the information is passed through the nerves to the central nervous system, which then decides what action to take.

Sensation and touch respond to texture, identifying rough or smooth, dry or wet, etc.

Pain extends sensation and touch beyond a limit that is comfortable. Sensors report the injury to the central nervous system which then takes appropriate action.

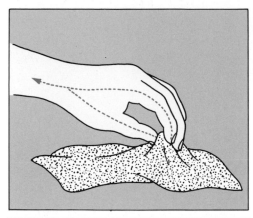

Sensation also responds to heat, warning the body if the temperature is too high or low.

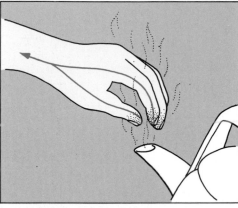

Pain in response to an outside stimulus is a major part of the body's defense system. The degree of response can be reduced by analgesics.

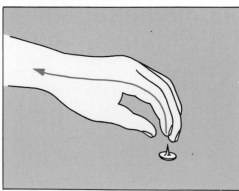

side. Researchers played a number of unkind pranks on the unfortunate Tom. On one occasion, they told him that his work was unsatisfactory; this made him angry and his stomach lining became flushed. Then they told him he was to be dismissed because of his 'unsatisfactory' conduct, and his stomach lining blanched with fear.

Many other experiments on human beings and animals support the general scientific belief that mental and physical events are closely interconnected. It follows from this that the way a patient thinks about his disease is bound to play a great part in how he responds to treatment.

The belief that such influences are important underlay the debate about 'psychosomatic' medicine. This was widely discussed some years ago, but seems to be out of fashion now, partly because the very term 'psychosomatic' implies the existence of *two* things, body and soul.

Such philosophical considerations aside, however, there is general agreement that mental factors are important in many, perhaps most diseases, though this is not to say they cause them. It follows that modifying the patient's attitude to his disease may play an important part in his recovery. And even if recovery is not possible — if the disease is incurable or fatal — the patient's attitude may make all the difference between a life that is tolerable, and one that is intolerable.

That this is true can be seen in the differences between the responses of individuals to an identical disability, for example, blindness. Of two people who become blind at the same age and in roughly similar circumstances, one may sink into apathy and depression, while another may take advantage of whatever opportunities are available and, perhaps, even launch out into a new career.

The same thing is true of many diseases. Often the therapist — orthodox or unorthodox — can make little or no difference to the illness itself, but he can do a great deal for the patient's attitude. And this, in turn, has all kinds of effects on the way the patient experiences his disease.

One can see this particularly clearly in the case of pain. Pain is an extraordinary complex phenomenon, which involves every aspect of the personality. It is wholly

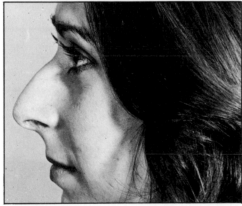

The Indian fakir can lie on a bed of nails without feeling pain (*above*). This has as much to do with the way his weight is distributed as with the pain presenting a threshold of sensation which can be overcome by his mental attitude.

Whether as the result of injury or heredity, dissatisfaction with a physical characteristic — a large or misshapen nose, for example — can severely undermine the self-confidence of someone who lives in a society that places overwhelming emphasis on physical appearance. The sophisticated techniques of plastic surgery include bone and tissue grafting, which can enlarge and decrease size and alter shape (*above left* before, *above right* after).

subjective — it cannot be measured by the outside scientific observer — yet for the patient himself, it may be his dominant experience. There are many causes of pain, but there is little or no correspondence between the degree of injury and the intensity of pain; indeed, some of the most severe forms of pain occur without any obvious injury at all. A serious wound received in battle may cause no pain, while a seemingly trivial injury may result in chronic intractable pain.

There are many forms of treatment for pain. They include drugs, various kinds of nerve stimulation, destruction of nervous pathways, and modification of the patient's attitude to his pain by meditation, imagery, and so on. Often, none of these is a complete answer in itself, and the best results are obtained by using several of them in combination. But even when the approach is primarily by surgery or drugs, the patient's own attitude is crucial. This is true when there is an obvious physical cause for the pain, such as arthritis, but it is also true when, as is commonly the case, there is no identifiable cause.

The importance of the patient's beliefs and attitudes is particularly clear in the case of pain, but it is also present in other instances. One person, for example, may suffer acute embarrassment from mild acne of the face which, to someone else, would be little more than a minor nuisance. Some people subject themselves to expensive and painful surgery to alter the length of their noses, the size of their breasts, or the amount of hair on their heads; sometimes there is a good reason for such operations, but more often the 'disfigurement' exists only in the mind of the patient, and is an expression of an underlying psychological disturbance. The operation may merely transfer the patient's focus of discontent from one feature to another. In such cases, the right answer is not surgery but a recognition of and an attempt to come to terms with the psychological problem.

Considerations of this kind underly a great deal of alternative medicine. In other words, most alternative medicine, of whatever kind, contains a large element of psychotherapy. With diseases that can, in principle, be cured or ameliorated, the psychotherapy will help to promote recovery, while if the disease is incurable, it will at least make the symptoms more tolerable.

There is no doubt that for a considerable number of people, the kind of psychotherapy offered by alternative practitioners is specially valuable. This pinpoints an important difference between orthodox and alternative medicine.

Orthodox medicine, whatever its success, has one drawback: it lacks a basic philosophy. In so far as it is scientific, this lack is inevitable, for the essential character of science is that it is empirical and provisional. Orthodox medicine is a collection of treatments that have arisen in many different ways, and its only underlying principle is that correct treatment depends on finding the cause of the disease.

Alternative medicine, on the other hand, takes its stand on principle. Some of the principles differ from one therapy to another: classic Chinese acupuncture, for instance, derives its principles from mediaeval Chinese ideas, while homoeopathy relies on the 'like curing like' principle enunciated by Samuel Hahnemann. There are, however, some fairly general principles which are common to most alternative practitioners, but which find no place in orthodox medicine. These philosophical

ideas are part of the appeal of alternative medicines for many people.

THE PHILOSOPHY OF ALTERNATIVE MEDICINE

Alternative medicine provides a meaning for symptoms. At one level, the idea, widespread among many practitioners, is that the symptoms of disease are somehow beneficial, in that they represent the body's attempt to heal itself; consequently, they should not be suppressed. A stronger version of this idea, originally formulated by Hahnemann, is that suppressing symptoms (for example, treating a skin rash with cortisone) will 'drive the disease inwards' and make it worse, or even incurable.

On another level, illness has, for some alternative practitioners, a more metaphysical, almost mystical, significance. They hold that it is telling the patient something important about his way of life; it is a warning to alter his habits, his diet, or his thinking. There are clear religious overtones to this belief, echoes of ideas going back to the Middle Ages and beyond, when it was held that an illness was a sign from God, and an opportunity for conversion to a new way of life. There are many cases recorded in which this happened; well-known examples occurred in the lives of St Francis of Assisi and St Ignatius Loyala.

Few modern patients interpret their illness in this way, but people suffering from a chronic or incurable disease often ask the doctor: 'Why has this happened to me?' The only honest answer the doctor can give is, 'I don't know', and, even if he does know the explanation, or part of it, this may not help the patient very much. Suppose the doctor says that the cause is an auto-immune reaction, and goes on to explain that this means the body is reacting against part of itself. Does this tell the patient what he wants to know? It says something about the mechanism of the disease, perhaps, but it does not answer the *why*? Yet many patients do want an answer to 'why?' rather than 'how?'

Sometimes they offer an explanation themselves, and these suggestions often reveal that they believe they are somehow to blame. Perhaps they had too much stress; they have eaten the 'wrong' foods or not

Saint Francis of Assisi (1181/2-1226), founder of the Franciscan order, considered anything natural as a reflection of God's purpose. He called his frequent illnesses 'sisters', seeing them as a mystical expression of God's will.

enough vitamins; and so on. It may not be logical to blame oneself for being ill, but few of us are wholly logical when we are ill and self-accusation is seen quite often in patients. Sometimes, paradoxically, it is made worse by the modern emphasis on positive health and self-care, which carries the implication that illness is partly one's own fault.

In more religious ages, disease was often ascribed to the anger of God for some fault committed. Today, most people reject this but seek instead a secular 'scientific' explanation. In consequence, the mantle of the priest has, to a considerable extent, descended on the shoulders of the doctor. But a medical training does not equip doctors to provide answers to the ultimate questions about the meaning of illness, suffering, and death, and many of them do not like being cast in the priestly role. Doctors may, of course, hold religious views just as anybody else, but it is probably true to say that the effect of a modern medical training is a sceptical or at least agnostic outlook on such

matters. Alternative practitioners, in contrast, usually subscribe to a more or less coherently metaphysical world view.

This tendency should not, of course, be over-stated: there are metaphysically-minded orthodox doctors and secular-minded alternative practitioners. And by no means every consultation in alternative medicine has a metaphysical dimension; it is often possible to relieve minor aches and pains by a quick manipulation or insertion of a needle, without any need to go into all kinds of abstruse considerations of a patient's lifestyle or mental attitude to his symptoms. It is mainly in the approach to relatively intractable problems or to psychological symptoms that metaphysical beliefs may play a part.

The philosophical content of much alternative medicine is either a strength or a weakness, depending on your point of view. To the scientifically minded, the philosophy largely removes alternative medicine from the realm of serious discussion, since it is not amenable to scientific testing. After all,

Some alternative techniques, notably acupuncture, homoeopathy and osteopathy, have found secure roles in orthodox medicine, eroding barriers between orthodox and alternative therapies. Acupuncture in particular has responded well to close scientific scrutiny.

you cannot disprove a philosophical theory scientifically. (Much the same criticism has been made of psychoanalysis, which has many of the features of an alternative psychiatric system.)

Partly for this reason, there is a tendency for some kinds of alternative medicine, particularly those which are also practised by orthodox doctors, to exist in two forms. One has a strong philosophical content and is marked by fairly strong antagonism to orthodox medicine, while the other places little or no emphasis on philosophy and tends to emphasize the similarities to, rather than the differences from, orthodox medicine. The first kind of alternative medicine might be called the extremist wing, and the second the moderate wing.

THE TWO FORMS OF ALTERNATIVE MEDICINE

The difference between the extremist and moderate forms can be seen particularly clearly in the case of acupuncture. There are today two versions of acupuncture, one traditionalist, which accepts the ancient Chinese ideas, and one scientific and Westernized. The division can also be seen in homoeopathy: there is an extreme form, which lays great emphasis on the use of highly dilute medicines and on certain philosophical, even semi-mystical, ideas about disease and its causation, and a moderate form, which is based on fairly orthodox notions of pharmacology and largely ignores philosophical notions. Similar divisions can be seen in other types of alternative medicine.

On the whole, the division between extreme and moderate versions of alternative medicine corresponds fairly well with the division between lay and medical practitioners. As a rule, doctors who take up the study and practice of an alternative system like to continue to practise orthodox medicine as well, and they tend to build bridges between the two kinds of approach. They emphasize the similarities between alternative and orthodox medicine rather than the differences, and they look for scientific explanations of the effectiveness of the alternative system. The only alternative systems practised on any considerable scale by orthodox doctors are acupuncture, osteo-

pathy and homoeopathy and, in the case of all three, numerous attempts have been made over the years to reconcile them with orthodox medicine.

Some doctors, however, have preferred to adopt a more extreme position, and have regarded the alternative and orthodox views as more or less irreconcilable. Thus, some accept the traditional Chinese version of acupuncture, and some hold to a strongly philosophical and antiscientific version of homeopathy. The great majority of lay practitioners are also extremists in this sense.

Does it matter in practice, so far as you, the patient, are concerned? The answer must be 'yes' and 'no'. On the purely practical level, the difference in techniques may not be great; as for results, it is meaningless to dogmatize about these in the near-total absence of figures. Uncontrolled impressions, however, suggest that there is not a great deal of difference between the two approaches in terms of results. Moreover, individual attitudes vary, and what matters is how you feel about the approach of the particular therapist you go to. The personal qualities of the therapist — how you relate to him and he to you — are of the utmost importance. There is a well-known saying in medicine that doctors tend to get the kinds of patients they deserve and vice versa, and the same also applies to non-medical therapists. On the whole, you are more likely to get good results if you are treated by someone whose general assumptions and attitudes you share. It is, therefore, important that you are aware of the differences in approach that exist among therapists, so that you can take these into account in deciding whom to go to for help.

THE PLACE OF ALTERNATIVE MEDICINE

One thing, at least, seems certain: alternative medicine is here to stay. Patients' demands will ensure this, if nothing else, but doctors themselves are also beginning to change their attitudes. It may be that we are witnessing what the philosopher of science, T. S. Kuhn, has called a 'paradigm shift'; scientists seldom change their minds radically, but new ideas are assimilated because younger, more open-minded scientists come on the scene and replace the old

Hydrotherapy (*left*) was used to treat illness by the ancient Greeks and Romans, and the spas that sprung up in Europe during the eighteenth and nineteenth centuries formed a major part of medical practice. Therapy involved either taking the waters for their special mineral content, or being immersed in them. Hydrotherapy is extensively used in Naturopathy (see page 193), and modern methods include saunas and massage by high-pressure water jets, to improve circulation and to stimulate liver and kidney activity in eliminating waste matter from the body

guard. Something of this kind may be happening in medicine today.

At any rate, no matter how much some people may lament it, a change in public attitudes seems to be occurring, and since, ultimately, it is the public who pays the bills, doctors cannot expect to remain aloof. Rather than rejecting these ideas outright or accepting them uncritically, we need to look at them coolly, and try to sort out what is valuable and what is useless, eccentric, and even harmful.

Some recent books on alternative medicine give the impression that their authors regard all the alternative methods available as equally valuable and efficacious. All are accorded a similar amount of respect, and are allotted similar amounts of space. Such an uncritical approach is self-defeating. It is undeniable that some of the treatments currently on offer can be of placebo value only, and though the placebo effect is certainly important, to place all the therapies on an equal footing is to devalue them all.

The policy adopted here is to discuss just a few of the many kinds of therapy that exist.

These are presented in some detail, to allow a clearer understanding of how they came into existence, why they are practised in the way they are today, and what are their strengths and weaknesses. The treatments chosen are all those in which appreciable numbers of doctors have been trained: acupuncture, osteopathy, homoeopathy, and various unorthodox or semi-orthodox psychological techniques, including hypnosis. Not only do doctors (as well as many lay therapists) use these techniques; there is already some research evidence to show that they work, though, admittedly, not as much as could be wished. Herbalism is, in some ways, the odd man out. Very few doctors practice herbalism as such today, but herbal medicine is probably the oldest kind of treatment in the world, and herbs are the ancestors of a great many modern drugs, including many of the most powerful and effective. After all, penicillin derives from a mold and is, thus, in a sense herbal, and the same is true of other antibiotics, all of which have been found in the world of nature. Herbal medicines are probably the commonest form of alternative remedy that patients buy across the counter.

The treatments described in this book are not the only ones that could help an individual patient, but they are the ones which, at present, seem to offer the most solid bridges across the gap between orthodox and alternative medicine. For this reason, if no other, they are arguably the most significant. As far as possible, it is important to avoid fostering a spirit of opposition between the two kinds of approach. Many people, on both sides, unfortunately, still wish to do so. It is worth remembering that orthodox and alternative practitioners tend to see the outcome of each others' mistakes, and to lose track of their own. It would be unrealistic and irresponsible to suggest that any form of alternative medicine will ever eliminate the need for orthodox medicine. In this respect, the term 'complementary' is preferable to 'alternative', for the unorthodox techniques should be thought of as filling in some of the gaps left by the orthodox approach. They can also provide a form of psychotherapy, especially for problems for which the 'medical model' of disease is not appropriate.

This does not mean that alternative medicine is necessarily always a second choice, something to turn to if orthodox treatment fails. There are many patients for whom some form of alternative treatment may well be best from the outset. The truly holistic practitioner of the future will be able to decide what kind of treatment is most suitable for each patient, and be qualified to use several of them himself.

The possible applications of alternative medicine are varied, and it is not practicable to give lists of diseases which are suitable for treatment. Not only would this contradict the basic view that each patient is an individual, so that what is right for one person may be wrong for someone else with the same diagnosis; it would also ignore the fact that many of the patients who come to alternative treatment have symptoms that elude the net of conventional diagnosis. Whether such a patient has a psychological disorder, or some physical problem that no orthodox doctor has managed to identify, is often uncertain, but in such cases the readiness of unorthodox practitioners to treat the symptom picture as the patient describes it,

without necessarily trying to penetrate to the underlying 'cause', may be very important.

The following categories are, therefore, intentionally broad and general. They are not meant to be exhaustive, but rather to give some idea of the kinds of problem that an alternative practitioner is likely to see.

1 You are suffering from symptoms that you yourself realize are due to 'stress' or other psychological causes.

In this case — and always with the proviso that serious organic disease has been excluded — you may well find help from an alternative practitioner. It is likely in such a case that the particular form of therapy used may matter less than the personality of the therapist himself, and how well it meshes with your own. In other words, the therapy used is almost certainly going to be an adjunct to psychotherapy — a grandiose word, which really means not much more than talking to the patient. In general, it is fairly easy to obtain some alleviation of symptoms in such cases, but complete cure is much more difficult. Indeed, it is probably difficult to define what 'cure' would mean.

2 No doctor has managed to find an explanation for your symptoms that you regard as acceptable.

Many patients who consult alternative practitioners fall into this category, and it is probably the most difficult to make any firm conclusions about. Some of these patients are suffering from psychological tension, but by no means all. Sometimes, there is an underlying organic problem that no doctor has yet spotted; this may eventually come to light, in which case it may be corrected by orthodox medical means. Sometimes no diagnosis can be reached, yet there does seem to be an organic problem even though an unknown one. In such cases, an alternative approach can at times succeed when everything else has failed; certainly, there is nothing to be lost by trying.

3 You are suffering from a known disease for which orthodox treatment does exist but it is relatively ineffective, unpleasant, or merely palliative.

This category again covers a large number of patients who consult alternative practitioners: they include people suffering from a number of common chronic or recurrent diseases, such as rheumatoid arthritis, osteoarthritis, asthma, and migraine, to name just a few. In such cases, the prospects for alleviation are quite good, but for complete cure are poor. Remember that most of these diseases are long-lasting, but are subject to largely inexplicable ups and downs. It is not unreasonable to expect that treatment will bring about an increase in the number or duration of good patches and, in practice, this often seems to happen. Naturally, the sceptics can and will say that this is just a placebo effect, but, as we saw earlier, the placebo response is in a sense perfectly 'real'. If, therefore, a given treatment seems to work for you, well and good. You may be able to reduce, or possibly even eliminate, your orthodox treatment. However, it is important not to be absolutist about this; there is no reason why you should not use both orthodox and alternative medicines simultaneously and, indeed, a great many patients do this.

4 You are suffering from a known disease for which there is no orthodox treatment at all.

Unfortunately, there are still a number of diseases for which there is no real treatment available. Many of these are progressive, leading to increasing disability and eventually death. Naturally, sufferers from such disorders, or their relatives, turn to alternative medicine in a desperate search for help. This puts the practitioner, if he is honest, in a difficult position. Should he tell the truth: that nothing he can do will make any real difference? Or should he give the patient treatment, even though he knows it is only of placebo value?

There can be no universally valid answer to this dilemma. On balance, it seems justifiable to give treatment, provided it is harmless, but without making any promises about what can happen. It is surely never justifiable to deny hope to anyone; after all, diagnoses can be wrong, no matter how certain they may seem. However, although it may be legitimate to leave the possibility of cure open so far as the patient is concerned, it is more questionable whether his relatives

should be left in the same uncertainty; as a rule, it seems best to tell them the truth.

5 Cancer

This requires separate consideration because of the special position it holds in many people's minds. There are many different kinds of cancer and the outlook varies enormously from case to case. At one extreme, some varieties are almost invariably fatal even today, yet an increasing number of cancers are becoming curable by modern methods. It follows from this that early diagnosis is vitally important, and that orthodox medical treatment should be given every chance. If treatment fails, however, or if the prospects of cure are known to be poor from the outset, there is certainly a case for considering an alternative approach. But it is important to be realistic about what such an approach can and cannot achieve. Beware of falling into the 'conspiracy' fallacy — the idea that some near-miraculous, alternative cancer treatment exists, which orthodox doctors are too prejudiced or ignorant to take up. There is no such miracle treatment.

A patient at the Laetril Cancer Clinic in Mexico collects medications from the clinic's dispensary. Laetril, which is derived from crushed apricot pits, is attracting attention from orthodox medicine.
A cure for cancer still eludes orthodox medical research. The alternative approach attempts to activate the body's natural defences, which for some reason have been suppressed. Treatment ranges from herbal medication to meditation and faith healing.

There is, however, a whole range of alternative treatments that can be used for cancer — homoeopathy, diet, and meditation, for example — many of which are used in combination at cancer clinics specializing in alternative therapies.

Are they effective? This depends on what criteria one uses. So far there is no good evidence that they prolong life or prevent recurrences. This does not mean that they may not do such things, only that it cannot be proved that they do. On the other hand, it does seem that patients' mental attitudes have a considerable influence on the outcome in cancer, and the best results occur in patients who either deny the existence of the disease, or adopt an aggressive angry attitude towards it (and sometimes towards their doctors!). Every doctor knows of patients with seemingly advanced inoperable cancer who have lived far longer than seemed possible at the time of diagnosis; in rare cases, such patients recover completely. Since such remissions or cures do occur naturally, it is possible that their occurrence may be favored by some of the alternative techniques. It has to be said, however, that such events are the exception rather than the rule, and the main effect of alternative methods of treatment in cancer seems to be to improve the quality of life, rather than its duration. This is by no means a negligible advantage. Whether it is worthwhile for any given individual is another question. Most forms of alternative treatment for cancer demand a considerable investment of time and attention by the patient, and not everyone feels that they want to use the life that remains to them in this particular way. The decision to do so must necessarily be a personal matter, for the patient to discuss with his relatives and his family doctor. Certainly, anyone who is disinclined to make this investment should not feel guilty; the possible benefits of alternative treatment are too uncertain to justify any such feeling.

It is a sad fact that many smokers start young. Increased awareness of the physical damage caused by smoking at last seems to be reducing the number of smokers.

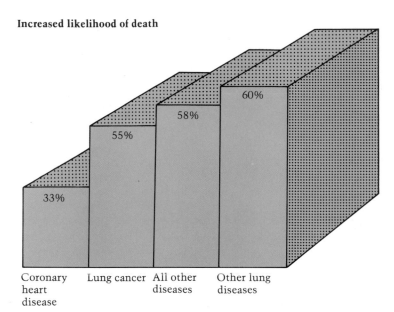

Increased likelihood of death

Coronary heart disease — 33%
Lung cancer — 55%
All other diseases — 58%
Other lung diseases — 60%

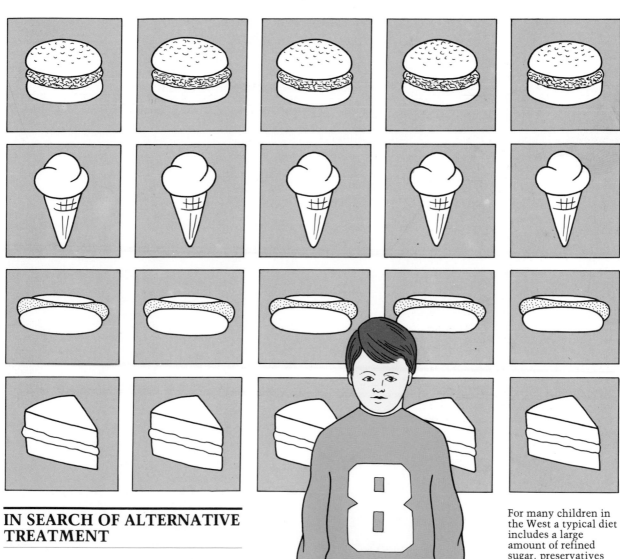

IN SEARCH OF ALTERNATIVE TREATMENT

Given that for one reason or another you are attracted to the idea of alternative medicine, how should you proceed? What form would be most likely to be helpful, and where should you look for it?

The first thing to understand is that, in deciding to look into alternative treatment, you have taken on a certain degree of responsibility for your own health. Indeed, this is one of the ways in which alternative medicine differs — or should differ — from the more authoritarian versions of orthodox medicine. Some doctors, and quite a few of their patients, still seem to prefer the older,

For many children in the West a typical diet includes a large amount of refined sugar, preservatives and artificial coloring with a correspondingly small proportion of fresh vegetables and natural fiber. Dietary patterns established in children tend to linger into adulthood.

more traditional therapeutic situation, in which the doctor provides all the answers, and the patient does what he is told. Quite a few doctors today, however, and also many patients, feel that the person who is being treated ought to have a better understanding of what is going on, and should cooperate intelligently in the treatment. Alternative practitioners usually make the same point, although it has to be said that some of them are as dogmatic and authoritarian as any orthodox doctor.

The process of taking responsibility for your own health often begins with the search for an alternative practitioner. Even before this stage, however, there is the possibility of improving your health on a do-it-yourself basis, and this is not necessarily a matter of taking medicines at all.

Diet Although it would be rash to make any confident pronouncements about the fine details of diet for the general population, some guidelines seems to be well established. Thus, it makes sense to reduce the intake of fat, especially animal fat, below that usually found in a Western diet. It is also advisable to reduce refined carbohydrates (that is, sugar, including brown sugar) as much as possible, while increasing the intake of com-

The importance of exercise to a sense of well-being is now firmly established. Its main effect is to improve the efficiency of the heart, thus diminishing the chances of heart attack and disease.

Whether you enjoy social sports like golf or football, or sports like running, swimming and dancing which can be performed on one's own, regularity of exercise is essential to maintain strength and suppleness.

The traffic jam is a potent symbol of everyday stress as experienced by millions of travellers. Breathing polluted air and feeling intense frustration represent an unhealthy combination.

plex carbohydrates (rice, potatoes) and fibre. There is no need to become a vegetarian on health grounds, but it is probably an advantage to reduce your meat intake; fish seems to be a safer source of animal protein. Alcohol in excess should certainly be avoid-ed but a *moderate* alcohol intake (say, a glass of wine daily) seems to be good for you.

Smoking At least it is possible to be dogmatic about this: smoking is bad for you. Not only is it the main cause of lung cancer;

The title page of an old edition of the Hippocratic collection (*below*), writings attributed to the great Greek physician Hippocrates who lived in the fourth century BC. His influence lives on in the Hippocratic Oath, which is still used at some medical school graduation ceremonies.

it is implicated in many other forms of cancer as well, it plays a major role in the production of chronic bronchitis and emphysema, and it is a 'risk factor' for various forms of arterial disease, including coronary artery disease. Stopping smoking is, probably, the most effective single step that any smoker who wants to improve his or her health can take.

Exercise Although opinion about the value of exercise is still not unanimous, most evidence suggests that regular exercise is beneficial in a number of ways. For men, it probably reduces the chances of a heart attack. It tends to lower the blood pressure. It also has a definite effect on the psychological state by reducing anxiety and helping to alleviate mild depression. Although it may not improve the chances of a long life — the evidence for this is still debatable — it will, for most people, enhance the quality of life. It also tends to reverse the trend towards replacing muscle with fat, which otherwise occurs with the onset of middle age.

The type of exercise chosen should be one you enjoy, otherwise you are unlikely to keep it up, and it should be one that uses the main muscle groups, especially the legs, in a rhythmic fashion. Walking, jogging, cycling, and swimming are among the best kinds. The optimum duration and intensity are still under debate among experts, but current thinking suggests that it is unnecessary to go to extremes; the kind of exercise that can be comfortably fitted into one's day-to-day routine is probably adequate, but regularity is important: three days a week is the minimum frequency, but four or five days are better.

Avoidance of stress Complete avoidance of stress is, of course, impossible. We all need a certain amount of challenge, but it should not cause more stress than we each can cope with. People's ability to tolerate stress varies widely, and only you can tell if what you have to cope with is excessive. If it is, you need either to modify your life in some way, or to adopt some means of neutralizing it. This could be one of the meditative techniques available, or it could be something as simple as a holiday.

There are some basic steps, advisable for everyone to take, whether or not they are ill and whether or not they are specifically looking for an alternative form of therapy. Even if you do have a definite health problem, for which you think an alternative approach is appropriate, it is not always necessary to seek out an alternative practitioner. There are several kinds of alternative medicine that are suitable for do-it-yourself use. Homoeopathy is a treatment of this kind, and so is 'acupressure'. Simple relaxation, again, is something that anyone can practise without going to a therapist.

If, however, you do want to receive treatment from a therapist, how should you go

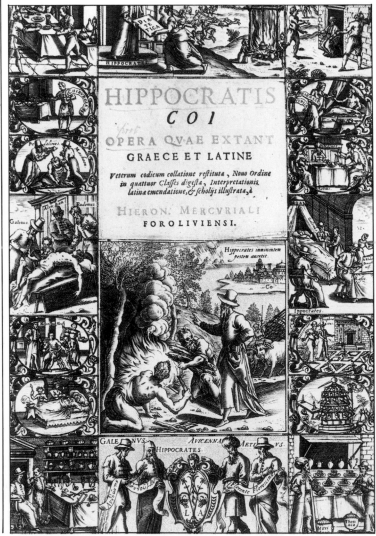

HIPPOCRATIS
COI
OPERA QVAE EXTANT
GRAECE ET LATINE
Veterum codicum collatione reſtituta, Nouo Ordine
in quattuor Claſſes digeſta, Interpretationis
latinæ emendatione, & ſcholijs illuſtrata, à
HIERON. MERCVRIALI
FOROLIVIENSI.

about it? What kind of treatment is most likely to help you, and how should you pick your practitioner?

The first thing to realize is that you should apply the same standards of caution and common sense to the choice of a therapy or a therapist, as you would when making any other important decision. Sometimes, people who order their lives in a reasonably prudent manner seem to abandon every critical faculty when they look for alternative treatment and consequently lay themselves open to disappointment and even deception. It is, unfortunately, true that there are a certain number of dishonest therapists about; indeed, the health industry sometimes seems to be particularly attractive to such people, perhaps because illness makes patients more gullible, and because patients, on the whole, are used to trusting their medical attendants, facts upon which the dishonest can capitalize. This is not to say that there are no dishonest doctors; there are, but for them there is a means of disciplinary control, through peer panels and State and local medical associations.

There is no such control over lay practitioners. As the law stands in Britain (it is much more restrictive in many other countries), anyone can practise any form of treatment, with or without qualifications; the only restraints are that practitioners lacking medical qualifications cannot prescribe many kinds of drugs, or sign death certificates and other official documents, and are not allowed to treat some diseases (including venereal disease, but not cancer).

Some forms of alternative medicine do have organizations concerned with training, and these keep a list of practitioners who have fulfilled their requirements. For example, the United States Homeopathic Association in Arlington, Virginia is the professional body of registered homoeopaths in the USA and keeps a list of doctors and lay practitioners who have trained to the standards set by the Association. However, these organizations do not have statutory recognition, so that anyone can practice without being a member. In Britain, as a rule, doctors who practice an alternative therapy belong either to no organization, or to one which is not open to lay practitioners, such as the Faculty of Homoeopathy or the recently formed British Medical Acupuncture Society.

The result of all this is that, with the better-established alternative therapies, such as homoeopathy, osteopathy, and acupuncture, there is a confusing variety of organizations — one or two (sometimes more) which are non-medical. There are also a number of practitioners of these therapies, both medical and lay, who are not members of any organization. This makes the task of selecting a practitioner more difficult. Another problem is that, whereas lay practitioners can advertise their services, doctors cannot, a difference which explains why some lay practitioners appear so successful.

HOW TO PROCEED

In the majority of cases, the initial step in looking for alternative treatment should be *to consult your family doctor*. Some patients are afraid to approach their doctor with a request for alternative treatment, but this fear is often unjustified. Only a small minority of general practitioners practise any form of alternative treatment themselves, but many are sympathetic or, at least, open to the idea, and will either make no objection or refer you themselves — usually to another doctor who does practise alternative medicine. Naturally, some general practitioners are hostile to alternative medicine, and it is possible that yours may be one of the relatively few who have a fixed objection to their patients receiving any form of alternative treatment. If so, your choice is either to acquiesce, or to make your own arrangements. Before doing so, try to find out why your doctor objects in your case. He or she may have a perfectly valid reason, in which case you should respect it.

If your problem is a minor though perhaps irritating one (for example, a persistently blocked nose), no great harm will be done if you seek alternative treatment without your doctor's approval. The same is probably true if you suffer from a chronic disease whose diagnosis is not in doubt, such as osteoarthritis. Even in such cases, it is better to obtain the tacit consent of your general practitioner or at least inform him of your decision, since he can remove you from his list of patients if he strongly disapproves of alternative treatment. This occasionally happens, although if relations are seriously strained, it may be advisable to find a new

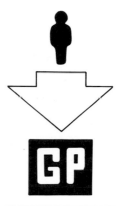

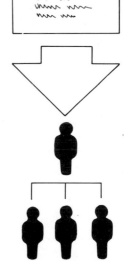

The referral system: the patient goes to the GP who then writes to an alternative practitioner who may suggest one or several therapists. As practised in Britain, the referral system affords greater safety than the patient referring directly to a therapist.

Carl Jung (1875-1961) was an ardent disciple of Freud, but went on to formulate his own analysis of psychology, which includes the basic classification of extrovert and introvert, and his definition of libido as the will to live.

general practitioner anyway.

The British system of referral has much to recommend it, although some patients feel that it is unreasonable that doctors should have the right to say whether their patients may, or may not, receive alternative treatment. There are many countries which lack GPs in the British sense, and there patients refer themselves to specialists directly. This may seem to offer patients greater freedom, but it is not always in their best interests. A common symptom like persistent backache, for example, may be due to a vast range of causes, some serious and others trivial, and the right person to treat it could be an orthopedic surgeon, a general practitioner, a gynecologist, an osteopath, an acupuncturist, or even a psychiatrist. In the absence of a GP referral system, the patient must make up his own mind whom to turn to, and if he chooses wrongly there could be a delay, possibly serious, in obtaining the correct treatment. In other words, what is needed at the outset is a generalist, not a specialist.

The weakness of the referral system is that some doctors are not as open-minded as they could be to the idea of alternative treat-

ment. However, on balance, the advantages outweigh the disadvantages. Moreover, in Britain, the rule that patients must be referred to specialists is applied less strictly than it used to be. Now a specialist can see a patient without a referral letter provided he informs the GP of the patient's visit, and of the treatment recommended.

In summary, then, the ideal way to find alternative treatment is through your family doctor. However, there will be cases when this is not possible and you will have to rely on your own resources. This is where caution and common sense should be exercised. One particular warning is important here: be wary of advertisements which offer diagnosis by post on samples of hair, and in other unorthodox ways. These advertisements are framed in pseudo-medical terminology, to suggest that the methods employed depend on the latest technological wizardry. These 'diagnoses' are, in almost all cases, worthless and sometimes positively dangerous. Some unscrupulous operators claim to be able to predict the future development of fatal or crippling diseases such as cancer, multiple sclerosis, and Huntington's and offer to cure these non-existent diseases — of course, at considerable cost. The mental suffering inflicted on the wretched recipients of these 'diagnoses' is appalling. It cannot be said too strongly that such claims to be able to predict serious illnesses long before they appear are bogus and should be ignored. Diagnosis should be left to doctors.

Assuming that your diagnosis is not in doubt, or, if it is, that serious organic disease has been excluded by a doctor, the next step is to decide on a therapy and a therapist. Once again your family doctor, if sympathetic, is the best person to consult. He or she may be able to recommend someone in the neighborhood and, if so, this would be ideal. Alternatively, at least in the case of homoeopathy, osteopathy, and acupuncture, your doctor can obtain a list of medically-qualified practitioners; it is likely that you will be referred to a medically-qualified colleague rather than a lay practitioner, even though it is now considered ethical to go outside the medical profession, if your doctor thinks it advisable. But is it, in fact, an advantage to go to a doctor who is practising alternative medicine, or might a lay practitioner be as good or even better?

LAY OR MEDICAL ?

Lay practitioners greatly outnumber medical practitioners in all the alternative therapies and, indeed, in the case of many therapies, there are no doctors practising at all. The question may, therefore, be decided in advance for you, either by the type of therapy you are interested in or by what is available in your area.

If a medically-qualified practitioner is available, this has certain advantages. It gives you the benefit of a further medical opinion on your diagnosis, should there be any doubt about this, and the doctor can prescribe orthodox treatment as well as alternative measures should it be advisable. In one sense, therefore, his or her approach may be more truly 'holistic' than that of a lay practitioner.

Against this, many lay practitioners claim that doctors are not the best people to practise alternative therapies, because their training has made them too mechanistic in their thinking and too problem-oriented. Very few doctors, it is alleged, survive the indoctrination they receive in medical school with their intuitive faculty intact, and they use alternative therapies in the way they do orthodox drugs — as a treatment for specific problems, rather than for the 'whole person'.

Lay practitioners also often complain that doctors are inadequately trained in alternative techniques. Most courses for lay practitioners in homoeopathy, acupuncture, osteopathy and so on last, full-time, for several years. Many doctors, on the other hand, practise these methods as an adjunct to their regular treatment after much shorter courses of instruction.

It is difficult to come to any conclusion about these differences. As so often in this field, a great deal depends on the individual therapist, whether medical or lay. On grounds of safety, you are likely to be better off with doctors, whose medical training has given them a knowledge of anatomy and pathology, the need for sterilizing instruments, and similar matters. Effectiveness is another question but, in the case of many therapies, success depends less on formal training than on experience and flair.

Sigmund Freud (1856-1939) approached psychoanalysis through medical studies and hypnosis; but it is his method of revealing the patient's repressed experiences through free association, that forms the basic technique of modern psychoanalysis

Chiropractic is similar to osteopathy; it is a method of manipulating the spine and other joints of the body to treat bone and muscle injury. It is more established in North America, Australia and New Zealand than in the United Kingdom.

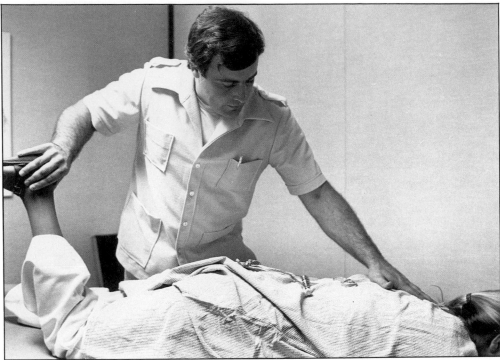

Many therapies rely largely on manual dexterity (osteopathy, acupuncture), or on intuition and experience (homoeopathy), and on the establishment of a good rapport between patient and therapist. An orthodox medical training does not guarantee these qualities, or prevent their acquisition.

One consideration is whether you feel more at home with a scientific or a philosophical approach. As a rule, a medically qualified practitioner is likely to be more scientifically minded, though there are exceptions, while lay practitioners are often indifferent or even hostile to science.

In summary, the question whether a therapist is medically qualified or not is of secondary importance. Much depends on the circumstances of each individual case. This is particularly true in relation to the psychological therapies. Both Freud and Jung were physicians, but neither insisted on analysts possessing medical qualifications. In the US all psychoanalysts must be medically qualified, but there are many 'therapists' and 'counselors' who have no qualifications at all and this does not seem to be a problem

Whether the therapist is medical or lay, you obviously want him or her to be good. In

the absence of a recommendation by your GP, the next best way of finding a good therapist is probably personal recommendation, but there are pitfalls here. What suits someone else may not suit you, and the fact that a friend suffering from a complaint similar to yours has been successfully treated by a particular therapist or therapy is no guarantee that you will be equally lucky.

Another method is to write to one of the professional organizations of the discipline you are interested in and ask for a list of practitioners. If he is a member of a profesional organization, a practitioner has probably attained a certain level of training; if in doubt, you should ask about this. Practitioners who are not members of an organization may have had no formal training at all and it is possible that they could have acquired expertise in an unconventional way. Remember that there is nothing to stop anyone from 'qualifying' as a therapist. Unfortunately, in the United States, not all the disciplines have managed to form national or State associations or to agree on standards.

Another way of classifying therapies is according to whether the therapist does some-

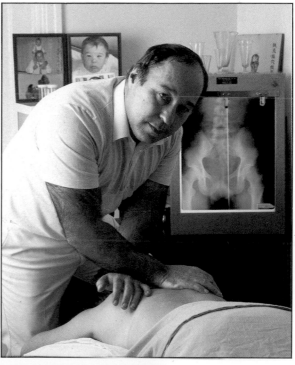

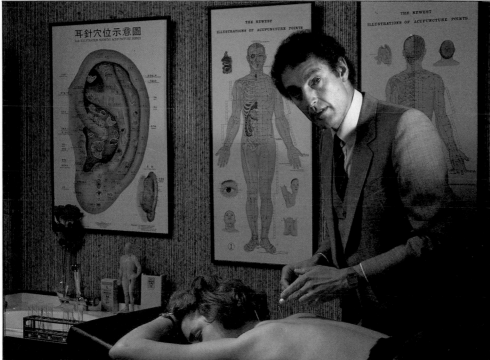

Peter Chappell (*above left*), chairman of the Society of British Homoeopaths. Homoeopathy is 150 years old, and is the only alternative medicine incorporated into the British National Health Service.

Michael von Straten (*above*) is president of the British Naturopathic and Osteopathic Association. Osteopaths have equal status with doctors in the USA and Australia, and the British School of Osteopathy treats some 50,000 patients a year.

Dr Alan Grant (*left*), a member of the British Medical Acupuncture Society. Of all alternative therapies, acupuncture's success is backed up with considerable scientific evidence.

49

HEALTH SERVICES AND SUPPLIES — PER CAPITA NATIONAL AND PRIVATE CONSUMER EXPENDITURES

In dollars. Based on Bureau of the Census data for total U.S. population.

OBJECT OF EXPENDITURE	1976	1977	1978	1979	1980	1981	1982
Total national	**633**	**714**	**792**	**893**	**1,024**	**1,169**	**1,305**
Hospital care	270	302	334	376	433	504	574
Physicians' services	124	142	158	176	202	234	262
Dentists' services	43	47	52	58	67	74	82
Other professional services	14	16	18	21	24	27	30
Drugs and drug sundries	59	63	68	75	83	91	95
Eyeglasses and appliances	15	16	18	20	22	25	24
Nursing home care	51	59	67	77	89	103	116
Other health services	17	18	20	22	26	29	32
Net cost of insurance and administration	23	31	33	41	46	48	54
Government public health activities	17	19	24	27	30	33	37
Total, private consumer	**366**	**416**	**458**	**514**	**586**	**664**	**740**
Hospital care	120	134	148	169	193	224	260
Physicians' services	92	106	117	129	148	170	189
Dentists' services	40	45	50	56	64	71	79
Other professional services	11	12	14	15	18	20	21
Drugs and drug sundries	54	57	62	69	76	83	86
Eyeglasses and appliances	14	15	17	18	20	22	20
Nursing home care	23	26	30	33	39	47	51
Net cost of insurance	12	21	21	25	29	27	33

thing to you (for example, by giving you medicine or by some form of physical manipulation), or whether *you* undertake most of the treatment yourself; for example, by modifying your diet, behaviour, or posture with the therapist's advice. Naturally, these two possibilities are not mutually exclusive, and a single therapist may well use both approaches simultaneously or successively. In general, many alternative therapists, whatever treatment they use, attach great importance to concomitant changes in their patients' lifestyle. Sometimes this advice is sound, but often it appears arbitrary and idiosyncratic.

The outcome of treatment in any individual case is so hard to predict that no firm statements about what kind of problems will do best with the various forms of treatment are possible. However, some therapies are, in principle, applicable to almost any kind of illness (for instance, homoeopathy) whereas others, such as the psychological methods, are really only suitable for functional and psychological disturbances. Manipulative treatments are, naturally, most suited to painful disorders of the muscles and joints, especially the back, though they also seem to be effective at times in certain other problems.

WHAT KIND OF TREATMENT?

To some extent, the choice of treatment will be determined by what is available locally. Some treatments are widespread, but the more esoteric practices are usually only to be found in large cities. The next question is personal preference. All things being equal, it is best to try something that appeals to you. If, for example, you have a deep-seated fear of 'needles', it makes no sense to consider acupuncture.

There is also the question whether your particular problem is more likely to yield to one kind of approach rather than another. Although alternative medical systems are of many kinds, it is possible to classify them according to the kind of approach used, which may be physical, medicinal, or psychological.

A physical method is one in which some kind of manipulation is used, or instruments of various kinds are used for stimulation. Physical methods include osteopathy, chiropractice, massage, rolfing, and the Alexander technique. They also include acupuncture, 'acupressure', and transcutaneous nerve stimulation.

A medicinal method is one in which medicines are given, usually by mouth. The principal examples are homoeopathy and its offshoots (tissue salts, anthroposophical medicine, the Bach flower remedies) and herbal medicine. Dietary modification could also be included here.

Psychological methods include a mixed group of practices, such as hypnosis, meditation, relaxation, biofeedback, and healing. Not all these are, strictly speaking, therapies at all; some are mainly intended as means of fostering psychological and spiritual development, and any benefits for health that may accrue are largely incidental.

THE FIRST MEETING WITH THE THERAPIST

This is an important encounter for both participants. It allows the therapist to assess you and your problem; it also allows you to assess the therapist, and you should make sure you do this. The initial session is likely to be longer (and, therefore, more expensive) than subsequent ones. The traffic need not be one-way; you are entitled to ask the therapist questions, and you should do so. You need answers to the following:
1 What kind of treatment will you get, and how is it supposed to work?
2 How long will treatment take?
3 What will it cost?
4 What are the chances of success?

The therapist should be willing to answer these questions frankly. Be suspicious of anyone who takes refuge in evasion or dogmatism, or who seems to resent being questioned. Some of the questions may be difficult to answer, especially those about the duration of the treatment or the chances of success, but even so an attempt should be made. No therapist should ask for payment in advance, since it is impossible to know how many sessions may be required in any given problem. In some cases, it may take a long time — after all, if an illness has been present for a number of years, it is unreasonable to expect it to be cured overnight; but it

is questionable to claim that no improvement at all can be expected for many weeks or months. Generally, there should be at least some perceptible improvement after about three or four sessions.

This is not to deny that some patients may build up a relationship with an individual therapist that they find helpful psychologically, and they may wish to continue seeing this therapist at intervals for a long time.

The chances of success are always hard to estimate at the outset. At times, a seemingly easy problem may prove intractable, while often the apparently impossible may respond brilliantly. Experienced therapists are, therefore, cautious about making predictions, although some are determinedly optimistic by nature, or in order to maximize the placebo effect (which is very important in both orthodox and alternative medicine). Others are non-committal at first, and prefer to wait and see what happens. Either policy is a reasonable one depending, to some extent, on the personality of the patient. However, a firm promise of success should be viewed with some suspicion.

The first meeting between therapist and patient is significant, not only because guidelines for treatment are worked out, but also because it establishes rapport between the two parties.

51

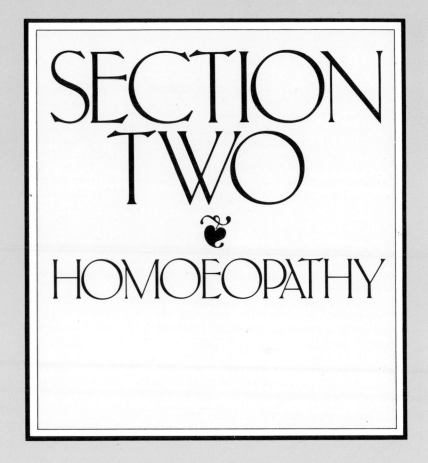

SECTION TWO
&
HOMOEOPATHY

OMOEOPATHY IS UNUSUAL among alternative therapies for at least two reasons. Firstly, its founder, Samuel Hahnemann, was an orthodox physician, and secondly, it is the only form of unorthodox medicine to be officially recognized in Great Britain by Act of Parliament, and to be formally included within Britain's National Health Service.

For these reasons, if for no others, one would expect most orthodox doctors to have at least a nodding acquaintance with the subject. However, this is far from being the case. Medical students learn nothing about homoeopathy during their training and, if they hear of it at all, it is usually when some inadequate dose of medicine is contemptuously referred to as 'homoeopathic'. Homoeopathy, in other words, is usually regarded as synonymous with the use of tiny doses, and this is as much as most doctors know about it.

Since it began in the early nineteenth century, in fact, homoeopathy has attracted derision and hostility from orthodox doctors and, as far as possible, they have tried to ignore it altogether. It is not possible to understand the reasons for this unless one goes back and traces the curious story of how homoeopathy developed.

AN OUTLINE OF HOMOEOPATHY

The story of homoeopathy begins with Samuel Hahnemann (1755-1843). He was an orthodoxly qualified German physician who, understandably, became dissatisfied with the medical practices of his day, which consisted largely in bleeding and the use of large doses of dangerous drugs. He, therefore, looked for alternative, better forms of treatment, but for a long time he was unsuccessful. Towards the end of the eighteenth century, however, he conducted an experiment on himself: he took some cinchona bark (quinine) to see what would happen. To his surprise, he experienced, for a few hours, the symptoms of malaria. This planted in his mind the beginning of an idea. Perhaps, he thought, quinine cures malaria because it can produce the symptoms of malaria in a healthy person.

He did not immediately make this theory public, but spent a number of years developing it and, almost certainly, carrying out further experiments on himself and his family, though we know little about these. Eventually, he encapsulated his idea in the Latin slogan *similia similibus curentur* — let likes be cured by likes. He later christened this principle 'homoeopathy', from two Greek words meaning 'similar' and 'disease'. He believed that a homoeopathic medicine produces an artificial disease that mimics the disease from which the patient is suffering. He held that it was impossible for two similar diseases to coexist simultaneously in the same patient; hence, by inducing a mild disease by means of a drug, the patient's own disease could be, so to speak, pushed out. This is something like vaccination, although not quite the same.

Some examples will clarify the idea. Belladonna — Deadly Nightshade — produces a hot, dry, flushed skin and hallucinations, both of which may occur in scarlet fever. Belladonna was, therefore, said by Hahnemann to be 'homoeopathic' to scarlet fever and was used by him both to treat and prevent it. Again, onions cause the eyes and nose to discharge profusely, so a homoeopathic medicine derived from onions is used to treat the common cold and hay fever.

The medicines that Hahnemann used at first were those in general medical use in his day, although later he added new ones of his own. For knowledge of their effects, he relied partly on his wide reading in several languages, but also on experimentation, testing medicines on himself, his family, and later his pupils. These experiments are called 'provings', from a German word meaning 'testing'.

The 'like cures like' principle was the basis of homoeopathy, but it was not the only feature that differentiated Hahnemann's practice from that of his contemporaries. For one thing, he soon began using much smaller doses than did the orthodox physicians of his day. Many people think of this as the essential characteristic of homoeopathy. Yet it was only at a comparatively late stage in his long career that Hahnemann emphasized it strongly, and began to claim that the homoeopathic method of preparing medicines gave them special properties.

A third point of difference with orthodox medicine was that Hahnemann used single medicines, rather than complex mixtures, on the very reasonable grounds that it was

Samuel Hahnemann (1755-1843) is the father of homoeopathy. He worked on the principle that like cures like, whereby he treated a patient's symptoms with a remedy that produced similar effects.

Overleaf: Hahnemann's desk is still in daily use. This, together with his medicine chests, chair and bookcases are preserved at the Royal London Homoeopathic Hospital, Great Ormond Street.

not possible to distinguish the effects of large numbers of drugs when they were mixed together. And finally, he did not give medicine for a set length of time or number of doses, but only as and when the patient's symptoms required it.

In summary then, and disregarding for the moment the many changes it underwent as it evolved, it can be said that classic homoeopathy has the following characteristics:

1　Medicines are chosen on the basis of *similarity* between the symptoms they produce in healthy people and the symptoms from which the patient is suffering.

2　The medicines are given singly.

3　The medicines are given in small doses.

4　Medicines are not repeated routinely, but only when the patient's symptoms demand it.

So much for the general principles of homoeopathy. Putting them into practice, however, proved to be another matter. Hahnemann himself modified his ideas a good deal as time went by, and so did his followers, and it is impossible to understand homoeopathy unless this development is taken into account.

THE EVOLUTION OF HANNEMANN'S THOUGHT

Hahnemann was, by any standards, an eccentric. Although he qualified as a doctor in 1779, when he was 24, he quickly found himself at odds with the conventional medicine of his time, which he was later to call 'allopathy'. For a long time, he ceased to practise his profession at all, and maintained himself and his large and growing family by translating medical texts. He also did much original work in chemistry. Another of his interests was the treatment of the mentally ill, a subject on which he held enlightened views; he advocated kindness and understanding, in place of the whipping and other harsh measures that were standard treatment in his day.

It was not until 1796 that he published anything on homoeopathy, and then not by name; and it seems that it was only in about 1805, when he was 50, that he began to practise homoeopathy seriously. Up until then, he had been constantly on the move, hardly spending a year in one place, but in 1811 he moved to Leipzig where, in the years after the Napoleonic Wars, he became very successful. In Leipzig, he lectured at the University and gathered about him a small but devoted band of followers, who studied homoeopathy under him and collaborated with him in his 'provings'.

From a modern standpoint, it is possible to criticize his research methods, but in intention at least he was thoroughly scientific. The 'provers' took the medicines, in doses that he judged suitable, and then noted down in their diaries the symptoms they experienced. Hahnemann would question them carefully about what they had recorded, and they had to swear to the accuracy of their descriptions. In this way, he accumulated an enormous amount of first-hand material, which he published in several volumes as the *Materia Medica Pura*. Even today, this work, together with Hahnemann's other writings, is the main source for homoeopathic practitioners; relatively little has been added since.

It is, therefore, rather unfortunate that Hahnemann chose to record his results in such a way that they were virtually unreadable. That is, he listed all the symptoms in an anatomical scheme of his own devising, so that they are about as digestible as a telephone directory. This led later homoeopaths to try to construct new kinds of reference books; and, even though Hahnemann's work is fundamental to homoeopathy, hardly any modern homoeopaths actually read the *Materia Medica Pura*, but make do instead with later compilations by others.

In addition to his practical work on medicines, Hahnemann also wrote a book on the theory and practice of homoeopathy; this is usually called the *Organon*. The first edition of the *Organon* was published just before he settled in Leipzig; further editions followed at intervals throughout his long life, while the sixth and last only came to light after his death; this final edition was published in 1920.

For a number of years, all went well for Hahnemann at Leipzig. True, he was at odds with the professor of medicine, but his prac-

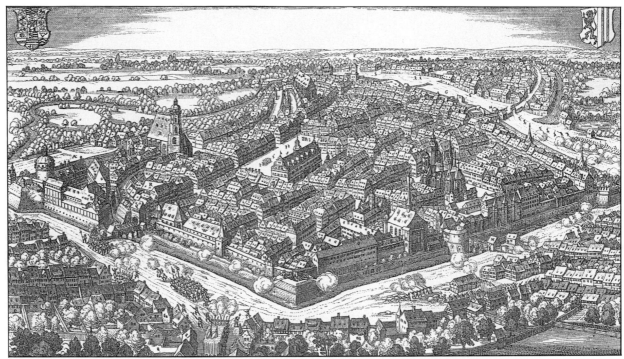

tice was booming and he was gaining adherents, although slowly. Then trouble came. He found himself attacked not only by the allopathic doctors but by the apothecaries as well, who resented the fact that Hahnemann made up his own medicines, and advised his disciples to do likewise. For a time, their criticisms were silenced by the arrival in Leipzig of Prince Schwarzenberg, who had recently defeated Napoleon just outside the walls of the city, and who now had come expressly for the purpose of being treated by Hahnemann. Unfortunately, after an initial improvement, the Prince died, and Hahnemann was blamed. The apothecaries took advantage of this to obtain an injunction preventing him from dispensing his own medicines, and since they were unwilling to dispense Hahnemann's medicines, his practice could not continue. He was, therefore, forced to leave Leipzig.

He accepted the post of Court Physician to the Duke of Anhalt Köthen, the ruler of a small German principality some 36 miles away. At Köthen he became something of a recluse, and seldom saw his disciples. But this did not prevent him from sending angry messages to Leipzig, criticizing those whom he referred to as 'half-homoeopaths' for adulterating the purity of the homoeopathic doctrine with allopathic ideas. His attitude led to considerable disharmony among the Leipzig homoeopaths and, eventually, led to the closure of the recently opened Homoeopathic Hospital.

Hahnemann's practice in Köthen was almost exclusively concerned with the treatment of chronic disease. This brought home to him the fact that, although homoeopathy worked well enough as a treatment for acute disease, it was much less successful for chronic disease. He finally formulated a new theory of chronic disease, and attributed its incidence, in most cases, to an all-pervasive 'miasm' that he called *psora*.

The *psora* theory led to fierce arguments among Hahnemann's followers and was widely ridiculed by his critics, but it became very influential among later homoeopaths. Hahnemann also introduced a number of new medicines for the treatment of chronic disease, many of which, such as cuttlefish ink *(Sepia)* and quartz sand *(Silicea)*, had never been used as medicines before.

While at Köthen, Hahnemann introduced another new idea that was even more revolu-

Hahnemann moved to Leipzig *(above)* in 1789. Professional hostility, especially from the city apothecaries, forced him to leave, and he lived subsequently in Köthen and Paris, where he died in 1843.

Memorials to Samuel Hahnemann in the Royal London Homoeopathic Hospital: Hahnemann in old age (*below*), portrait (*right*) and statue (*bottom*) of Hahnemann, and model of a Hahnemann monument (*bottom right*), now in the USA.

tionary in homoeopathy than his theory of chronic disease: this was the doctrine of 'dynamization' or 'potency'.

Up until this time, Hahnemann had advocated the use of small doses, but not infinitesimal ones. Now he went further, and claimed that, if medicines were diluted in a special way, they became more powerful instead of weaker. The crucial part of the preparation was the 'dynamization', which consisted in hard shaking or (in the case of insoluble substances such as sand) grinding in a mortar. Such dynamization, according to Hahnemann, made active medicines more active, and rendered active some substances (such as sand and common salt) that were not usually regarded as medicines at all.

The method of preparing homoeopathic medicines, which is still in use today, is based on this idea. In the case of a herbal medicine, the starting point is an alcoholic extract called the 'mother tincture'. One drop of this is mixed with 99 (or sometimes nine) drops of water *and shaken hard* to give the 'first potency', written 1c (first centesimal dilution). One drop of this preparation is then mixed with 99 drops of

water and shaken to give the 'second potency' (2c), and this process is repeated as many times as desired. Some commonly used potencies in Britain are the 6th, 12th, and 30th centesimal. Insoluble substances, such as metals, are prepared by a similar method, being ground up in a mortar with an inert substance (milk sugar).

It will be apparent that this procedure yields extremely dilute preparations. A 30th centesimal potency, for example, is the equivalent of 1 drop of medicine in 10^{60} (1 followed by 60 zeros) drops of water. As one contemporary critic commented, this was like putting a drop of medicine into Lake Geneva and using the lake water to treat patients! Hahnemann replied, however, that the hard shaking — dynamization — made all the difference.

Modern molecular theory suggests that the 12th centesimal potency is the limit beyond which no molecules of the original substance would be present. This is, therefore, taken as the boundary between 'low' and 'high' potencies. For any homoeopath who follows Hahnemann's later teaching, 'high' potencies are more powerful than 'low' ones; in other words, although

A display of homoeopathic preparations at Nelsons, Britain's foremost homoeopathic chemist, in London. Nelsons also supply a number of self-treatment homoeopathic remedies to many pharmacies and health shops throughout the country.

they contain less of the original medicine, or even none at all, they have been dynamized to a greater extent and this makes them more powerful.

This idea did not seem so absurdly paradoxical in Hahnemann's day. Hahnemann lived just before the modern molecular theory was established, so it was not unreasonable for him to believe that, no matter how much a substance is diluted, there must always be *something* left. Later scientific developments made this idea seem implausible, and posed considerable difficulties for the more scientifically-minded homoeopaths, some of whom rejected the dynamization theory altogether.

For Hahnemann himself, however, it became an indispensable part of his system, and he laid down the rule that the 30th centesimal potency was to be used for all medicines and also for provings.

By now he was an old man, and growing increasingly frail. However, he still had surprises in store for his followers. When he was 75, his wife died; they had been married for nearly 48 years and had produced eleven children. It seemed unlikely that Hahnemann would survive her for long. Four years later, however, he contracted a most unexpected second marriage to a fashionable young French portrait artist, who had arrived in Köthen disguised as a young man. Three months later, Melanie took her husband to Paris, where he set up a most successful practice and lived, apparently very happily, until his death on 2 July 1843, at the age of 87. Melanie continued to practice homoeopathy after his death, and her adopted daughter married Clemens Boenninghausen, one of Hahnemann's most assiduous disciples.

HAHNEMANN: SCIENTIST OR MYSTIC?

It is not possible to understand Hahnemann or the system of medicine he founded without realizing that his thought contains two separate but intertwined strands. In some ways he was a scientist but, in others, he was a metaphysician or even a mystic. To a large extent, these two aspects of his character can be associated with different phases of his life: up to the time he left Leipzig, he was chiefly a scientist, while at Köthen, he became more extreme and metaphysical.

To his Leipzig period belong his main 'provings', which were scientific attempts to discover the effects of medicines. At this time, too, his theories about homoeopathy were expressed more or less within the framework of current scientific thought. After he moved to Köthen, he not only formulated the theories of chronic disease and potentization that seemed so strange to his contemporaries, but he also adopted the view that disease is caused by disturbance in what he called the 'dynamis', a difficult term that is usually translated as 'vital force'. This was not a new concept — indeed, it was very much in the air at the time — but Hahnemann took it up and made it the cornerstone of his theory.

He held that life is sustained by the vital force. Disease is due to some outside influence that disturbs the smooth functioning of the vital force, and this gives rise to symptoms. The task of the physician is to remove the obstacles, so to speak, that impede the natural flow of the vital force, which will then bring about healing. Allopathic medicine is undesirable because it merely masks the symptoms; homoeopathic medicines, on the other hand, bring about a true recovery.

Hahnemann often speaks of dynamization as releasing 'spiritual' forces in the medicines; for him, the medicines were somehow able to act at the level of the vital force itself.

Some of his successors found these references to the vital force, dynamization, and spiritual properties dangerous and undesirable, since they made homoeopathy into a kind of metaphysical system. For others, however, this was precisely its appeal; they adopted Hahnemann's suggestions enthusiastically, and soon took them much further than the Master himself had done. Hence, there soon grew up two schools of homoeopathy, one scientific and 'moderate', the other metaphysical and 'extremist'.

To a considerable extent, the subsequent development of homoeopathy is the story of the interplay and rivalry that occurred between these two schools.

THE DEVELOPMENT OF HOMOEOPATHY

Homoeopathy spread widely throughout many parts of the world in the second half of the nineteenth century. By about 1875, homoeopaths were to be found in most European countries, and homoeopathy had become firmly established in India, still one of its main strongholds. It reached the United States as early as 1825, and was so influential there that, by 1875, it seemed likely to become the accepted form of medicine.

Homoeopathy was brought to Britain by Frederic Hervey Foster Quin, a well-connected doctor who is thought to have been the illegitimate son of the Duchess of Devonshire. In spite of fierce opposition from orthodox doctors, homoeopathy was taken up by members of the Royal Family and other eminent people, and this ensured its survival.

There were considerable differences in the ways in which homoeopathy was practised in the various countries. French homoeopaths, for instance, used — and still use — 'low' potencies, and also adopted the practice of mixing remedies. British homoeopaths also used low potencies and, under the leadership of Richard Hughes, who came to dominate the British homoeopathic scene in the last two decades of the nineteenth century, largely rejected Hahnemann's more extreme ideas. Hughes and his colleagues were sceptical about potentization and the miasm theory of chronic disease, and they rejected Hahnemann's views of the 'vital force'. Instead, Hughes emphasized the ideas that homoeopathy had in common with orthodox medicine, and he looked forward to a day when homoeopathy and orthodox medicine would be combined.

American homoeopathy, meanwhile, was developing in a different way. The most influential (though not the most numerous) school of American homoeopathy was the 'high potency' group. These homoeopaths took the potency idea much further than Hahnemann had done, and soon were claiming to have made the 200th, 1,000th, and even higher *centesimal* potencies! To do this by hand would have taken literally months of work, to say nothing of many gallons of water, but the Americans had in-

Frederic Quin (1799-1878) was the first president of the British Homoeopathic Society. His championship of homoeopathy was considerably strengthened, when in 1854 the Board of Health tried to suppress information on the homoeopathic hospital's much lower mortality rate in the treatment of cholera.

vented machines which, they claimed, produced the same effect as Hahnemann's technique. These high-potency enthusiasts also set a great deal of store by Hahnemann's more extreme views and, in particular, by his theory of chronic disease and the vital force. In adopting these ideas, they were considerably influenced by the ideas of the Swedish mystic Emmanuel Swedenborg, whose teachings were popular in the United States at that time.

Thus, a split developed in American homoeopathy between the small but vocal band of high-potency enthusiasts, who were holding out for the 'pure' Hahnemannian teaching, and the larger but less 'committed' body of low-potency prescribers. This split, in the end, played a large part in the decline of American homoeopathy. The low-potency homoeopaths eventually merged with the ranks of orthodox medicine and ceased to be distinguished as homoeopaths, while the high-potency school gradually dwindled away. By 1900, American homoeopathy was already on the decline, and, by about 1920, it had all but disappeared.

The last important high-potency homoeopath in America was James Tyler

Kent (1849-1916). He was one of the most influential figures in twentieth-century homoeopathy. In the early 1900s, a British homoeopath, Margaret Tyler, studied under Kent in Chicago. On her return to Britain, full of enthusiasm, she and her mother, Lady Tyler, set up a scholarship to send doctors to the USA to study Kent's teaching. An early beneficiary was Dr (later Sir) John Weir, who soon after his return was appointed Compton Burnett Professor and Honorary Secretary of the British Homoeopathic Society.

A decisive change in British homoeopathy was now inevitable. Under Margaret Tyler, Weir, and other Kentian enthusiasts, Hughes's books and ideas were swept away. The emphasis shifted to the use of high potencies and to those ideas of Hahnemann that isolated homoeopathy from mainstream medicine. The result was that British homoeopathy became a medical backwater, growing more introverted as time went by.

Nevertheless, the tradition of royal patronage of homoeopathy continued and, when the NHS was set up in 1946, the homoeopathic hospitals were included, with guarantees of their continued existence. In 1948, the Homoeopathic Trust, a charity with responsibility for raising and administering charitable funds for education and research, was formed. In 1950, the British Homoeopathic Society became the Faculty of Homoeopathy, established by Act of Parliament.

Partly as a result of this official recognition, British homoeopathy became known world-wide, with students coming to the country from all over the world. Teaching was almost entirely Kentian, the main books used being those of Kent himself and of Margaret Tyler, who was a prolific writer. Because the Kentian approach was anti-scientific and metaphysical, it also appealed strongly to the large number of existing lay practitioners. Instruction in lay schools of homoeopathy is still Kentian today. Among doctors practising homoeopathy, however, there has been a trend, in recent years, towards reconsidering the bases of homoeopathy and re-examining the writings of the older British homoeopaths, such as Hughes, who, despite their relative antiquity, seem more in tune with the modern medical approach.

MODERN HOMOEOPATHIC PRACTICE

In practice, there are wide variations in the ways Hahnemann's ideas are interpreted. This makes it difficult to describe what goes on in a 'typical' consultation, since a good deal will depend on the orientation of the particular homoeopath.

If the homoeopath is a doctor, he or she starts by taking standard medical history and, if possible, reaches an orthodox medical diagnosis. This enables the homoeopath to assess the likely outcome of treatment and, indeed, to decide whether homoeopathic or orthodox treatment — or a combination of the two — is most likely to be helpful. Then, if appropriate, the patient and his or her symptoms are reconsidered from the homoeopathic angle. This actually requires retaking the history, which means that a homoeopathic consultation involves nearly twice as much time as an orthodox one.

The professed aim of a homoeopathic consultation is to find 'the totality of the symptoms'. This is true of all the various homoeopathic schools, but differences arise over the exact meaning of the phrase totality of symptoms'. Does it, for example, include the physical manifestations of disease (pathology), as Hughes maintained? Or are the psychological aspects of overwhelming importance, as Kent taught? Each practitioner has his own views about such questions.

In practice, the approach varies considerably, according to the individual problem and, in particular, according to whether the illness is acute or chronic. Acute disease is easier to deal with, if only because most acute illnesses tend to get better by themselves. The homoeopath's main task is to accelerate recovery.

The essence of the homoeopathic approach is individualization. This means that the homoeopath is interested in features of the case which, from an orthodox medical point of view, are of little or no importance. Thus, an orthodox doctor, confronted by a patient suffering from an acute sore throat, examines the throat itself, the neck, and the ears, and perhaps takes a swab to examine bacteria that may be causing the illness. The doctor is then able to diagnose the patient as

Bottles in Nelsons homoeopathic pharmacy in London (*opposite*) containing tinctures from natural sources such as plants, animal material and natural chemicals

The Swedish mystic Immanuel Swedenborg (1688-1772) whose theories gained popularity in the USA at the end of the last century and influenced American homoeopathic practice at that time (*above*).

suffering from an acute pharyngitis or tonsillitis, and the examination is complete. It is of no importance whether the symptoms are worse on the left or right side, or whether the patient is or is not thirsty, or whether drinking cold water causes vomiting almost at once; such matters are irrelevant, or even distracting, in reaching an orthodox diagnosis.

To the homoeopath, however, they are vitally important because it is such things that point to one medicine rather than another. The homoeopath is relatively uninterested in common symptoms — pain, for example, is the rule in an inflamed throat and, by itself, does not help much in finding the right remedy, whereas the localization of symptoms to one or other side is more significant. In general, the more unusual and distinctive a symptom is, the greater its potential value to the homoeopath, since what he or she is trying to do is to narrow down the choice of possible remedies — ideally, to just two or three, or even one. If you look up 'pain in the throat' in a homoeopathic repertory, you find hundreds of remedies listed, which is not very helpful; it is, therefore, necessary to look for features of the individual case that will identify the remedy more precisely.

Because it is not always possible to find unusual or distinctive symptoms, homoeopaths have introduced another principle, called 'concomitance'. If two or three major symptoms are found together, especially in a rather unusual combination, this will also help to narrow the field of choice, since relatively few medicines will include all these symptoms. For example, a combination of sore throat, hot, dry skin, dilated pupils, and delirium would strongly suggest *Belladonna*.

In summary, then, the homoeopathic approach to an acute illness consists in: looking for any unusual symptoms; looking for factors that modify symptoms — that is, make them better or worse, such as warmth, cold, eating, drinking, moving about, lying down, and so on; and looking for characteristic grouping of symptoms — concomitance.

This may all sound rather complicated but, in practice, an experienced homoeopath can usually arrive at a prescription in an acute case without much difficulty. Moreover, although individualization is always the aim, it often happens that a particular illness is common in a given population at certain times, so that the same prescription can be given to a great many patients.

In treating chronic disease, the same general principles apply, but there are a number of special problems. For one thing, the mere fact that the illness has gone on for a long time means that it is probably difficult to cure. For another, the essence of the homoeopathic approach is to identify changes from the patient's normal state. But if a patient has been ill for many years, how is one to know what is his or her 'normal' state? For these and other reasons, the approach to chronic disease is more complicated than the approach to acute disease, and there are more divergences of opinion about it.

The homoeopath's first move, in chronic as in acute disease, is to observe the patient's appearance and demeanour. The homoeopath observes the way the patient speaks and answers questions; whether emotions are show or held back; how the patient behaves during the consultation. The homoeopath notes these and many other things, probably half-consciously, as clues to the remedy.

Next, the patient's history is taken. This is done on much the same lines as in an orthodox consultation but the purpose is different, since the homoeopath wishes to individualize the case as much as possible. The homoeopath asks first about the patient's complaint, and inquires in detail about the particular symptoms, seeking all the time to find characteristics that are 'strange' or 'peculiar'. What makes the symptoms worse or better? How does the patient feel about his illness — angry, resentful, depressed?

Next, the questioning turns to the history of the illness. How did it begin? Did anything special happen to the patient shortly before the onset — an accident, a bereavement? How has the disease altered and progressed with time?

Then comes a general review of the patient's health throughout life — ideally, as far back as childhood. Have there been any serious illnesses or operations in the past? If so, these may provide further clues to the remedy.

The homoeopath also inquires about the family history — illnesses in parents, brothers and sisters, and other close relatives. Individual homoeopaths attach variable importance to this; for the Kentian school, family history is of considerable significance because they believe there is a hereditary tendency for certain types of illness to recur in later generations of affected families.

Another feature of the modern Kentian approach is 'constitutional' prescribing. The idea here is that certain homoeopathic remedies, especially the most commonly used, are associated with particular types of people. For example, *Sepia* (cuttlefish ink) is said to be best for tired women with a sallow complexion, exhausted by childbearing and the strains of looking after their family, to the point where they are depressed and indifferent to husband and children. *Arsenicum album* (white arsenic), on the other hand, is suited to obsessively tidy people who feel the cold and are anxious and fearful. A number of detailed descriptions of this kind were given by Kent and even more elaborate, indeed almost lyrical, versions were contributed by Margaret Tyler. In treating chronic disease, the chief aim of some homoeopaths is to try to fit the patient into one of these descriptions. Others have been more cautious about this idea, and still others do not use the 'constitutional' approach at all.

Homoeopaths who do prescribe constitutionally pay a great deal of attention to those personal characteristics of the patient that are unrelated to the present illness. The principal category here is the psychological one: fears, moods, and emotions. Considerable attention is also directed to food preferences, and to reactions to different kinds of weather.

Having accumulated all this information, the homoeopath now has to analyze it and use it to arrive at a remedy. Some homoeopaths do this largely from their memory and knowledge of the medicines. Others use a repertory, and there are a number of more or less elaborate ways of doing this. These days, the repertories are being computerized, and several computer programmes are already available.

Whatever means are used, the result is usually a 'short list' of, perhaps, four or five remedies that seem possible. The homoeopath has to make the final choice among

A homoeopathic doctor in his consulting room with some of the preparations used in treatment. Remedies prescribed by a homoeopath are individually prepared for each patient.

these by using his or her own discretion; at this point, choosing perhaps to refer to one of the major compilations of homoeopathic *materia medica*. These works are voluminous and mostly date from the late-nineteenth or early-twentieth century; their main sources are Hahnemann's writings and, to a lesser extent, those of his early successors.

Having selected the remedy, the homoeopath must now choose the *potency* and the *form* in which to give it. This is where considerable divergences in practice begin to appear. The Kentian school favors high or 'ultra-high' potencies; that is, 30c or above. (There is, however, some doubt about exactly how high the 'ultra-high' potencies really are, since they are mostly prepared mechanically in quite a different way from that advocated by Hahnemann.) The Kentians also advocate giving a single dose and waiting for some time — at least a couple of weeks — before repeating it. This was what Hahnemann taught in the fifth edition of the *Organon*, though the sixth edition, which was not published until after Kent's death, contained a quite different scheme. British homoeopaths, at the turn of the century, used low potencies repeated daily or twice daily for several weeks, and every other possible combination has been used at one time or another. Everything is, therefore, at the discretion of the individual prescriber.

The Hahnemannian method of preparation generally produces medicines in liquid form, and some homoeopaths prefer to prescribe liquids whenever possible — for example, five drops to be taken in water once or twice a day. Many, however, feel it is more convenient to use tablets; these are made of sugar of milk, with a few drops of the medicine added to the bottle or container in order to medicate the tablets. Another alternative is to medicate powders made of sugar of milk.

Whatever methods are used, the homoeopath will, if possible, review the patient after one or two weeks (in the case of chronic disease), and then decide whether to repeat the dose, change the potency or even the medicine, or simply to do nothing and watch developments. In acute diseases, naturally, the patient may need to be seen more frequently, and usually the doses are given more often as well — perhaps even hourly to begin with, the frequency being reduced as improvement occurs.

THE HOMOEOPATHIC MEDICINES

A great many medicines have been used by homoeopaths at one time or another — about 2,000 in all — but, in practice, far fewer are commonly prescribed today. Those most commonly used were described by Hahnemann and, as in the parlor game, they may be animal, vegetable or mineral.

The vegetable remedies — the largest group — are typically prepared from the whole plant — leaves, stem, roots and all. An alcoholic extract is prepared and forms the 'mother tincture', which is subsequently potentized by alternate dilution and succussion (shaking up).

The mineral remedies include some elements, such as gold and sulphur, salts such as common salt itself and various others, and also some complex substances such as quartz sand. Since most are insoluble in water, they are first ground up with sugar of milk until they become sufficiently finely divided to form what modern chemists would call a colloidal solution. They can then be potentized as liquids.

The animal remedies, like the plant remedies, are mostly derived from the whole creature. *Apis mellifica*, for example, is the honey bee, used to treat swellings and stinging pains; other animal remedies include snakes, spiders, cockroaches, and other unusual creatures. Patients who learn that they are being given medicines derived from such sources sometimes feel apprehensive, but the homoeopathic method of preparation yields such extremely high dilutions that there is no danger. The same applies to the vegetable and mineral substances, some of which would be seriously poisonous in their undiluted form. For this reason, the prescription of certain medicines in low potencies is restricted to doctors.

An important group of homoeopathic medicines, not described by Hahnemann but introduced by the American school, is the *nosodes*. A nosode is a homoeopathic preparation of diseased tissue or diseased products, for example, tuberculous lung tissue or gonorrheal pus. These substances — which again are only given in high potencies

Medicine	Ailment or Condition	Remarks
Aconite (Aconitum napellus)	Sudden, violent and brief symptoms Exposure to drafts or a cold wind Dry suffocating cough Asthma Sore throat after exposure to cold dry winds High temperature with great thirst Great pain Bereavement Animal bites Anxiety, restlessness, fear, grief	*Symptoms worsen:* *around midnight* *when lying on affected side* *in a warm room* *in tobacco smoke* *when listening to music* *Symptoms improve:* *in the open air* *with bedclothes thrown off*
Actaea rac. (Actaea racemosa)	Headache Neuralgia Painful muscles after strenuous exercise Shooting pains	*One marked symptom is a feeling of depression, confusion and despondency. May be due to over-exertion or fright.* *Symptoms worsen:* *in cold, damp conditions* *when moving* *Symptoms improve:* *in warmth* *when eating* *headache improves in open air.*
Apis mel. (Apis mellifica)	Effects of insect stings Burning stinging pains Swelling of lower eyelids	*Apis mel. is advised in cases where irritability and despondency result from fright, jealousy, anger or grief.* *Symptoms (mostly on the right side) worsen: during late afternoon* *after sleeping* *from heat* *when touched* *in closed and heated rooms* *Symptoms improve:* *in open air* *from cold bathing*
Belladonna (Atropa belladonna)	Great heat, redness, throbbing Brightly flushed face Dilated pupils Pounding pulse Facial neuralgia Severe throbbing earache Throbbing boils Throbbing headache Tendency to catch cold after having hair cut or exposure to cold wind Dry hacking cough Sunstroke	*Suited to lively, congenial individuals who nevertheless may display violent temper when unwell.* *Symptoms worsen:* *in the afternoon and at night* *from noise* *from touch* *when lying down* *Symptoms improve:* *with warmth* *while sitting erect*
Bryonia (Bryonia alba)	Irritability Chestiness — colds often go down into the chest Dryness Dry, painful, often violent cough Dry lips Excessive thirst, especially for cold drinks Food lies like a stone in the stomach which is painful to touch Sits with knees up Diarrhea after eating overripe fruit	*Suited to individuals with dark hair and complexion who may be subject to rheumatism or bilious attacks.* *Symptoms worsen:* *with any movement* *with warmth* *Symptoms improve:* *with cold* *with cold food and drinks* *from pressure (except on the abdomen)* *with rest* *while lying on the painful side*
Calc. Carb. (Calcarea Carbonica)	Excessive appetite Craving for eggs and sweets Aversion to milk A problem with being overweight May feel generally better when constipated	*Suited to quiet, shy, sensitive people who are subject to depression.* *Often a feeling of being looked at by everyone and a fear of being laughed at. Embarrassment when entering a room full of strangers.*

Medicine	Ailment or Condition	Remarks
	Tendency to feel the cold and to catch cold easily Profuse periods in young girls	*Symptoms worsen:* *in cold weather* *in damp weather* *at night* *when standing* *at full moon* *Symptoms improve:* *in dry weather* *from warmth (avoid sun)* *while lying on the painful side*
Calc. Fluor. (Calcarea Fluorica)	Head colds with thick greenish-yellow discharge Catarrh Cough with tiny lumps of tough mucus Piles — bleeding, protruding, itching Varicose veins	*Symptoms worsen:* *after rest* *in damp weather* *Symptoms improve:* *after moving about a little* *from warm applications*
Calc. Phos. (Calcarea Phosphorica)	Headache following change of weather Severe stomach pain after eating Fractures slow to heal Rheumatic pain following exposure to drafts Periods too early and excessive Acne	*Suited to individuals who tend to be absent-minded and touchy.* *Symptoms worsen:* *with any change in the weather*
Cantharis (Cantharis vesicatoria)	Burning pains Burns and scalds before blisters form Sunburn Burning pain in the bladder, before, during and after passing water Urine scalds and is passed drop by drop Constant urge to pass water Gnat bites	*Symptoms worsen:* *from touch* *while passing water* *after drinking cold water*
Carbo. Veg. (Carbo vegetabilis)	Indigestion and flatulence where bringing up wind gives temporary relief Mild food poisoning after eating fish Car exhaust or mineral gas poisoning Ailments following cold damp weather Hoarseness Loss of voice Cold limbs at night Collapse or other ill-effects of exhausting illness	*Symptoms worsen:* *after eating fatty foods* *during warm damp weather* *in the evening and at night* *Symptoms improve:* *on bringing up wind* *from cold*
Cuprum Met. (Cuprum Metallicum)	Cramp in fingers, legs or toes Nausea with stomach pain Spasmodic cough and shortness of breath Metallic taste in the mouth	*Symptoms worsen:* *in the evening and at night* *in cold air* *after vomiting* *Symptoms improve:* *after a cold drink* *while sweating*
Drosera (Drosera rotundifolia)	Coughs Whooping cough or any sudden, violent cough which may end in vomiting Deep hoarse barking cough with retching Constant tickling cough Laryngitis with a dry throat making it difficult to talk Sensation of having a feather in the throat	*Symptoms worsen:* *with warmth* *after drinking* *when laughing* *when lying down* *after midnight*
Euphrasia (Euphrasia officinalis)	Colds with watering eyes and streaming nose Inflamed eyes which sting and burn Conjunctivitis Inability to bear bright light Hayfever First stage of measles	*Symptoms worsen:* *in the evening* *in bed* *when indoors* *from warmth* *in bright light* *Symptoms improve:* *in dim light or darkness* *from cold applications*

Medicine	Ailment or Condition	Remarks
Gelsemium (Gelsemium sempervirens)	Influenza Symptons of flushing, aching, trembling 'Tight headache' Heavy eyes Shivering Weary with heavy aching muscles Sneezing Sore throat Absence of thirst even with high temperature Difficulty in swallowing Running nose	*Suited to excitable people who suffer from 'nerves', have great difficulty in coping with life's problems and by whom even the simplest tasks are anticipated with nervousness and worry.* *Symptoms worsen:* *about 10 a.m.* *in hot rooms* *when exposed to the sun* *before thunderstorms* *on receiving bad news* *Symptoms improve:* *in the open air* *after passing water*
Graphites (Graphites)	Unhealthy skin Cracked weeping eczema Tendency for injuries to suppurate Cracked finger tips Overweight a problem Constipation Curious symptom of being able to hear better in noisy situations Sensation of cobwebs on the face	*Suited to individuals who are extremely cautious by nature and who find difficulty in making decisions.* *Symptoms worsen:* *at night* *during and after periods* *in draughts* *Symptoms improve:* *in the dark* *after wrapping up as protection against draughts*
Hepar Sulph. (Hepar Sulphuris)	Skin highly sensitive to touch (even clothing on affected parts is very painful) Injuries tend to suppurate Body odor Intense chilliness Cough brought on by the least exposure to cold air Choking Sensation of a splinter at the back of the throat Wheezing Crack in the middle of the lower lip	*Suited to acutely sensitive individuals of fair hair and complexion, who speak quickly, dislike fuss and prefer to be left alone* *Symptoms worsen:* *in cold air* *when lying on the painful side* *when affected parts are touched* *Symptons improve:* *with warmth* *from wrapping up (especially the head)* *in damp wet weather*
Hypericum (Hypericum perforatum)	Very painful cuts and wounds Lacerated wounds involving nerve endings Falls injuring spine, especially coccyx Headache with a floating sensation as a result of a fall Blows on fingers or toes Horsefly bites	*Symptoms worsen:* *from the cold and damp* *from touch* *in a closed room* *Symptoms improve:* *while bending head backwards*
Ipecac. (Ipecacuanha)	Any illness where there is constant nausea and sickness Morning sickness during pregnancy Bronchitis Asthma Rattling of mucus in the bronchial tubes with nausea and sickness	*Symptoms worsen:* *periodically* *while lying down*
Kali. Bich. (Kalium Bichromicum)	Complaints brought on by a change to hot weather Catarrh with a stringy discharge Sinus troubles Hard cough with stringy sputum or in plugs Sore throat Migraine — blurred vision before headache Pains move rapidly from place to place Nausea and vomiting after alcohol	*Symptoms worsen:* *in the morning* *from alcohol* *during hot weather* *Symptoms improve:* *from heat*
Kali. Phos. (Kalium Phosphoricum)	Mental tiredness from overwork Nervous exhaustion Nervous indigestion Indigestion following a 'working lunch' Exhaustion following long periods of preparation for examination	*Suited to shy individuals with a poor memory* *Symptoms worsen:* *from noise* *from mental exertion*

Medicine	Ailment or Condition	Remarks
	Headache with humming in the ears following mental effort Loss of voice or hoarseness after overexertion and constant use of the voice Giddiness from exhaustion and weakness Bad breath Dry tongue in the morning	*Symptoms improve:* *during gentle movement* *from warmth* *after nourishment*
Merc. Sol. (Mercurius Solubilis)	Feverish head cold (with weakness and trembling) Sore throat with excessive saliva Tongue flabby and indented Thirst Bad breath Body odor Metallic taste in the mouth Diarrhea with straining Toothache made worse from hot or cold food or from external heat but improved with the cheek is rubbed Ulcers on gums or elsewhere Abscesses	*Symptoms worsen:* *at night* *in a warm room* *in bed* *during wet or changeable weather*
Nat. Mur. (Natrium Muriaticum)	Colds with sneezes Nose runs like a tap (treat quickly at the onset) Sinus troubles Migraine — hammering headache preceded by misty vision or zigzag lights Eczema at the borders of the hair Herpes of lips (cold sores) Use of a lot of salt on food Continuous thirst Dislike of bread	*Suited to those of a pale complexion and oily skin who tend to feel insecure, worry about the future and are easily moved to tears. They are irritable and quarrelsome, do not wish to be ignored but dislike consolation* *Symptoms improve:* *in mid-morning* *near the coast* *while lying down* *Symptoms improve:* *in the open air* *while lying on the right side* *with cold bathing*
Phosphorus (Phosphorus)	Bronchitis Hard dry cough Hoarseness, laryngitis, loss of voice Craving for cold food and drink (e.g. ices and cold water) which is vomited as soon as it becomes warmed by the stomach Vomiting Tendency to bleed easily (bright red blood)	*Suited to people who are usually tall and slender with delicate skin and fair or red hair. They are physically and mentally hypersensitive and are often young people who are growing rapidly* *Symptoms worsen:* *in the evening* *while lying on the left side* *after warm food and drink* *Symptoms improve:* *while lying on the right side* *after cold food* *in the open air*
Pulsatilla (Pulsatilla nigricans)	Catarrh (yellow-green thick discharge) Styes (especially on upper lids) Mumps Measles Change of life Periods suppressed or delayed Periods scanty yet protracted Aversion to fat or greasy food Absence of thirst (even in fever) though the mouth may be dry Rapid change in symptoms—from feeling well to feeling miserable Pains shift rapidly	*Suited to females with fair hair, blue eyes and fair or pale complexion (often with pink patches.) They are affectionate, easily moved to laughter or tears, shy, never obstinate but like and seek sympathy. They are sensitive to reprimand and tend to put on weight easily. They dislike extremes of weather.* *Symptoms worsen:* *in the evening* *from heat* *after eating rich foods* *from sudden chilling when hot*

— can be used to treat patients who have suffered from the relevant disease in the past, especially if they say that they 'have never been well since' a particular illness. In some cases, there is no history of the illness in question, but the patient's symptoms, nevertheless, suggest that a particular nosode is indicated. In other words, some of the nosodes have acquired the status of independent homoeopathic medicines.

It is also possible to make up new nosodes on an *ad hoc* basis for particular patients — for example, by potentizing pus and other substances from that patient.

Another possible source of new homoeopathic medicines, so far little explored, is the field of modern pharmacology. The side effects which frequently occur with orthodox drugs can be used as indications for their *homoeopathic* use. Thus, any modern drug can be potentized in the Hahnemann way and used to treat patients suffering from the relevant symptoms, including the side effects of the drugs themselves; for example, a skin rash caused by a drug might be treated by a potentized preparation of the same drug.

A similar idea has been applied to the treatment of allergies. Hayfever sufferers, for instance, have been treated with potentized preparations of grass pollen.

OTHER HOMOEOPATHIC REMEDIES

There are several other kinds of alternative medicine that have something in common with homoeopathy but are not identical with it; they are mentioned briefly here.

Tissue salts (biochemics)
This treatment derives from a nineteenth-century German physician, Dr W H Schüssler, who was influenced by the scientific discoveries in his time about the relevance of chemistry to living things. He conceived the theory that disease is due to deficiency in various minerals, and on this basis he developed 12 'tissue salts'. These are given, on the basis of the patient's symptoms, in a low-potency form. All of them are also used in homoeopathy, and the only difference between the two systems is in the underlying theory.

The tissue salts are often used for self-medication by patients, and are widely available in pharmacies and health stores selling herbal and homoeopathic medicines.

The Bach flower remedies
Dr Edward Bach (1880-1936) was, at one time, bacteriologist at the London Homoeopthic Hospital, where he worked on the development of a special class of medicines known as the bowel nosodes. Later, he left the hospital to embark on a semi-mystical quest for flowers, which he believed would have healing powers. Eventually, he identified 38 flowers that he said could be used. The indications for selecting the right medicine was the patient's emotional state, and the medicines were prepared in a special way, the flower heads being placed on the surface of water in sunlight for three hours before bottling.

There are few practitioners of Bach's method nowadays, but a number of homoeopaths and others use some of the Bach remedies, especially the 'rescue remedy' derived from five different flowers and advised for 'panic, sorrow, shock, terror, sudden bad news and accidents'. The remedies themselves are widely available and can be used for self-treatment.

Anthroposophical medicine
This is a complex form of medicine that is based on the work of the Austrian philosopher and mystic, Rudolf Steiner (1861-1925). Steiner was originally a Theosophist but broke with Theosophy in 1909 to found his own movement, which he called Anthroposophy. Steiner's medical ideas have a good deal in common with those of Hahnemann, although there are also differences; Steiner drew much more on ideas derived from symbolism and occultism. Many anthroposophical medicines are the same as those used in homoeopathy, but they are often given as mixtures instead of singly. The Hahnemannian method of potentization is sometimes used but Steiner also invented more complicated procedures. For example, metals are often 'vegetablized': the metal is added to the soil in which a plant is growing; the following year the plant is composted and used to fertilize a second generation of plants, and the process is repeated for a third year. This is said to 'dynamize' the metal very effectively, while the influence of the metal causes the plant to

Dr Bach grouped negative states of mind into seven categories: apprehension, uncertainty, loneliness, lack of interest in the present, oversensitiveness, despair, and feelings of extreme care for others.
Top — left to right:
Wild clematis — indifference and absentmindedness.
Aspen — anxiety and fear of the unknown.
Wild Rose — apathy, lack of ambition.
Bottom — left to right:
Crab-apple — self-hatred.
Honeysuckle — nostalgia, dwelling on the past.
Rockrose — panic, extreme terror.

direct its action to a particular organ or system.

One important anthroposophical medicine does not form part of the homoeopathic list, but was a new contribution by Steiner. This is *Iscador*, which is derived from mistletoe and is used for the treatment of cancer. Mistletoe is grown on a number of tree species, and is combined with various metals to give a range of *Iscador* types which are used to treat different kinds of cancer.

In Europe, there are a number of hospitals using Steiner's methods and some hundreds of doctors trained in anthroposophical medicine, but this form of treatment is much harder to find in Britain. However, a number of homoeopathic doctors in Britain use, at least, some anthroposophical medicines, including *Iscador*.

THE SCOPE OF HOMOEOPATHY

Hahnemann and many of his followers believed that homoeopathy was a complete system of medicine and, indeed, would ultimately supplant allopathy, athough they did acknowledge the need for surgery in some cases. A few modern lay homoeopaths adopt such an extreme position today, but the majority, and certainly almost all medically-qualified homoeopathic practitioners, recognize that there are many illnesses that demand orthodox treatment.

It remains true, however, that homoeopathy can theoretically be prescribed as a supplementary form of treatment in almost any situation. This is because homoeopathic medicines are classically prescribed on the patient's symptoms, rather than the medical diagnosis. (Notice that this means, strictly speaking, that there can be no homoeopathic treatment for an abnormality that does not produce any symptoms, such as mildly raised blood pressure.)

In practice, therefore, homoeopathy is used today for acute illnesses, such as colds and sore throats, and for chronic diseases when there is either no orthodox treatment or only treatment that is not wholly satisfactory for one reason or another.

Homoeopathy lends itself well to self-treatment, especially for acute disease. It is possible to buy an emergency kit containing medicines that can be used to treat colds,

The Homoeopathic First Aid Set contains six medicines, three ointments and two tinctures which treat common problems such as fever, rheumatic pains, colds and vomiting and also bruises, cuts, burns and stings. Safe and free from toxic effects, the treatments can be taken by children as well as adults.

coughs, sore throats, and so on, as well as minor burns, bruises, and sprains. These are available from homoeopathic chemists. There are also some booklets written for people who wish to treat themselves in this way.

Another field of application is the psychological one. Hahnemann did not distinguish between mental and physical disease, and held that most physical diseases had a mental aspect, and most mental disorders had a physical one. Most of the homoeopathic medicines have psychological as well as physical indications for their prescription, and can therefore be used to treat psychological disorders. There is certainly a place for this form of treatment in mild anxiety, depression, and other minor disturbances, but it is not suitable for severe depression or schizophrenia, except in the hands of a suitably experienced doctor or psychiatrist.

Children seem to respond particularly well to homoeopathy and they enjoy taking the medicines, which are mostly sweet.

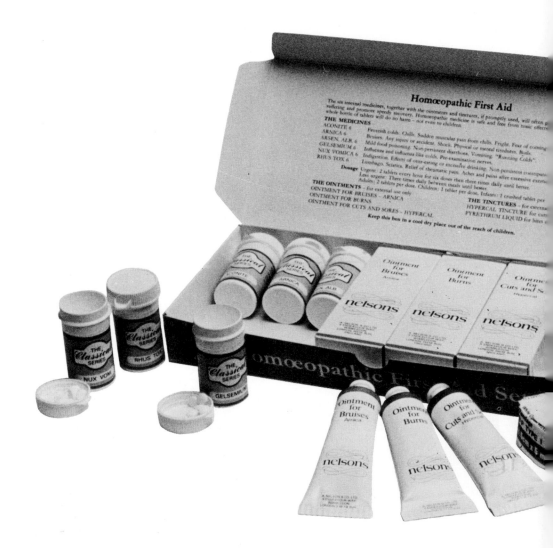

Homoeopathy can be specially useful in the treatment and prevention of recurrent colds and sore throats, for which antibiotics are usually ineffective.

Homoeopathy's principal claim is that it is safe, and this is true. Provided no serious disease has been overlooked, there are very few risks attached to homoeopathy. In theory, repeated doses of a low potency might induce symptoms attributable to the medicine in question but, in practice, this very rarely occurs; indeed, a recent experi-

ment carried out at the Royal London Homoeopathic Hospital, in which volunteers took up to 32 drops daily of three commonly used homoeopathic medicines in an undiluted form, produced hardly any symptoms.

There is also the question of the 'aggravation'. Hahnemann taught that if the right homoeopathic medicine was given, the patient would always become a little worse temporarily before improving. Some modern homoeopaths also believe this, and report that they quite often see 'aggravations' of this kind. However, others, equally experienced, hardly ever see them. In any case, even if aggravations do occur, they are short-lived and never cause serious or long-lasting damage to health.

But if homoeopathy does no harm, what about good? Is it effective?

EFFICACY

For a number of reasons, partly historical, there has been very little scientific research into the efficacy of homoeopathy. Indeed, only two or three clinical trials that satisfy modern criteria have been published, and it is impossible to draw any firm conclusions from them.

The most elaborate trial was carried out in Glasgow in the late 1970s. This was in two parts. The first was a pilot study and was 'uncontrolled', and so not acceptable to orthodox critics. The second part, however, was 'controlled'; 50 patients suffering from rheumatoid arthritis were prescribed homoeopathic medicines, but half of them, in fact, received placebo. Neither the patients nor the homoeopathic doctors knew which was which. All the patients continued to take their orthodox treatment as well. After three months, the results in the two groups were compared, and the patients who received placebo were found to have done significantly worse than those who received the homoeopathic medicines. The two groups were then switched and the trial continued for a further three months, after which the patients receiving homoeopathic treatment were again found to have done better than those receiving placebo. This was a joint trial in which doctors from the Glasgow Homoeopathic Hospital, the University Department of Medicine, and the

Cholera killed thousands in the epidemics that ravaged the undernourished slum dwellers of nineteenth-century industrial cities in England. Fortunately for them, the working classes could not afford the services of orthodox doctors whose remedies included bleeding, purging and huge doses of toxic drugs, and many turned to the advice of Dr Albert Coffin, the larger-than-life American herbalist who had revolutionized the attitude of the poor to health care. Although his treatment of the severe dehydration and loss of bodily chemicals caused by cholera was demonstrated again and again to be successful, this was covered up by the medical establishment. That the disease could be caused by contaminated water was demonstrated by a Dr Snow, who halted an outbreak in London simply by removing the handle of the local water pump.

BOARD OF WORKS
FOR THE LIMEHOUSE DISTRICT.
COMPRISING LIMEHOUSE, RATCLIFF, SHADWELL & WAPPING.

In consequence of the appearance of **CHOLERA** within this District, the Board have appointed the under-mentioned Medical Gentlemen who will give **ADVICE, MEDICINE, AND ASSISTANCE, FREE OF ANY CHARGE, AND UPON APPLICATION, AT ANY HOUR OF THE DAY OR NIGHT.**

The Inhabitants are earnestly requested not to neglect the first symptoms of the appearance of Disease, (which in its early stage is easy to cure), but to apply, WITHOUT DELAY, to one of the Medical Gentlemen appointed.

The Board have opened an Establishment for the reception of Patients, in a building at Green Bank, near Wapping Church, (formerly used as Wapping Workhouse), where all cases of Cholera and Diarrhœa will be received and placed under the care of a competent Resident Medical Practitioner, and proper Attendants.

THE FOLLOWING ARE THE MEDICAL GENTLEMEN TO BE APPLIED TO:--

Mr. ORTON,
56, White Horse Street.

Dr. NIGHTINGALL,
4, Commercial Terrace, Commercial Road, (near Limehouse Church.)

Mr. SCHROEDER,
53, Three Colt Street, Limehouse.

Mr. HARRIS,
5, York Terrace, Commercial Road, (opposite Stepney Railway Station.)

Mr. CAMBELL,
At Mr. GRAY's, Chemist, Old Road, opposite "The World's End."

Mr. LYNCH,
St. James's Terrace, Back Road, Shadwell.

Mr. HECKFORD,
At the Dispensary, Wapping Workhouse.

BY ORDER,

THOS. W. RATCLIFF,
Clerk to the Board.

BOARD OFFICES, WHITE HORSE STREET,
26th July, 1866.

Royal Infirmary took part.

More recently another 'double blind' trial was conducted jointly between King's College Hospital, London, and The Royal London Homoeopathic Hospital. Patients suffering from osteoarthritis of the hip or knee were studied, the effects of one homoeopathic medicine *(Rhus toxicodendron)* being compared with those of an orthodox drug and a placebo. In this trial, no difference was found between the homoeopathic medicine and the placebo, both of which were significantly less effective than the orthodox drug.

This trial attracted considerable attention, and was widely criticized by homoeopaths on the grounds that it was not a true test of homoeopathy, in that all the patients received the same medicine. It is important to understand that all the *Rhus tox* trial showed was that the particular medicine used was ineffective in the setting of this particular trial; further generalization is unwarranted, and there are many possible explanations for the negative result.

An interesting animal experiment was carried out a few years ago to test the effectiveness of a homoeopathic preparation in eliminating lead from the body. Rats were experimentally poisoned with lead, and were then divided into groups which were given placebo, a drug that is known to cause lead to be excreted, or the homoeopathic medicine. The homoeopathic medicine and the orthodox drug were found to be equally effective in eliminating the lead.

These results are potentially important. If the homoeopathic medicines were found to be equally effective in eliminating lead from children with increased lead levels in their blood, it would provide a uniquely safe way of treating this distressing problem. So far, unfortunately, it has not been possible to carry out a clinical trial in human patients.

It is worth emphasizing that whatever the outcome of any clinical trial, or even of many trials, it cannot amount to a 'proof of homoeopathy' (or a disproof, for that matter). This is because homoeopathy is as much a philosophy as a branch of science. It is a way of looking at patients, and of thinking about their problems, quite as much as it is a collection of medicines. What is possible, however, is to test whether individual medicines, or groups of medicines, work in particular situations. Until this is done, doctors will continue to be sceptical about homoeopathy.

As well as tests of the clinical efficacy of medicines, the potency idea can also be investigated as a separate scientific question. That is, experiments can be devised to see whether the homoeopathic method of manufacture yields results that can be measured in the laboratory. Many attempts to do this have been made from the nineteenth century onwards, but few would stand up to modern criticism. A notable exception was important research carried out some 30 years ago in Glasgow by Dr W E Boyd, who studied the effects of homoeopathic preparations of mercuric chloride on an enzyme, diastase; Boyd was able to demonstrate a clear effect. Research is currently under way at The Royal London Homoeopathic Hospital, where the effects of various potentized substances on the growth of yeasts are being investigated.

The results so far achieved are by no means conclusive, and they need to be repeated and extended, but they suggest that potentized solutions have measurable effects, even at high dilutions. To this extent, Hahnemann has been vindicated. However, they do not support his idea that medicines become more effective the further they are diluted; rather, the effects seem to wax and wane alternately as dilution and 'potentization' are continued.

In conclusion, then, the question of the efficacy of homoeopathy is still unproved. Certainly, that it has survived for over 150 years, often in the face of strong opposition from orthodox medicine, must mean that a great many practitioners and their patients have been convinced that it works, and this is an important fact. Critics, however, can always reply that the long detailed history-taking, the attention to the patient as an individual, the ritual of looking up the symptoms in the repertory or with the computer, are all powerful placebos and that this explains why the treatment works. Against this, homoeopaths can only point to the few trials carried out so far, and their own clinical experience.

The question whether homoeopathy works is not merely academic. Under EEC legislation, the manufacturers of homoeopathic medicines in Great Britain and

Europe have only a few years in which to provide evidence that some of their medicines work otherwise the product licences will be withdrawn. There is now a good deal of urgency to carry out some research.

There is also the problem of the supply of practitioners. Although many general practitioners are interested in the subject, and the training courses run by the Faculty of Homoeopathy in Britain are always full, this will not by itself ensure the continuation of homoeopathy within the NHS. There is also a need for doctors at consultant level, and the difficulty here is that there is no recognized training framework for a young doctor hoping to become a consultant in homoeopathy; indeed, homoeopathy is not officially recognized as a speciality.

For these and other reasons, it is now essential to present homoeopathy in a way that will make it acceptable to the main body of doctors. If this is not done, it will disappear from the NHS by default, which would be a great pity, for the homoeopathic hospitals represent one of the main bridges across the gulf that still separates orthodox from alternative medicine.

THE AVAILABILITY OF HOMOEOPATHY

In most parts of Great Britain, Europe and the United States it is easy to find a lay practitioner of homoeopathy. There has been a tradition of lay practice almost from the beginning: Melanie Hahnemann learned homoeopathy from her husband and practised it after his death, while Boenninghausen, one of the most prominent of the early-nineteenth-century homoeopaths, was originally a lawyer. Today, there are lay practitioners in many countries; some are self-taught, but others have attended one of the lay colleges that offer homoeopathic instruction. The teaching at these establishments is almost invariably Kentian, and

Patients in a ward in the Royal London Homoeopathic Hospital. Treatment is available under the NHS and the hospital's physicians prescribe both orthodox medical treatment and homoeopathic remedies, as appropriate. Other forms of treatment such as osteopathy and acupuncture may also be used.

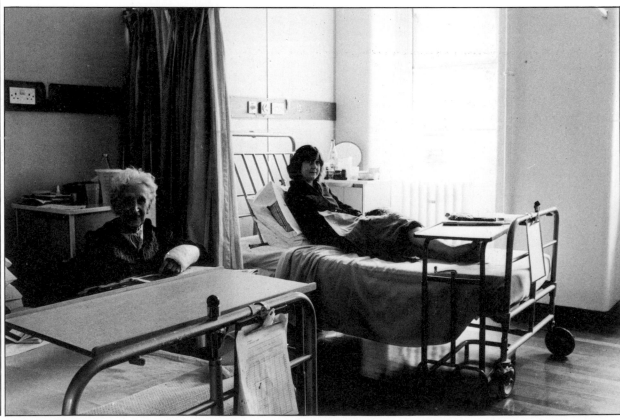

The Royal London Homoeopathic Hospital, one of the five NHS homoeopathic hospitals in Britain. The others are in Glasgow, Liverpool, Tunbridge Wells and Bristol. Between them, they treat more than 86,000 people a year as outpatients.

Over 2,000 homoeopathic substances have been listed and in a large homoeopathic hospital such as in London, the pharmacist will have most of these on hand for the preparation of individual medicines for the thousands of patients who visit the hospital.

there is often a strong metaphysical element, with claims that homoeopathy does not only cure diseases, but also favor the 'spiritual evolution' of mankind.

It is sometimes more difficult finding a doctor who practises homoeopathy. In Britain, there are about 300 Fellows and Members of the Faculty of Homoeopathy, though many more doctors have attended courses of instruction and use homoeopathy to some extent in their practices. British doctors wishing to learn homoeopathy are well catered for by the full-time and part-time courses organized by the Faculty in London, Glasgow, and elsewhere. Membership of the Faculty involves passing a postgraduate examination in homoeopathy, while the higher diploma, the Fellowship, is usually awarded for a thesis. Any doctor is eligible to become an Associate.

There are five NHS homoeopathic hospitals in Britain — in London, Glasgow, Liverpool, Tunbridge Wells and Bristol; between them they have seven consultants on

their staff, and a considerable number of assistant physicians. Some of these hospitals are small, but the London and Glasgow hospitals are large and see thousands of patients annually. For example, the Royal London Homoeopathic Hospital sees some 2,500 patients each year and the total number of consultations is more than 16,500. In most cases, it is the patient who asks for referral to the hospital, but patients are asked to bring a letter from their general practitioner.

When the London hospital was founded over 100 years ago, its doctors only prescribed homoeopathic medicines. Today, such a policy would not be practicable; doctors in British homoeopathic hospitals are physicians who practise homoeopathy. This means that they prescribe homoeopathic or orthodox medicine, as seems appropriate. In addition, other kinds of treatment, such as acupuncture or osteopathy, may be used. Thus, the aim is to offer a truly comprehensive and 'holistic' kind of medicine.

Biochemic tissue salts, such as calcium phosphate (Calc. Phos.), potassium phosphate (Kali. Phos.), sodium chloride (Nat. Mur.) and silicon oxide (Silica), are among the many homoeopathic substances shown here (*left*). The 12 tissue salts recommended by Dr Schussler are all used in homoeopathy but are also widely available as self-treatment remedies in pharmacies and health shops.

A number of homoeopaths and other alternative practitioners use Bach flower remedies (*below left*) and they are widely available in drugstores and health shops. They can be used to relieve ordinary physical conditions and the 'rescue remedy', derived from five different flowers, is said to be effective for 'panic, sorrow, shock, terror, sudden bad news and accidents'.

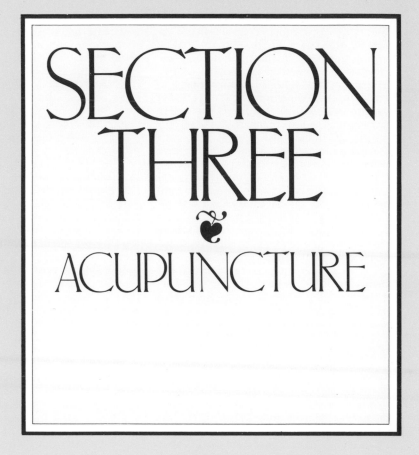

SECTION THREE
ACUPUNCTURE

CUPUNCTURE originated in China and the basic Chinese concept of disease is that it entails an imbalance in the system of flow within the body in one part or another. Treatment is intended to restore equilibrium, and may consist in performing acupuncture, or moxibustion (the application of warmth to acupuncture points). The aim in every case is to restore balance to whatever has become imbalanced.

Among the various forms of alternative medicine, acupuncture is of special interest in at least two ways. Firstly, in its traditional form, it has probably the most detailed and elaborate philosophical basis of any system, for the ideas that underly it are not peculiar to acupuncture but are part of the whole Chinese world outlook. Secondly, Westernized scientific acupuncture has been the subject of a certain amount of research and theorizing, which has brought it at least part of the way along the path from alternative medicine to orthodoxy.

TRADITIONAL CHINESE MEDICINE

Traditional acupuncture is only one method of treatment used in traditional Chinese medicine, which also includes an enormous range of herbal medicines. Indeed, in the last 2,000 years, much more has been written in China about herbal medicine than about acupuncture, yet this vast herbal literature is almost unknown in the West. Common to both herbal medicine and acupuncture, however, is a great body of theory about disease, and a most elaborate system of diagnosis. In order to understand traditional acupuncture, therefore, one has first to get a grasp of the main ideas of traditional Chinese medicine.

The fundamental difference in attitude between Western science and traditional Chinese thought must be emphasized at the outset. Western science typically tries to look behind phenomena to find their cause. This leads to a search for scientific 'laws' that will explain why things happen as they do. Some writers have traced this attitude to the Judeo-Christian concept of a Creator God, or First Cause. In any case, the consequence has been a view of the world as a hierarchical structure. It follows that the way to control events is to penetrate as deeply as possible behind appearances to reach this cause, and to act at that level. As applied to medicine, this means that the symptoms of the disease are important only in so far as they provide clues to what is happening at the biochemical, cellular and, increasingly these days, at the molecular levels. In an ideal world, medicine could dispense with symptoms altogether, and proceed entirely on the basis of objective tests and measurements.

This way of thinking is foreign to traditional Chinese thought. The key concepts here are not causation and law, but *order* and *pattern*. This emphasis derives, in part, from Eastern religions, which do not embody the idea of a Creator. In an important sense, for the Chinese, there is nothing behind phenomena: the medium *is* the message. The quintessential symbol of the Western conceptual system might be William Blake's Divine Lawgiver, measuring out the cosmos with his dividers; for the Chinese, it is a seamless web, woven by no one, that represents the endless rhythmic ebb and flow of the 'Ten Thousand Things'.

Western thinkers have often spoken or written as if they thought of the universe as a giant cryptogram, a secret text written in code by the Creator, which it is the scientist's task to decipher. For Chinese thinkers, on the other hand, there are, in a sense, no mysteries; the truth is there for everyone with eyes to see. Wisdom consists in attuning oneself ever more finely to the rhythm of the universe — the Tao.

Another characteristic Western image of the scientist is as an explorer, ever seeking to push back the boundaries of knowledge (the metaphor is significant). The nearest Chinese equivalent to the scientist is the sage, who sits quietly in his mountain hut, and observes the rhythm of the unfolding seasons.

YIN AND YANG

The yin-yang polarity is fundamental to Chinese thought and medicine. These terms are impossible to translate. Originally, yang meant the sunny side of a slope or the south bank of a river, while yin meant the shady side of a slope or the north bank of a river. These meanings were later extended to include, for yang, heat, movement, vigor, in-

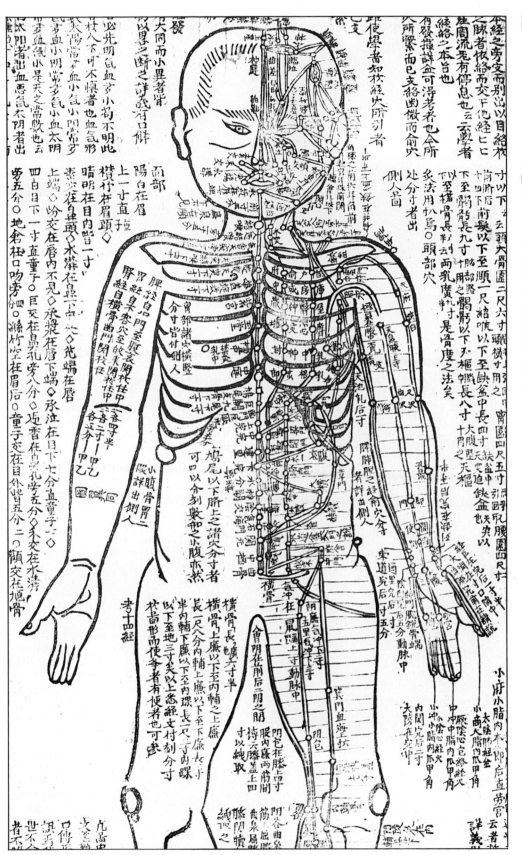

The Chinese yin-yang symbol (*above*) expresses the delicate balance of dark (yin) and light (yang), which embraces all opposites: female and male, cold and heat, passive and active, repose and motion. The black and white dots show the flow of one aspect into another.

The nineteenth-century Japanese acupuncture chart (*left*) shows the course of some of the 59 meridians or channels which direct the flow of Chi (vital energy, life force). There are twelve main pairs of meridians.

The Chinese charts (*right*) show the body's acupuncture points, of which there are more than 300. Acupuncture was introduced to Europe in the seventeenth century, but has only been taken seriously in the last 40 years.

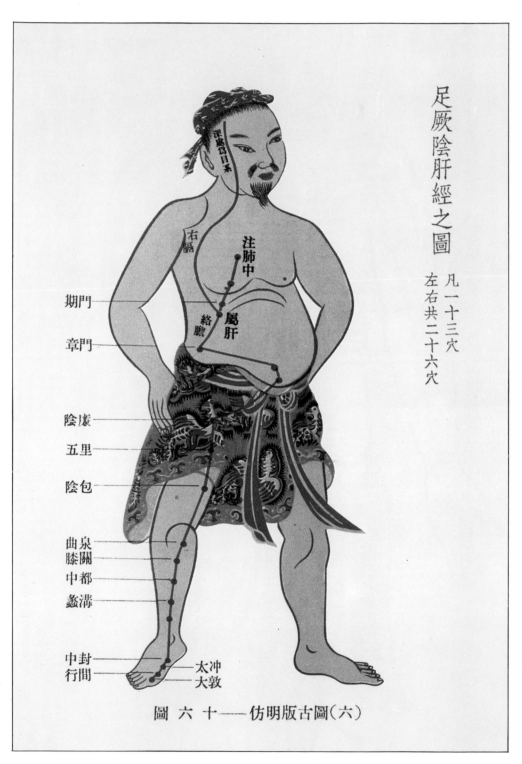

足厥陰肝經之圖

凡一十三穴
左右共二十六穴

注肺中
屬肝
絡膽
右扇
深盛昌目系

期門
章門
陰廉
五里
陰包
曲泉
膝關
中都
蠡溝
中封
行間
太冲
大敦

圖 六 十 —— 仿明版古圖（六）

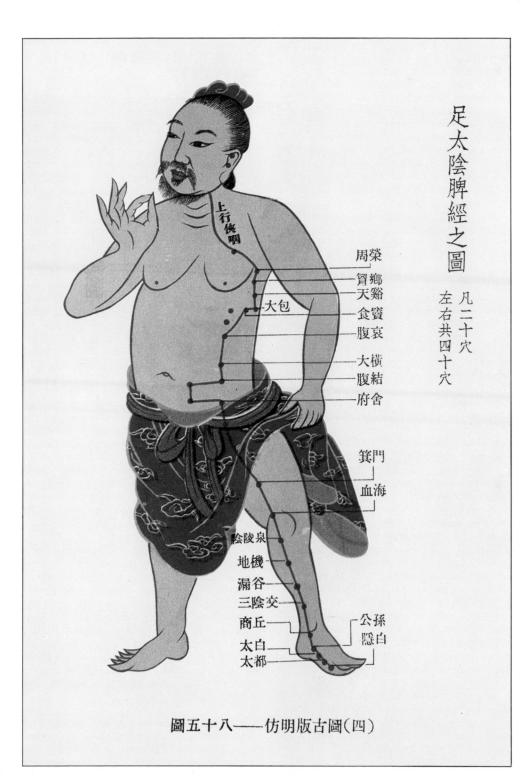

足太陰脾經之圖

凡二十穴
左右共四十穴

上行俠咽

周榮
胷鄉
天谿
食竇
腹哀
大包
大橫
腹結
府舍

箕門
血海

陰陵泉
地機
漏谷
三陰交
商丘
太白
太都

公孫
隱白

圖五十八──仿明版古圖（四）

89

crease, upward or outward movement; and for yin, cold, rest, passivity, decrease, and interior and downward movement.

Yin and yang are inextricably mixed together in Nature and in ourselves. Thus, male is yang and female yin, day is yang and night yin, summer and spring are yang, and winter and autumn, yin. However, it is never possible to isolate yin and yang completely; yang always contains a little yin and vice versa, which is why the yin-yang symbol has a white spot in the black part and a black spot in the white.

The categories of yin and yang are not permanent but dynamic; yin is always transforming itself into yang, and yang into yin. This is the basis of change. Ideally, yin and yang compensate for each other and preserve equilibrium; if this harmony is lost, so that one tendency increases at the expense of the other, the consequence is *dis-ease*.

The yin-yang concept leads to a different kind of logic from that characteristic of Western thought, derived ultimately from Aristotle, which regards opposites as mutually exclusive. In Chinese philosophy, there is no absolute black or white, only different shades of grey, and every statement contains the seed of its own contradiction.

Nevertheless, it is important not to exaggerate the differences between traditional Chinese and Western medicine. Both Chinese and Western medicine are characterized by a rejection of earlier supernatural explanations of disease, and regard it as a natural phenomenon that can be studied, understood and, up to a point, controlled. In a very important sense, therefore, traditional Chinese medicine is, like Western medicine, scientific.

The essential source book for Chinese medical theory is the *Inner Classic of the Yellow Emperor* — the *Nei Jing*. This is a collection of texts by unknown authors compiled between 300 and 100 BC. Later writers commented on the *Nei Jing* to bring out and clarify its ideas, or sometimes to add new ones; without such later commentaries, the *Nei Jing* would be almost incomprehensible to modern readers. Modern textbooks are based on works written in the Ching (Manchu) period (1644-1911), which in turn are based on commentaries in the Ming period (1368-1644) and, beyond that, in the Han period (202BC-AD220).

SOME BASIC MEDICAL CONCEPTS

The fundamental substances There are five Fundamental Substances in Chinese philosophy: Chi, Blood, Jing, Shen, and other fluids (sweat, saliva, gastric juices, urine, and so on). For acupuncture, the most important of these are Chi and Blood, which circulate in the channels called meridians. As usual, it is difficult to find Western terms for these concepts. Chi, for example, is sometimes rendered as energy, but Chinese thought does not distinguish between matter and energy. Chi could, perhaps, best be thought of as lying at the border between matter and energy, but it is impossible to define the concept clearly, because the Chinese do not think in terms of definitions. Instead, they describe Chi by what it does. Chi has various functions: it sustains all kinds of movement and change, it protects against harmful influences, it transforms food into other substances including Chi itself, it holds organs in place and prevents excessive loss of fluids, and it warms the body.

In Chinese physiology, blood is not the same as the blood recognized in Western physiology. It flows through the blood vessels, but also through the channels or meridians. The other Fundamental Substances are more difficult to categorize in Western terms and, since they do not play much part in acupuncture, they need not be discussed here.

The organs Chinese medicine recognizes a number of internal organs, but, though their names correspond, in most cases, to organs described by Western anatomists, their supposed functions differ a good deal, and the approach to the two systems is not comparable. There are five yin organs (heart, lungs, spleen, liver, and kidneys; the pericardium is sometimes included as well). There are six yang organs (gall bladder, stomach, small intestine, large intestine, bladder, and Triple Warmer).

The channels (meridians) and points The term meridian, though widely used, is misleading, since the concept is of channels or pathways that are supposed to link together

Tab. VI

Delineatio cavitatum vel locorum pulsuum et trium partium corporis.

Fūm fū. i.e. ventorum urbs: locus in occipitis parte ima, ubi extremi capilli statum pulmonis indicant.

Feù pē. i.e. natans albedo. locus in occipite infra aures.

Kí mūen. i.e. extremorum: locus infra mammillam, prodit originem intestini magni.

Kí Keu. i.e. spirituum os in dextra ante locum Quān.

Kí hái. i.e. spirituum mare, uno et dimidio infra umbilicum digito distans locus.

Quān yūen. i.e. limes originum, infra umbilicum tribus et dimidio digiti articulo: perfectorum spirituum receptaculum. Prodit originem ad vesicam.

Chùm yàm. i.e. penetratio viarum caloris primigenii in pedum superiore parte, ab imo et extremo osse tribus digiti articulis distans. Prodit originem ad ventriculum.

Tā Kì. i.e. magna lacuna, ad latera pedum supra talum, sunt illi pulsus. Mares in pede sinistro, fæminæ in dextro habent.

Xám ciāo. i.e. suprema pars corporis à vertice usq; ad os supremum stomachi infra cor et pectus.

Chùm ciāo. i.e. media pars corporis à stomacho ad ventris medium: continet fel, hepar, stomachum et ventrem.

Hià ciāo. i.e. infima pars corporis, à ventris inferiore ore ad plantas pedum.

Gùn yìn. i.e. hominis obviantis seu viarum humidi radicalis et caloris primigenii occursus in sinistra: prodit originem epatis et fellis.

Tàn hèn. i.e. rubeus ager, locus tribus infra umbilicum digitis.

Tài chùm. i.e. magna penetratio in ipso plantæ pedis medio. Dicitur et porta vitæ, quia cessante illic pulsu, moritur æger.

The Chinese diagnosis by pulses (*left*) is central to the acupuncturist's preliminary examination. Each meridian has its own pulse, associated with a particular organ, and there are six in each wrist. The pulses give the acupuncturist information on the balance, or imbalance, of yin and yang.

Traditional acupuncture diagnosis can differentiate between 28 categories of pulse, organized by depth, speed, rhythm, width, strength and length.

all the Fundamental Substances and Organs, and carry chi and blood. Diagrams of the channels represent them as if they ran on the surface of the body but, in reality, they are sometimes on the surface, and sometimes deep within the body, as they descend to reach the organs to which they are related. The acupuncture points mostly lie on the channels on the surface of the body, although some do not lie on channels at all.

A total of 59 channels is described but, of these, only 14 — those having acupuncture points — are of practical importance in treatment. Of these 59, 12 are paired and two unpaired, because they lie in the midline.

The body is usually said to have 365 acupuncture points in all but, in practice, less than these are used. The points all have their own Chinese names (such as Crooked Spring, Sea of Blood) but Western acupuncture books use a more or less standardized numbering system. In addition to these regular points lying on the channels, there are also a number of 'extra' points that do not lie on any channel. Furthermore, the Chinese recognize the existence of 'ah shi' points — areas that may become tender in disease, although they are not related to established acupuncture points.

The five phases or elements The yin-yang theory is the foundation of Chinese medical thought. There is, however, another theory which, though of lesser importance, needs to be mentioned briefly, because it usually receives considerable emphasis in Western books on traditional acupuncture. This is the theory of Five Phases, usually rendered as Five Elements, a mistranslation that illustrates the difficulty of trying to interpret Chinese ideas in a Western context.

Mediaeval Western thought followed antiquity in adopting the theory that there are four 'elements', or ultimate constituents, of matter: earth, air, fire, and water. The Chinese have five 'elements': wood, fire, earth, metal, and water. However, in keeping with the Chinese tendency to think in terms of processes, rather than of things, the concept here is not of substances, but of changes. Hence, the right translation is not elements but phases. Wood is associated with growth, fire with the peak of activity (and hence with incipient decline); metal with decline; water with rest (and hence incipient growth). Earth is more difficult to classify, but seems to be necessary as an intermediary between the other phases and to complete the system.

The Five Elements theory was first described in the fourth century BC, although it was probably formulated before this. During the fourth and third centuries BC, the yin-yang theory and the Five Phases theory existed simultaneously without being connected with each other, but, as time went by, attempts were made to reconcile the two. The Five Phases theory applied to medicine as a means of describing clinical processes and interactions. For example, wood is related to the liver, earth to the spleen, water to the kidneys, fire to the heart, and metal to the lungs. This scheme can then be used to illustrate how impairment of function of one organ has a knock-on effect on another: for example, if fire fails to produce earth, this means that the heart (fire) is unable to warm the spleen (earth); the corresponding symptom is an aversion to cold. The correct treatment might be to 'tonify' the heart.

Much of Western literature on traditional Chinese medicine describes diagnosis and treatment exclusively in terms of the Five Phases, and refers to the 'Law of the Five Elements'; this reveals a mistaken belief that traditional Chinese thought recognized scientific 'laws' in the Western sense, and exaggerates unduly the importance of the theory.

Traditional Chinese concepts of disease The Chinese regard disease as being associated with or caused by, three classes of influences: environment, emotions, and way of life. The principal environmental influences are wind, cold, heat, and dampness. Way of life includes diet, sexual activity and physical activity. There is almost no correlation between this conceptual system and that of Western medicine, which is one reason why it is almost impossible to equate a traditional Chinese diagnosis in a given case with a Western one, or vice versa. A Western doctor, for example, would be

According to Hippocrates, the balance of the four humors (*right*) — choleric (with lion and sword), sanguine (with ape), phlegmatic (with sheep and quill) and melancholic (with boar) — affected temperament and behavior, a concept similar to the equilibrium of yin and yang.

puzzled if told that a patient was suffering from Internal Cold and required his kidney *chi* to be strengthened; equally, a traditional Chinese physician would not understand a diagnosis of chronic bronchitis.

Methods of diagnosis Chinese medicine describes four methods of examination used by physicians: looking, listening/smelling (the same word is used for each in Chinese), asking, and touching. These are quite similar to the routine taught to Western medical students: taking the patient's history followed by physical examination consisting of inspection, palpation (examination by touch), percussion (tapping upon the body to find the condition of an organ by the sound), and auscultation (examining the chest and heart by applying a stethoscope).

Like his Western counterpart, the Chinese doctor starts by noting the patient's general demeanor and appearance. The most important inspection, however, is that of the tongue. The appearance, color, type and quantity of coating, size, mobility and so on are all noted and interpreted. The tongue is regarded as a prime indicator of the state of health.

Next, the doctor amplifies his or her impressions by questioning the patient, paying particular attention to sensations of heat and cold, pain, and the patient's medical history. Then comes feeling the pulse, conventionally regarded as the most important examination of all.

The pulse is usually felt in the radial artery at the wrist. The physician does this using three fingers on each wrist, giving a total of six pulses. Moreover, each pulse is felt at three degrees of pressure: superficial, medium, and deep.

A whole range of pulse qualities can be assessed. In addition to the depth, there are rate, rhythm, width, strength, length, and over-all quality. Various categories of pulse — usually 28 — are described. A skillful physician is said to be able to derive an astonishing amount of information simply by feeling the pulses, but learning the art requires thorough training, much experience, and the gift of intuition or sensitivity. Perhaps for this reason, the art of pulse-taking seems to receive relatively little attention in modern Chinese schools of traditional medicine.

As well as the pulses (*below*), the condition of the tongue (*left*) — its size, coating, color and moistness — plays an important part in the therapist's initial examination.

A patient receives pressure point analgesia before a tooth extraction (*right*). Much publicity has been given to the analgesic effects of acupuncture in surgery, but it is far from being proved a reliable pain reliever.

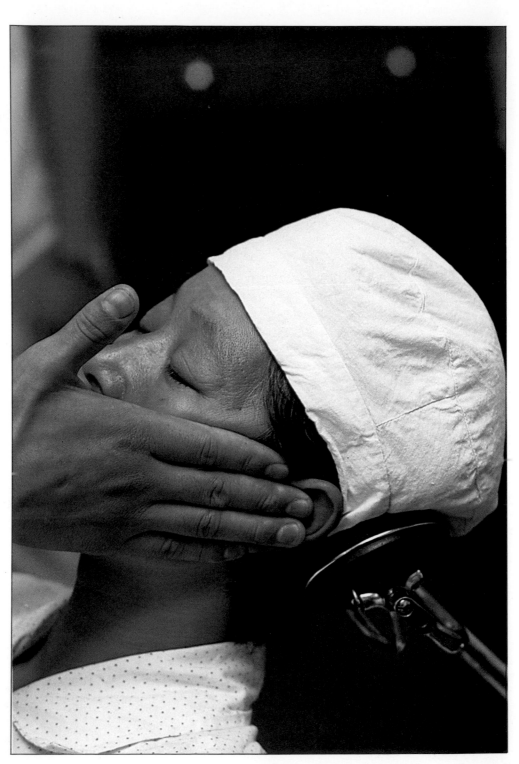

EAST V WEST

Traditional Chinese medicine is undoubtedly 'holistic'; far more so, indeed, than any other system of alternative medicine in the West. It provides an exceedingly sophisticated and comprehensive framework for medical practice, and the fact that it has served an extraordinarily intelligent and subtle civilization for over 2,000 years certainly means that it 'works'. When it comes to transposing it to the West, however, considerable problems arise. These are of many kinds — conceptual, cultural, and linguistic. Westerners and Chinese have different mental concepts, and often there are no terms in Western language to render these concepts; this has repeatedly led to serious misunderstandings. Apart from these difficulties, there are the scientific questions of whether such things as acupuncture points and channels do actually exist, and whether pulse diagnosis gives any objective information.

Attempts have been made to answer questions of this kind but the results have been inconclusive. Concerning the pulses, for instance, machines have recorded the pulses objectively, and it is claimed that many of the classic pulse categories can be detected. This has been disputed, however, and, even if the pulse patterns do exist, there is still the question of what, if anything, they mean. The interpretation of the pulses is necessarily in terms of traditional Chinese diagnosis, and it is difficult or impossible to translate this into Western concepts and terminology.

The existence of acupuncture points and channels is equally problematical. Early claims, that structures corresponding to these entities could be seen under the microscope have proved unfounded, and the most recent research has been based on the idea that the electrical resistance of the skin is reduced over acupuncture points. A large number of machines now exist for 'point detection', working on this principle.

Unfortunately, most people who have looked into this critically have come to the conclusion that 'point detection' does not work. It is very easy for the experimenter to mislead himself unconsciously; for example, pressing a little harder or longer with the probe will produce an 'acupuncture point'. Using a careful technique, it is possible to demonstrate areas of lowered electrical resistance objectively at various places on the skin, but these do not necessarily correspond to classic acupuncture points.

Experiences of this kind have led a number of Western doctors to feel considerable scepticism about much of the theoretical underpinning of traditional acupuncture. In spite of this scepticism, however, they have found that acupuncture does work in practice in a number of diseases, though by no means in all. Indeed, it often works astonishingly well in cases where there is no effective orthodox treatment, so that in such instances it could reasonably be considered the treatment of choice. But they have also found that it need not be practised in the classic Chinese way. To the more radical, this suggests that it may not be necessary to use the conceptual system of *chi*, points, channels and the rest, and that the theory of traditional acupuncture, though valid for the Chinese, may not be ideally suited for Western doctors wishing to practise acupuncture. Hence, there has grown up what might be called a form of scientific acupuncture.

SCIENTIFIC ACUPUNCTURE

Scientific acupuncture is a new branch of Western medicine. The ideas and practices are constantly changing and evolving, as new theories and techniques are introduced, and only some general indications of the scientific approach are possible here.

Scientific acupuncture ignores the concepts of yin-yang, chi, and so on. It also rejects the existence of channels or points. Instead, it assumes that acupuncture works via the nervous system, and that its effects can, in principle, be explained in terms of scientific anatomy and physiology, although, admittedly, the phenomena of acupuncture will probably require the introduction of some new concepts about how the body, and especially the nervous system, works. At present, it is impossible to put forward a comprehensive scientific theory of acupuncture; the best that can be done is to indicate some of the theories and pieces of practical information that may eventually come together in a more comprehensive picture.

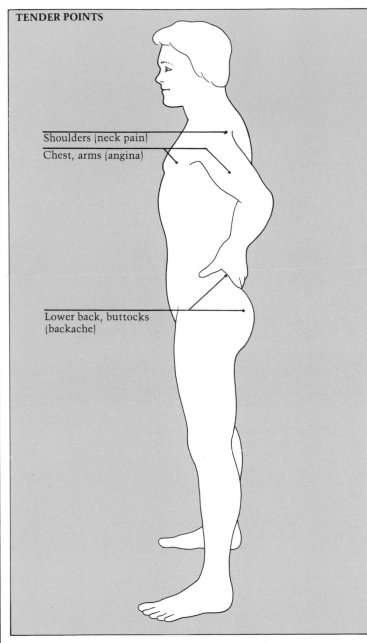

TENDER POINTS

Shoulders (neck pain)

Chest, arms (angina)

Lower back, buttocks (backache)

Tender points (*above*) refer pain from a specific source to the surface of the body. When the point is treated, the pain is relieved. Tender points are often the same as acupuncture points.

The 'tender points' It has been known for many years that disease of the internal organs, or deep structures, may be associated with 'tender points' or 'trigger points' at the surface of the body. Sometimes, nodules can be felt in the tissues under the skin at these places; sometimes, there is nothing much to feel but the patient experiences pain, which may be quite severe, when they are pressed. Tender areas of this kind occur in many kinds of disease. For example, in heart disease (angina), they may be found in the muscles on the front or back of the chest, and sometimes in the arm muscles. In backache, they often lie in the back muscles or the buttocks. If the neck is painful, they are commonly found in the muscles on top of the shoulders. Menstrual disorders may be associated with tender areas on the inside of the shins.

There is no general agreement about what causes these tender points. In many cases, they seem to correspond to the places where the main nerve supplying a muscle enters it; sometimes they overlie nerve complexes elsewhere in the body. Whatever their cause, however, it has been recognized for a long time that treating them — massaging them, freezing them, or injecting them with various substances — can relieve pain in the appropriate associated structure or organ, either temporarily or permanently. This was known long before acupuncture became popular in the West. Some doctors also realized that there was no need to inject anything at all to produce this effect — merely inserting a plain needle was enough. This is acupuncture by definition, for the word merely means puncturing the skin with needles.

A very important part of scientific acupuncture, therefore, is the treatment of tender points wherever they may be found, and much of the skill of the scientific acupuncturist consists of knowing where such points are located, and how best to stimulate them when found. Comparison of the common trigger or tender points with classic acupuncture points shows that they are often the same, and it does not seem unreasonable to believe that, in many cases, this is how the classic acupuncture points were discovered.

An interesting observation is that, when a needle is put into a trigger point, the patient

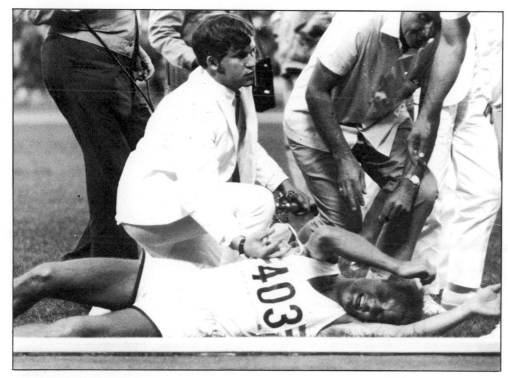

Athletes (*left*) often suffer injuries — a pulled muscle or a sprained tendon, for example — while in action but do not feel pain until the race is over. This illustrates the 'gate' theory, where gates in the spine can inhibit the flow of pain messages.

often experiences various types of sensation spreading up or down the limb in a pattern that recalls the distribution of the relevant acupuncture channel. This could explain how the channel theory came into existence in the first place. The scientific acupuncturist, however, prefers to believe that such effects are due to the spread of excitation patterns within the nervous system, which are then 'projected' to the body, rather in the manner of a 'referred pain' or 'phantom limb pain'.

Endorphins and enkephalins Another piece of the puzzle may be found in the recently discovered fact that acupuncture causes the release of endorphins and enkephalins.

Some years ago, it was discovered that the body produces substances whose effects include, among other things, reduction in pain perception. They appear to act in the same way as morphine and have, therefore, been called internally-produced opioids. Two main classes have been studied: beta-endorphin and met-enkephalin.

Acupuncture took a large step towards scientific respectability when it was dis-

covered that it caused the release of these substances. More precisely, fast stimulation (performed electrically) causes release of beta-endorphin, while slow stimulation, including the manual manipulation of the needles which is most commonly used in practice, causes release of met-enkephalin.

These discoveries are very interesting, but it is not yet clear what they mean. Release of endorphins and enkephalins may play a part in acupuncture analgesia, and probably help to explain the euphoric dreamy state that some people experience during treatment, but it is hard to see how it could account for the prolonged and even permanent relief of pain that can be achieved, sometimes after just one brief treatment. The solution to this conundrum will come only from improved understanding of how the nervous system works. The 'gate control theory' of the scientists, Melzack and Wall, may be relevant here.

The 'gate' theory The details of the theory are somewhat complicated but the basic idea is fairly simple. It is that the spinal cord possesses 'gates' or 'valves', that can open to

A more dramatic example of the 'gate' theory is the phenomenon of injuries sustained in battle, which, temporarily at least, cause no pain. (Illustration: 'At bay', the Battle of Isandula, January 22, 1879.)

allow pain messages or close to shut them off. The gates are thought to close and open in two ways. Firstly, they are affected by messages arriving at the spinal cord from the rest of the body — that is, via the peripheral nerves. Acupuncture presumably acts on the gates in this way.

Secondly, the gates can also be opened or closed by messages coming *down* the spinal cord from the brain stem and other higher centers, including those concerned with awareness and memory. This explains why a patient's attitude to acupuncture plays a considerable part in determining the patient's response.

This theory represents pain perception as a dynamic concept. Our ability to perceive pain is not a fixed mechanical thing but constantly fluctuates, according to the net balance of information arriving from all quarters. The gate mechanism in the spinal cord could be compared to a railway signalman, who has to decide whether to let the train through or not, on the basis of information reaching him both from down the line, where the train is at present, and from up the line where there are other trains and the central control office, which may wish to override his local decision.

The gate theory can account for the well-known fact that an injury received on the football field or in battle may produce no pain at the time, yet a similar injury suffered in different circumstances would be agonizing. It may also explain the analgesia induced by hypnosis and other forms of trance. It also seems relevant to acupuncture. None of this, of course, proves that the theory is right; it may, in the end, prove entirely mistaken. For the present, however, it does provide some kind of rational explanation for acupuncture-induced pain relief.

However, acupuncture seems to work for other kinds of disease as well as painful ones, and this is harder to explain in scientific terms. Provided that these effects are not entirely due to placebo, it may be that they depend on stimulation of the autonomic, immune, and endocrine systems via the hypothalamus. Given that acupuncture causes release of endorphins and enkephalins, it seems probable that it might have other more widespread effects as well. Such ideas will have to await further research to be refuted or confirmed.

WHICH KIND OF ACUPUNCTURE?

Since there are two versions of acupuncture, one traditional and one scientific, it is natural to ask which is better. In many cases, oddly enough, it may not make much difference. This is because a non-specific benefit can be obtained from inserting a needle anywhere. This is partly a placebo response, but physiological effects from random needling can also be demonstrated in animals. The task of the acupuncturist, therefore, is to improve on this basic non-specific effect.

Traditional acupuncturists claim that precise identification of acupuncture points and selection of treatments, according to classic Chinese theory, give better results than ignoring points and theory and using a scientific approach. They do admit that the difference is small — a figure of ten percent is sometimes quoted. The trouble is that a small difference of this order is almost impossible to demonstrate, even with an elaborate clinical trial, and since even simple comparative trials of the required kind are lacking, assertions about which system is better are meaningless. What scientific acupuncturists can say is, firstly, that there is no prospect of getting the vast majority of Western doctors to study traditional Chinese medicine, even if the means were available, which they are not. However, if acupuncture is presented in a way doctors can understand, more will be prepared to study it and use it.

Secondly, a scientific approach can throw up new ideas of treatment which do not exist in the traditional approach. One example is periosteal or bone acupuncture, which has been pioneered by a British doctor practising acupuncture, Felix Mann. This consists of needling the periosteum (the membrane covering the bones), the ligaments, and other deep structures around the joints to relieve arthritis and other painful disorders. The technique appears to give considerably better results in such cases than are achieved by the classic methods. Another example is the use of electrical machines to stimulate the nerves through the skin via conducting pads instead of needles.

To some extent, the opposition between

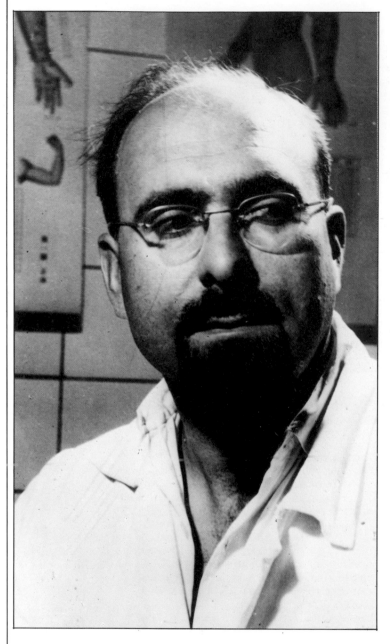

traditional and scientific acupuncture is an artificial one. Today, the Chinese themselves are open to new ideas and new techniques, and do not cling obstinately to the ideas of the past. It is among some Western practitioners that one finds the most extreme and intransigent attitudes. It remains true, nevertheless, that there is a fairly clear difference in the approach of the two schools. So what does this mean to you, the patient?

In some cases, you will get successful results from either a traditional or a scientific acupuncturist. However, nearly all scientific acupuncturists are also qualified doctors, which means that you are in the hands of someone who is familiar with anatomy and the need for sterilization of needles. Good lay acupuncturists are also familiar with these things, but remember that anyone can call himself an acupuncturist, at least in Britain. With acupuncture particularly, it is essential to make sure that your therapist knows what he is doing. Success with acupuncture depends more on manual skill and dexterity than on theory, and these qualities may be possessed by both types of therapist. But a scientific acupuncturist may be able to call on techniques not in the repertoire of most traditionalists.

None of these remarks should be taken to mean that traditional Chinese ideas are primitive or unsophisticated, lacking any relevance for us. On the contrary, they are fascinating and profound, and few people who have studied them in any depth doubt that the West has much to learn from them. Indeed, the ancient sages anticipated some fundamental ideas of modern science. For example, it is not difficult to see the yin-yang polarity reflected in the concept of positive and negative electricity. Later Chinese thought contains a remarkable anticipation of modern physicists' view that wave phenomena are an essential clue to the nature of matter, and a central place is accorded to what we would now call field theories.

Fascinating though these correspondences are, however, it is arguably in psychiatry, sociology, philosophy, and even politics and economics, that Chinese ideas can be most illuminating. Thus the concept of yin-yang polarity can be extraordinarily fruitful when applied to problems of per-

While acupuncture now has considerable authority in Western medicine, its 'scientific' application rejects the traditional Eastern philosophy behind yin and yang, meridians etc, and tries to explain itself in terms of the nervous system and traditional anatomy. Dr Richard Umlauf (*above*) has pioneered the use of acupuncture in surgery in Czechoslovakia.

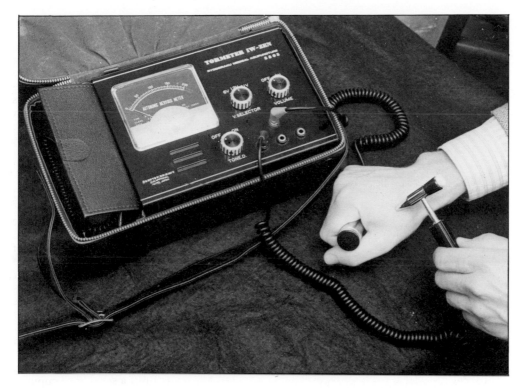

The point detector (*left*) was developed in an attempt to detect and monitor the electrical discharge of acupuncture points.

sonal development and interpersonal relationships, and to both small- and large-scale industrial relations.

Granted that the traditional ideas are relevant in such ways to our modern world, it may seem perverse and unreasonable to say that they are unnecessary for the practice of acupuncture, which, after all, originated in China. It is perfectly possible for Westerners to practise acupuncture on the traditional basis, but is it necessary to do so? Experience in the West suggests that acupuncture works equally satisfactorily in practice whichever theory is used. Practitioners with a Western scientific education usually feel happier using a scientific approach, and this appears quite justifiable, though it does not, of course, preclude them from adopting traditional insights whenever they think it advisable.

On the whole, an eclectic approach of this kind seems to be the best to adopt. It is as well to remember that all our theories are bound to be partial one-sided versions of reality, and it would be unwise to set too much store by any of them.

ACUPUNCTURE IN PRACTICE

It would not be practicable or desirable to give a complete list of disorders suitable for acupuncture treatment, since each case is different. Some rather broad generalizations, however, can be attempted.

The commonest group of disorders to be treated with acupuncture are painful conditions of the muscles and joints. These include arthritis of various kinds, 'wear and tear' in the spine (spondylosis), and a whole range of other painful disorders, including backache, which lack a proper diagnostic label, because their real cause is unknown. (Some were often called 'fibrositis' in the past.) Patients suffering from such problems constitute the bulk of an acupuncturist's work, and the results are good. For most of such disorders, there should be a 'good' or 'very good' response (considerable relief or complete cure) in about two-thirds of the cases, perhaps more. (Remember that this means one third will *not* respond; this can be disappointing if you happen to fall into this group.)

Among disorders other than those affecting muscles and joints, the results are variable. Some gynecological disorders, especially menstrual problems, respond well; menopausal symptoms can also be helped in some cases. Allergic disorders, including hay fever and nettle rash, can quite often be improved. Acupuncture is always worth trying for headaches. It can often relieve pain due to incurable disorders such as diverticulosis and, indeed, pain relief in general is one area where acupuncture is often successful. This can include unexplained pain of various kinds and even pain from cancer, although it is important to understand that acupuncture cannot cure the underlying problem in such cases. Psychological tension can often be relieved, at least temporarily. Sometimes in such cases, acupuncture produces a remarkable emotional release: the patient may cry for several hours after treatment and then feel much better. Asthma often responds very well, but usually the results are only fair. Skin diseases, such as eczema and psoriasis, also sometimes improve but again not predictably.

There is also an interesting group of patients who complain of feeling generally unwell, although they have no very definite symptoms — perhaps slight nausea, fatigue, lack of energy. Sometimes this is attributed to a persistent viral infection. Many of these patients are labeled as neurotic or depressed, and a few of them do, indeed, have a primarily psychological disturbance, but not all. Such patients can often be helped dramatically by acupuncture, and this is important, because conventional medicine really has little to offer people who feel generally run down, but who have no definite diagnosis.

With any kind of complaint, what seems to decide the outcome of treatment is often the responsiveness of the individual patient, rather than the precise diagnosis. Some people do much better than others. A few (about two to five percent of the population, depending where the line is drawn) can be classified as *strong reactors*. These are patients who do exceptionally well with acupuncture. They almost always find acupuncture a pleasurable experience. Usually within a few seconds of the needles' insertion, they feel deeply relaxed, even drowsy, or alternatively they feel unusually alert and awake. They may feel strange but not unpleasant sensations in the opposite limb to that being treated, or in another part of the body. After acupuncture, they may want to go to sleep. These effects do not seem to be due to suggestion and strong reactors are usually perfectly normal psychologically. Possibly, the phenomenon is caused by release of metenkephalin. Whatever the explanation, it means that the patient is likely to do well with acupuncture, provided he or she is treated lightly; if stimulated too much, a strong reactor may feel ill for a day or so.

It is often, though not always, possible to recognize strong reactors before treatment. They are usually under 35 and have a bright-eyed look. They often have a bad history with a wide range of conventional drugs. They may also be subject to allergies. Children should always be regarded as strong reactors and treated lightly; often they do well with acupuncture.

The converse of the strong reactor is the patient who is afraid of acupuncture. Such people do badly with acupuncture and should not be treated with this method, a fact long recognized by traditional Chinese physicians.

It is also wise to avoid treatment during pregnancy. This is not an absolute rule and there may be cases in which treatment is justified but, on the whole, the potential risks outweigh the benefits.

WHAT HAPPENS IN ACUPUNCTURE?

If you go to an acupuncturist for treatment, he or she will first take a history of your complaint in the usual way and then probably take your pulses. The details of the technique may vary from one practitioner to another.

In traditional acupuncture, from five to 15 points are usually stimulated in a session. The needles are inserted and usually left in place for about 20 minutes, during which time they may be manipulated at intervals. Manipulation consists mainly in either twirling the needle back and forth, or in

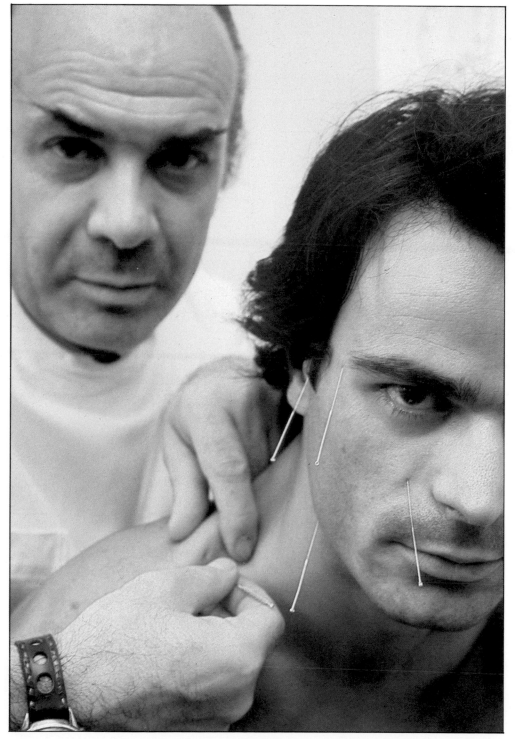

Needles are pushed into the surface of the skin, sometimes to a depth of an inch or more. The tip is rounded, so that it tends to push aside blood vessels rather than break them and cause bleeding.

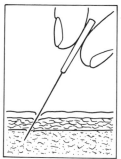

Three ways of applying moxibustion: Small moxa cones (*above*) made of dried mugwort and slow burning, are placed over acupuncture points to gently warm them.

may be used, and these are not necessarily tender. In such cases, the practices of scientific and traditional acupuncture resemble each other, and the main difference between the two approaches lies in the underlying theoretical concepts.

It is natural to ask whether acupuncture hurts. The answer is that it usually does, though not excessively. The amount of pain depends partly on the thickness of the needle and quite a lot on where it is inserted, since some sites are much more painful than others. It also depends on the sensitivity of the individual patient. Usually, there is a quick stab of pain as the skin is pierced, followed some time later by a deeper duller ache and possibly other sensations, which many patients find difficult to describe. At the same time, the needle, if it is in a muscle, may be firmly gripped so that the acupuncturist feels a definite resistance to twirling it. The phenomena are known collectively as 'Teh Chi' (obtaining chi) and are regarded as a favorable sign — indeed, some acupuncturists believe that the treatment will not succeed if they do not occur, though this is probably an exaggeration.

Many patients are surprised that acupuncture does not cause bleeding. Actually, it sometimes does, but more often not. This is because of the type of needle used. Acupuncture needles, which are usually of steel, have relatively blunt points, unlike the typical hypodermic needle which has a cutting edge. Acupuncture needles usually push blood vessels and other structures aside instead of piercing them, and this tends to minimize both bleeding and internal damage.

EFFECTS OF ACUPUNCTURE

Patients frequently report a sense of relaxation soon after the needles have been inserted. In a strong reactor, this may amount, as already described, to feelings of well-being or floating; patients familiar with the effects of marijuana sometimes say the sensations are similar, while others compare acupuncture to taking alcohol.

If the patient is suffering from pain, this may be relieved dramatically and completely, in some cases, almost as soon as the needle or needles are inserted. Such a happy outcome is impressive for both patient and

gently lifting it in and out.

Some scientific acupuncturists use a very similar procedure to the traditionalists as regards numbers of needles and duration of treatment. Others tend to stimulate fewer points — perhaps only two or three, occasionally only one — and for much shorter periods, often only a minute or two. An important part of the approach used by the scientific acupuncturist is the search for tender points. These may or may not correspond to classic acupuncture points, but this is irrelevant. In the case of painful disorders of the muscles or joints, the tender points may lie in the nearby structures. But if a more generalized illness is being treated, such as a menstrual disorder or simply a general lack of well-being, points on the limbs, for example, in the hands and feet,

The heat generated by moxa travels down the needle (*left*) into the point and along the meridian.

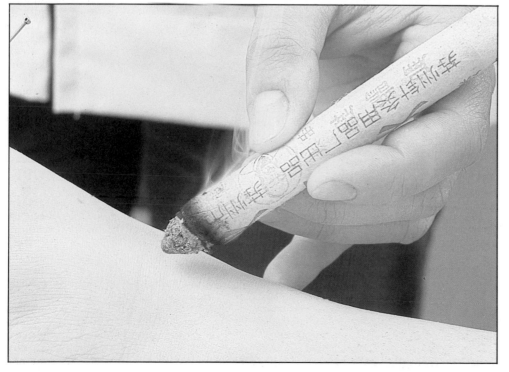

The hot tip of a moxa roll (*left*) is held close to a point until the heat becomes uncomfortable. This process is then repeated.

Patients often experience a sense of deep relaxation during treatment, and sometimes their symptoms completely disappear, with a subsequent feeling of release and exhilaration.

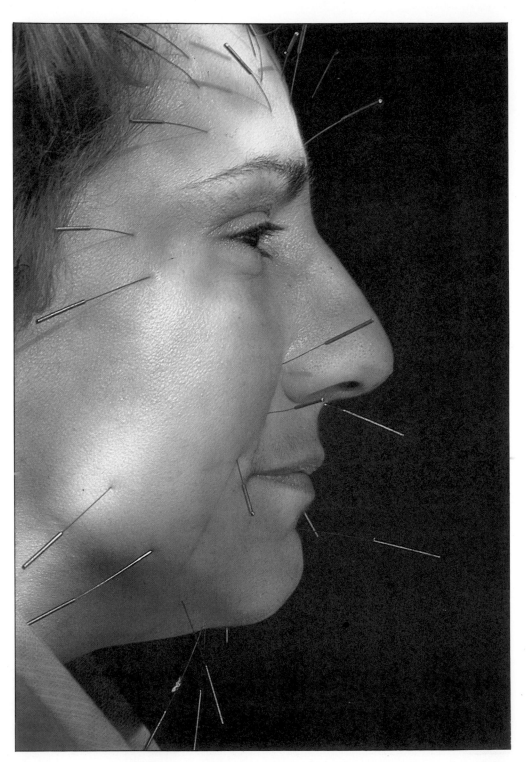

therapist. In other cases, improvement takes some hours or even days.

Some patients, on the other hand, experience a temporary worsening of their symptoms, which can last for a few hours or even a day or two. Such worsening is usually, though not invariably, followed by an improvement. It may indicate that the patient has been treated too strongly, but for some patients it happens regularly and they come to expect it.

The duration of any improvement varies from patient to patient. Usually, the initial treatment produces some improvement, often only partial, which lasts for a few days. After this, the patient returns more or less to his original state. Further treatments produce improvements that last longer, until ideally, a complete cure is achieved. The effects of any individual treatment, however, are unpredictable: some treatments help some ailments considerably, others less, and some not at all.

Likewise the number and frequency of treatments needed vary from case to case. In China, patients often have acupuncture daily for ten days at a time but, in the West, treatment is usually given at weekly intervals to start with. As a rule, at least some improvement should be apparent by about the third treatment; if this has not occurred, acupuncture is probably not going to work. In a favorable case, the intervals between treatments can be lengthened progressively until a complete cure is achieved.

However, in many cases, complete cure is not possible, but acupuncture can produce variable lengths of remission. The patient and therapist must then decide jointly whether it is worthwhile continuing the treatment at intervals. There can be no generalizations about this, but a reasonable working rule is that remission should last eight weeks to make it worth continuing with treatment. There are, however, some exceptions to this. For example, some patients suffering from cancer have obtained considerable pain relief from acupuncture, but this does not last very long and, as the disease advances, the pain-free intervals may get shorter. Such patients have sometimes been taught to treat themselves with self-acupuncture. The same approach is often used in patients suffering from hay

Acupressure, or cupping (*left*) involves making a vacuum within a cup by burning off the air inside with a swab of methylated spirits and quickly inverting the cup over an acupuncture point. This area of skin is drawn into the cup.

fever, who may also obtain good but short-lived relief. However, self-treatment of this kind is usually carried out not with needles but with pressing on appropriate areas of the body. In fact, it is not essential to use needles for stimulation; in principle, any method can be used, and simple pressure works fairly well, though it is less effective than needling. Popular books sometimes call this 'acupressure'.

DANGERS OF ACUPUNCTURE

For obvious reasons, acupuncture is potentially more dangerous than most other forms of alternative medicine. The main risks are infection and damage to the internal organs. The most serious form of infection that may occur is hepatitis, which can be transmitted from one patient to another by microscopically small quantities of blood. As boiling the needles does not eliminate the risk of transmitting hepatitis, all reputable practitioners use a more effective means of sterilization, such as autoclaving.

Avoiding damage to internal organs depends on a knowledge of anatomy. Acupuncture in the limbs is relatively safe but the head, neck, and chest are potential danger areas.

These risks, though real enough, should not discourage people from receiving treatment from a properly trained therapist. Some books by traditional acupuncturists give the impression that wrong selection of points can damage a patient's health for long periods, or even permanently. This fear, fortunately, is unfounded. It is true that over-vigorous treatment can produce a temporary worsening of symptoms, and it is also true that such treatment can make a strong reactor feel distinctly unwell for a day or two, but there is no convincing evidence for long-term deleterious effects.

In summary, therefore, acupuncture is a safe form of treatment, provided it is competently carried out.

SPECIALIZED FORMS OF ACUPUNCTURE

There are several specialized techniques or

In another form of acupressure the cups are equipped with a needle that enters the skin as it is drawn into the vacuum.

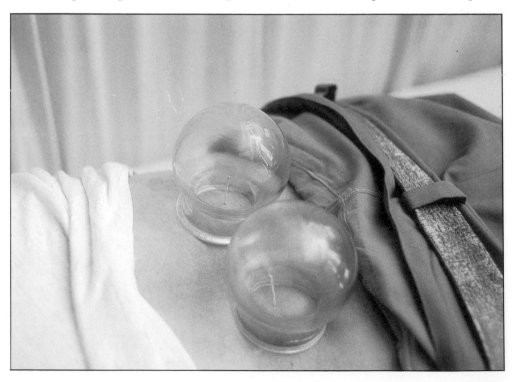

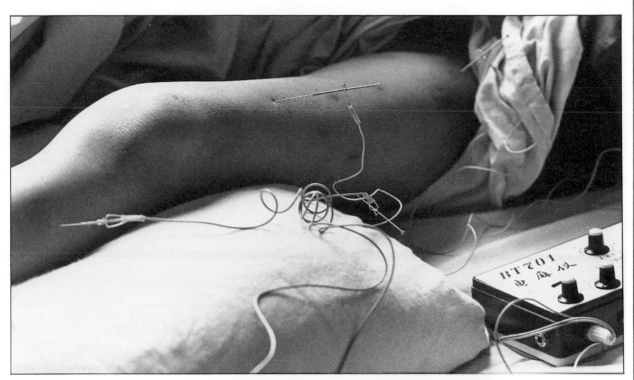

Instead of heat, a seven-volt electric current is passed down the needles (*above*) to stimulate and reeducate the muscles of a polio victim. Electroacupuncture can also be used in treating the ear (*left*).

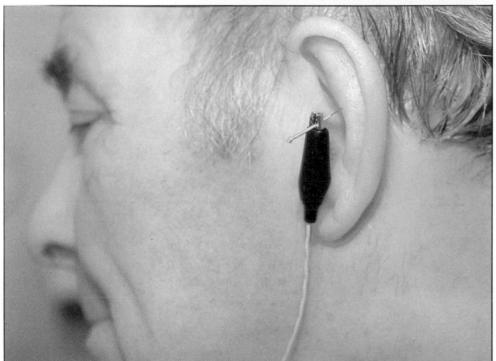

As well as electroacupuncture, which is only useful in long periods of needle manipulation, the use of low-power laser beams has also been developed recently.

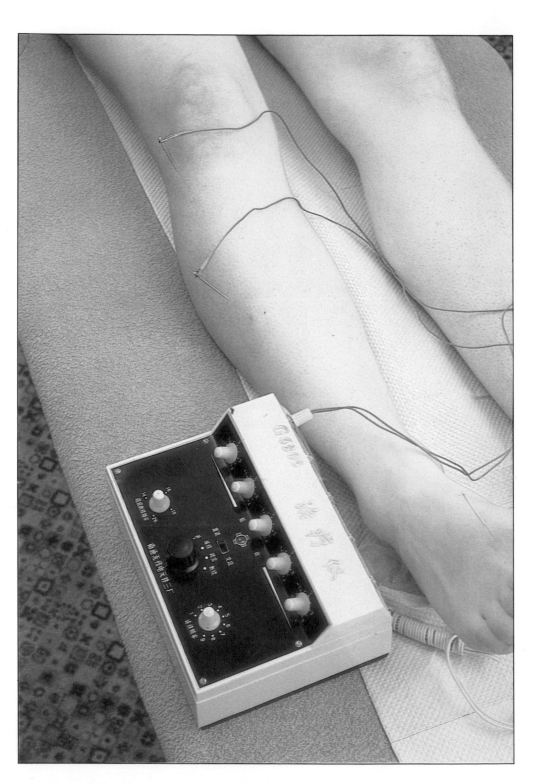

applications of acupuncture that need to be discussed separately.

Electroacupuncture and laser acupuncture

In addition to machines that purport to detect acupuncture points, there are also many that are used for stimulation. These work by feeding a small electric current through a pair of needles inserted in different sites; usually several pairs can be supplied from the one instrument. For technical reasons, the current used is alternating, the frequency being either slow (from about 3 to 100 Hz) or less frequently, fast (above 200 Hz). As mentioned earlier, fast and slow stimulation give rise to different kinds of physiological response; slow stimulation is generally regarded as the more useful form.

Opinions of the value of electrical stimulation vary, but many experienced therapists think that it offers no real advantage over manual acupuncture, and has some disadvantages. Manual manipulation of the needles allows the therapist to gauge the effect on the patient more accurately, and to adjust the intensity of stimulation to the patient's response. It also allows feedback to the therapist from the 'feel' of the needle in the tissues, and this can be a valuable supplementary means of judging the results. Certainly, for acupuncturists who use only short (one to two minutes) stimulation at a few places, there is no purpose in using electrical methods. If several needles are put in and left for 20 minutes or so, there may be some reason to use these machines.

The recently introduced technique of laser acupuncture is more controversial. The only real advantages claimed for it is that there is no risk of infection and, since it is pain-free, it can be used on children and others who are afraid of ordinary acupuncture. The lasers used are relatively low-power and penetrate only a short distance below the skin. They thus appear to be fairly safe (though they should not be directed at the eyes) but whether they work is another matter. Some acupuncturists have been impressed, contrary to their initial expectations, while others have found them ineffective. In view of the high cost of the apparatus, it does not seem likely that they will come in to widespread use, at least for some time to come.

Transcutaneous nerve stimulation

This technique is related to acupuncture and probably works in much the same way. It is a method of pain relief in which a small alternating electric current passes through the tissues between two conducting pads. The current is produced by a small portable battery-powered machine that works on the same principle as those used for electroacupuncture. The units are often quite small, something like a pocket radio receiver.

The frequency of stimulation is usually set at about 60 to 100 Hz, and the patient can adjust the power output to a level that he or she finds comfortable. The pads are placed either over the painful area or over a major nerve supplying the area; conducting jelly is used to provide maximum contact. If the treatment works, pain relief often begins soon after the machine is switched on. Treatment usually continues for about half an hour, although, if necessary, it can be longer. After the machine is switched off, pain relief can last sometimes for a few hours, sometimes till the next day. However, transcutaneous nerve stimulation is not a cure; sooner or later, the pain will return, but it can be eliminated or reduced again by further stimulation. This is, therefore, best thought of as a drug-free method of pain relief.

Some kinds of pain do well with this kind of treatment: they include osteoarthritic pain, trigeminal neuralgia, back pain, the kind of pain that can follow shingles, and pain in amputation stumps. With certain other kinds of pain, it is ineffective. Transcutaneous nerve stimulation sometimes works in patients for whom acupuncture has failed, though the converse is also true. It is usually worthwhile for patients who only respond well to acupuncture for short periods. The treatment is safe and does not lose its effectiveness with time. There are a number of different machines on the market, nearly all of which work satisfactorily. Prices are not exorbitant and are roughly comparable to those of a portable personal stereo recorder.

Acupuncture and surgery

Western interest in acupuncture began in the early 1970s, when visitors to China brought back extraordinary reports of operations being carried out without anesthetics, pain relief being induced by means of acupuncture. At first sceptics dismissed these reports, suggesting that perhaps the patients were hypnotized. Later, however, surgery under acupuncture analgesia was actually witnessed by Western surgeons and anesthetists, and moving pictures of such operations were brought back to the West. It became clear that there was something in the travellers' tales.

Nevertheless, as time passed, a somewhat less dramatic picture emerged. There was, indeed, some exaggeration in the earlier Chinese claims. In the first place, even when acupuncture was used, ordinary anaesthesia was always on hand as an additional aid. Patients also received orthodox premedication with conventional drugs before surgery. Secondly, the number of patients considered suitable for acupuncture analgesia was much smaller than original reports suggested — less than five percent, in fact, which corresponds in an interesting way with the proportion of the Western population who are strong reactors to acupuncture.

Some research in the West carried out by Dr Mann among others shed further light on this fascinating enigma. In most people, acupuncture analgesia simply does not work. It does, however, work in some strong reactors. What is interesting is that there seems to be no obvious relationship between where the needles are inserted and where the pain-free areas are located. For example, inserting a needle in the hand or foot may produce analgesia almost anywhere. In one subject, it did so in the tonsils; in another, the analgesia was in the upper gums. The subjects themselves are usually unaware that they have lost pain sensation, and it can only be detected by pricking them here and there with a needle.

Acupuncture analgesia does work for a small number of people, but it is not reliable or predictable. Thus, its practical importance is small and acupuncture analgesia has not been adopted to any great extent in the West. It is, however, of great theoretical interest; it does not seem to be due to suggestion or hypnosis and the explanation for why it occurs at all poses a considerable challenge to neurologists.

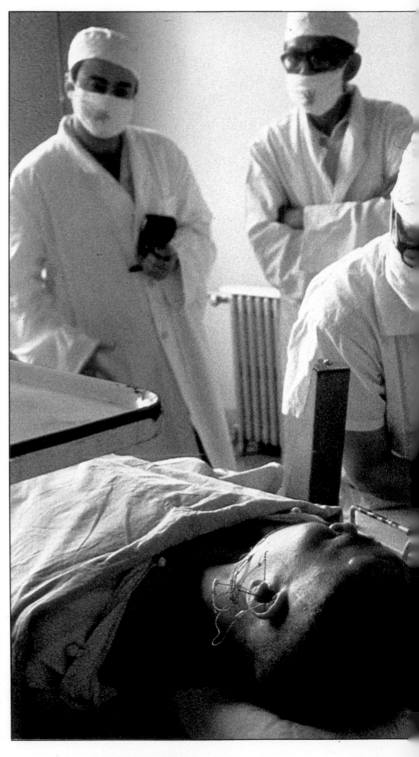

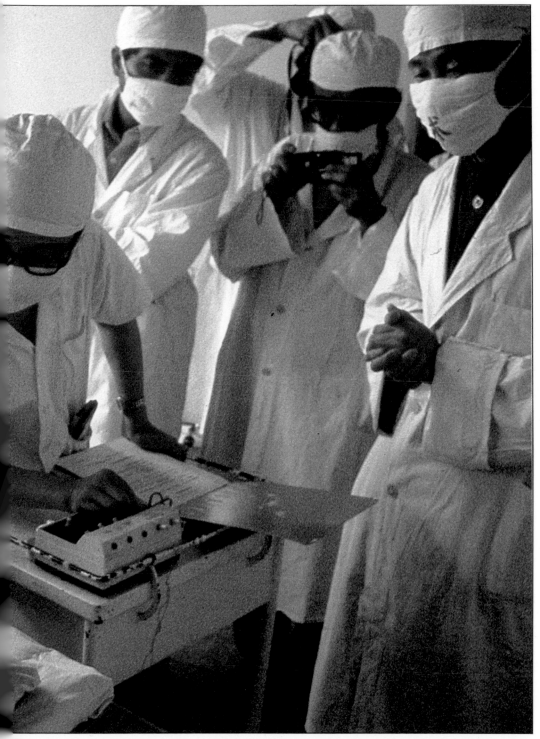

An operation being carried out under electroacupuncture in a Chinese clinic. During the Cultural Revolution, Chairman Mao was eager to promote the traditional techniques of Chinese medicine, and many doctors trained in the West were branded as elitist and lost their jobs.

Ear acupuncture

This is a curious and fascinating byway in the story of acupuncture in the West. It originated about 30 years ago in the work of a French doctor, Paul Nogier. His curiosity was aroused by finding some patients whose sciatica had been relieved by having the upper part of their ear lobes cauterized by a lay practitioner. He found references to this treatment in French medical literature of the nineteenth century and also in Egyptian tomb paintings, and this prompted him to examine the ears of patients suffering from painful disorders. He found that many of them had acutely tender points in their ears, and needling these removed the pain.

Nogier eventually mapped out the areas of the ear that correspond to various organs and parts of the body, and he was led to conclude that the ear contains an upside-down representation of a fetus, with the head represented by the ear lobe, the spine by the middle part (antihelix) and the legs and feet by the upper part (navicular fossa). The Chinese have claimed that some ancient texts support this idea. They soon took up Nogier's theory and transcribed his ear charts into a Chinese version, from which they have been re-transcribed into English. The present position is, thus, somewhat confusing. There are at least two sets of charts, some based directly on Nogier's work, and others on the Chinese interpretation of his work. Not surprisingly, a number of discrepancies exist between the two versions.

Meanwhile, Nogier has gone on to develop new ways of examining the ear. His original method was quite simple, for it was nothing more elaborate than pressing the ear with a probe to look for the tender points.

His next method was to examine the ear for areas of altered electrical resistance. Nogier designed a special instrument, the Punctoscope, for this purpose.

In recent years, Nogier has explored other treatments. The basis of these is the 'auricular cardiac reflex'. Nogier claims that the quality of the radial pulse at the wrist alters in certain subtle ways when light is shone on the ear; different colored lights are used to diagnose various kinds of disease.

As this very brief summary will indicate, Nogier's system of ear acupuncture is very complex. It has been taken up widely in France and Germany but only to a limited extent in Britain, where many medically-qualified acupuncturists are sceptical about it, especially its more esoteric aspects, such as the auricular cardiac reflex. A conservative assessment would be that there are some patients who have tender points on their ears; needling these does sometimes relieve pain, though usually only for a short time. It is not possible to be more definite about this form of acupuncture at present.

Acupuncture to stop smoking and control weight

Advertising columns nowadays frequently contain offers of acupuncture to help you give up smoking or lose weight. These claims sound almost too good to be true; and, unfortunately, they usually are.

The use of acupuncture to control addiction to food or smoking is really a spin-off from ear acupuncture. Usually, a semi-permanent needle, shaped like a small thumbtack or a tiny hatpin, is inserted into an area of the ear supposed to be related to the lungs or stomach. Whenever you feel like having a cigarette or a chocolate, you press the pin; this, allegedly, switches off your wish to smoke or eat.

Unfortunately, research has shown that, although these methods work quite well in the short term (up to about three months), by a year they have ceased to have any effect. This indicates that they have placebo value only and, in so far as they work at all, this seems to be the explanation. In such cases, acupuncture reinforces suggestion. A friend may tell you that he has lost weight or given up smoking since having acupuncture, and this could well be true. But remember that it requires a good deal of motivation to pay for a course of acupuncture, and to submit to the treatment in the first place, and anyone prepared to do this must be fairly determined to stop smoking or lose weight, as the case may be. In other words, what has helped him is willpower, rather than acupuncture.

There can also be some dangers in this kind of treatment. Ordinary acupuncture very seldom causes infection, provided the needles are properly sterilized, but leaving needles in place for a week or more does provide an opportunity for infection and, should this involve the cartilage of the ear, it may be very difficult to clear up. Even more worry-

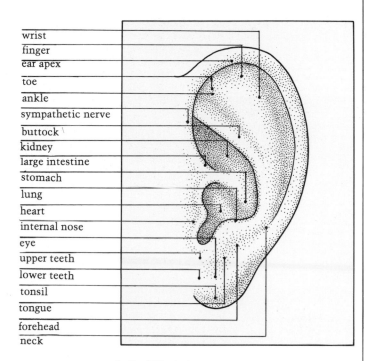

wrist
finger
ear apex
toe
ankle
sympathetic nerve
buttock
kidney
large intestine
stomach
lung
heart
internal nose
eye
upper teeth
lower teeth
tonsil
tongue
forehead
neck

In Paul Nogier's conclusions about ear acupuncture (*above and left*) — or auriculotherapy — the outer ear is shaped like an upside-down fetus. Acupuncture points — about 120 of them — refer in mirror image to areas of the body.

Nogier's findings were taken up by the Chinese, who combined it with their own ancient practice of ear acupuncture (*right*).

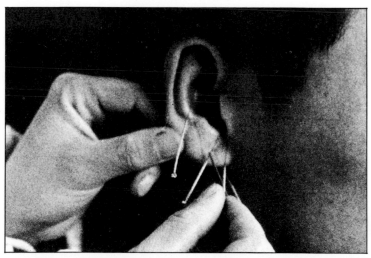

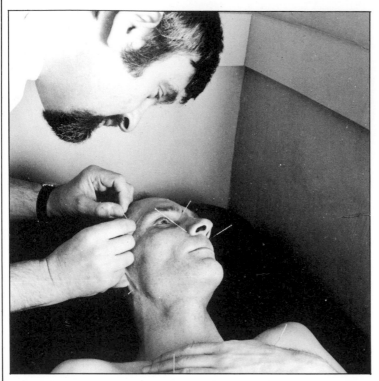

More than seven hundred doctors practise acupuncture in Britain, but most use it as an adjunct to orthodox treatment. The formation of the British Medical Acupuncture Society indicates how seriously the therapy is taken in the United Kingdom.

ing is a recently reported case, in which the use of such needles led to an infection of the heart valves. Admittedly, this is a very rare occurrence and is only likely to happen to someone with valves that were already damaged or abnormal. But it is not always possible to detect such abnormalities in advance, and infection of the heart is such a serious affair that the risk of it constitutes a good reason for avoiding this form of treatment altogether.

Acupuncture in animals

Some veterinary surgeons use acupuncture to treat animals. It is not easy to correlate acupuncture points in human beings with animal anatomy, but this does not matter too much if one is not strongly committed to the traditional system. At any rate, the results of acupuncture in animals appear to be astonishingly good; reports have even appeared of cures of long-lasting paralysis. It is difficult to explain these away as placebo responses. So far, however, too little has been published about veterinary acupuncture to allow any firm conclusions about its possible value.

THE AVAILABILITY OF ACUPUNCTURE

It is fairly easy to obtain acupuncture treatment on the east and west coasts of the United States, but not so easy in some parts of the south and mid-west. There are many lay practitioners, and an ever-increasing number of doctors are also learning the technique. A surprisingly large number of hospitals have one or two doctors on their staff who practise acupuncture. In most cases, this is not done in an acupuncture clinic as such, but forms part of the work of a Pain Clinic. In the last ten years or so, numerous clinics of this kind have been set up in hospitals. They use a variety of techniques — drugs, nerve injection, psychotherapy — and sometimes acupuncture and transcutaneous nerve stimulation as well. These clinics are staffed by anesthetists. Rheumatologists are another group of specialists, some of whom have taken an interest in acupuncture; this is understandable in view of the fact that most of their patients suffer from long-term painful disorders, and the drugs at present available for treatment all have a high incidence of side effects.

PROSPECTS FOR THE FUTURE

The future of acupuncture in the West, at least in a scientific non-traditional form, looks bright. Several acupuncture courses for doctors are held at regular intervals and are well attended, mainly by GPs but also by a number of hospital doctors. It may not be over-optimistic to believe that, within a decade, some instruction in practical acupuncture will be included in the undergraduate curriculum in medical schools. There is, however, a need for more research and clinical trials to convince sceptics that acupuncture is more than a placebo.

Traditional Chinese acupuncture will also continue in the West. The lay colleges of acupuncture teach this form almost exclusively, and there are also some doctors who both practise and teach it.

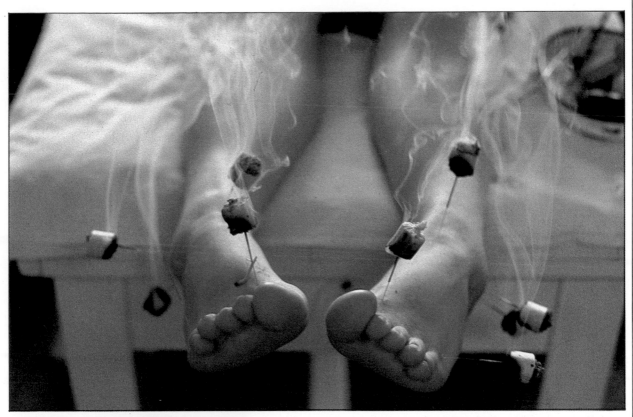

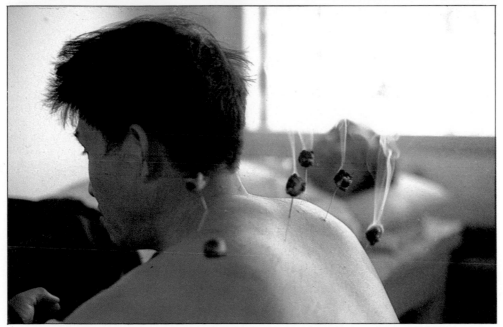

A more general way of treating acupuncture points is to warm them with slow-burning cones of moxa, illustrated here on the feet (*above*) and on the back (*left*).

This barefoot Chinese doctor is confronted by his patients with a directness difficult to imagine in a Western doctor's waiting room.

Cupping treatment (*bottom*) uses bamboo cups to draw up acupuncture points into the vacuum.

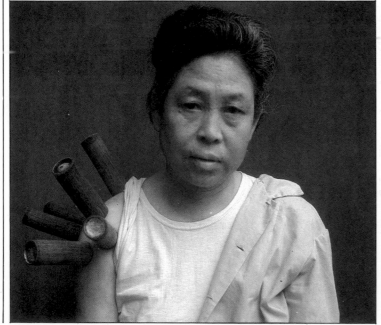

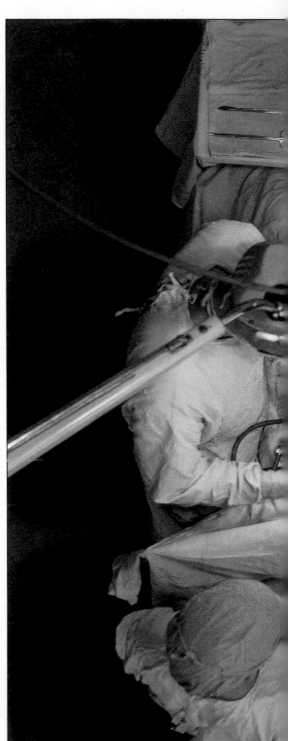

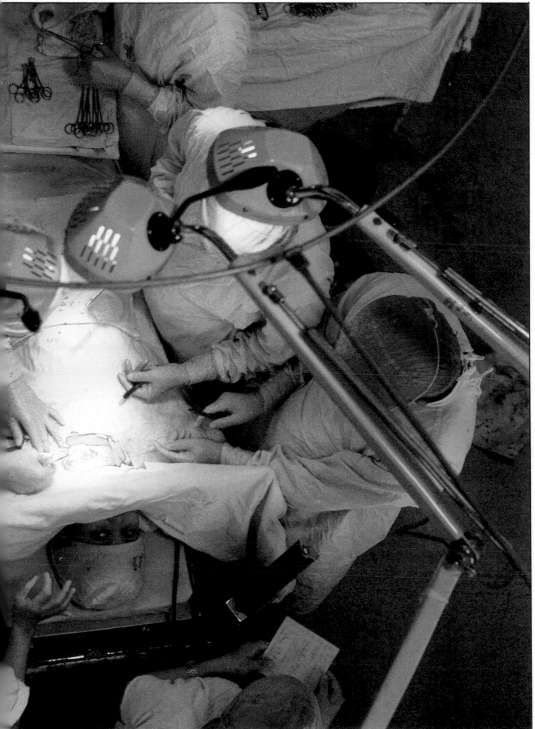

Surgery (*left*), for example Caesarean section and appendectomy, has been carried out with great success in China, using acupuncture for its pain killing effects.

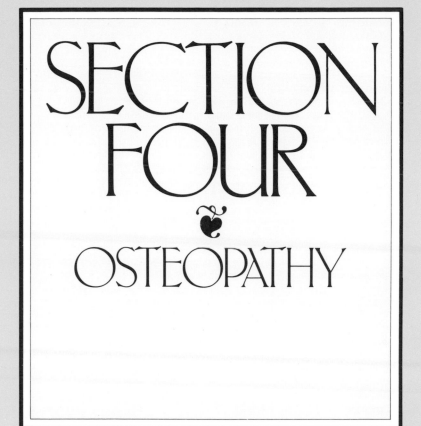

SECTION FOUR

OSTEOPATHY

OSTEOPATHY IS a form of diagnosis and treatment which is concerned with establishing and maintaining the structural and mechanical efficiency of the body's framework. Osteopaths believe this is vital for good health. Treatment is essentially the manipulation of the body, the spine in particular, in order to restore the normal mobility and function of joints and muscles. The word 'osteopathy' comes from two Greek words — *osteo*, or bone, and *pathos*, disease.

ORIGINS OF OSTEOPATHY

Osteopathy was first developed over 100 years ago by an American doctor, Andrew Taylor Still. Still was a qualified engineer as well as a practising doctor, and through his own experiences came to believe that a great many ailments could be explained on a mechanical malfunction basis.

In his early years Still had helped his father, a missionary in a small town in Kansas and had become disenchanted with the inefficacy of conventional medicine to heal or help the sick. This was later reinforced by the death of three of his children from meningitis. Still became convinced that a healthy body was

Andrew Taylor Still (1828-1912), the founder of osteopathy (*right*), believed that the correct alignment of the spine was essential to good health.

dependent on the proper functioning of the body's framework (or musculoskeletal system). He argued that many illnesses affecting the internal organs arose because of problems in the musculoskeletal system. Headaches, skin disorders, digestive troubles and many other ailments which seemingly had nothing to do with the spine were, according to Still, the result of the spinal cord being slightly out of position. By manipulation of the spine in the right place to restore alignment, the condition could be alleviated.

Central to Still's philosophy was the holistic nature of disease. He insisted that disease is related to the whole body, not just to a local part of it, and he believed not only that many ailments were related to spinal disorders but that manipulative therapy also cured other types of non-structural diseases. Gradually through Still's writing and teaching, his methods became known and others took up osteopathy (the word Still coined for his treatment). Still established the first teaching courses in osteopathy at Kirksville, Missouri, in 1892 and not long after Kirksville College, one of America's foremost centers of osteopathic education and research, was founded.

From 1902 American trained osteopaths began to practise in London and rapidly established themselves around the British Isles. Growing demand for treatment led to the establishment of training schools for osteopaths: the British School of Osteopathy in 1917 followed in 1946 by the London College of Osteopathic Medicine and in 1965 by the European School of Osteopathy. Because many other schools were set up with varying standards an attempt was made to get Parliament to set up an official register of trained osteopaths. When this failed the American trained osteopaths set up the Register of Osteopaths to which subsequently the graduates of the three schools named above have been admitted.

WHAT IS OSTEOPATHY?

Most people, including doctors, think of osteopathy as the practice of a range of manipulations to relieve painful problems, mainly of the spine and neck. It might surprise people to know that these treatments are not seen by the contemporary osteopath as the most important part of the contact with a patient. To those who have trained in and practise it, osteopathy is the knowledge, experience, and skill which enables a practitioner to assess how well a particular human body is functioning, as its complex machinery interacts with the demands and stresses imposed by the individual's environment, personality and lifestyle.

Once that assessment is made, the osteopath's function is to provide information and advice which will enable the individual to adapt, so that he or she copes more comfortably and with less risk of harm in the future. When the osteopath has diagnosed a disorder as a response to 'mis-use' of the body, the osteopath expects the adaptations that have been advised to bring about comfort, eventually by natural processes of recovery. Manipulation is seen as a safe, effective way of aiding those natural processes, and so hastens recovery. This is

Dr J. Martin Littlejohn (*left*), a pupil of Still, founded the British School of Osteopathy in 1917.

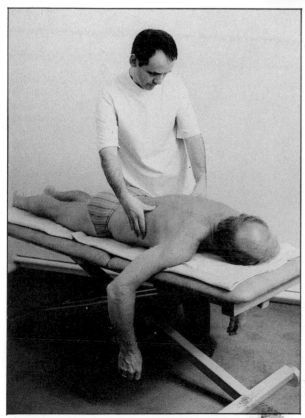

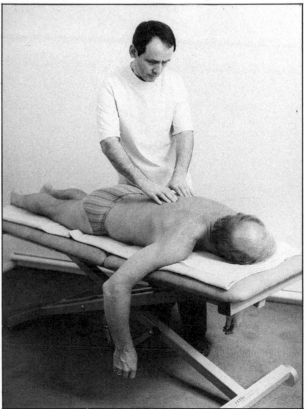

The osteopath must have a thorough knowledge of those structures in the body associated with joints — the bones, the muscles, the ligaments and the nerves.

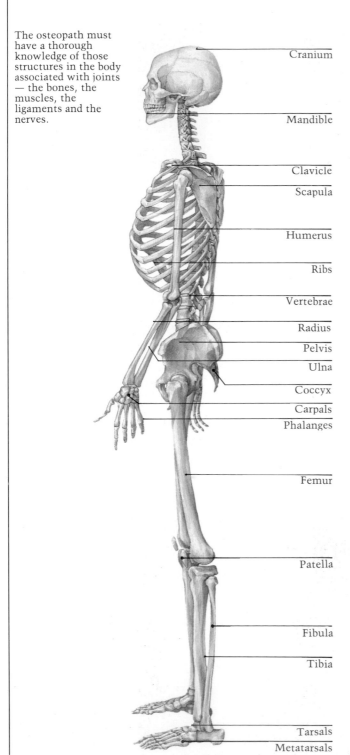

Cranium

Mandible

Clavicle

Scapula

Humerus

Ribs

Vertebrae

Radius

Pelvis

Ulna

Coccyx

Carpals

Phalanges

Femur

Patella

Fibula

Tibia

Tarsals

Metatarsals

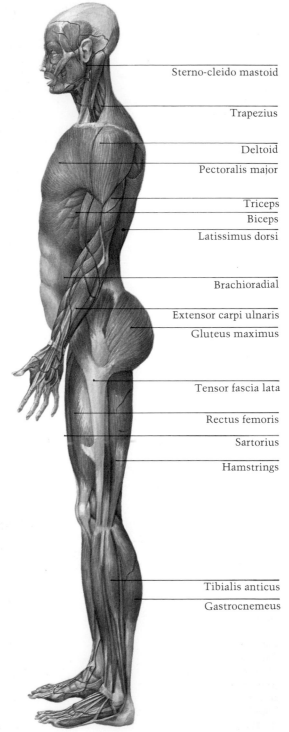

Sterno-cleido mastoid

Trapezius

Deltoid

Pectoralis major

Triceps

Biceps

Latissimus dorsi

Brachioradial

Extensor carpi ulnaris

Gluteus maximus

Tensor fascia lata

Rectus femoris

Sartorius

Hamstrings

Tibialis anticus

Gastrocnemeus

especially true when it is difficult for a patient to change certain aspects of his or her way of life. While manipulation, therefore, is seen as a useful aid to recovery, in the long term the most effective measures to maintain well-being are thought to be those that the patients have been guided into making themselves. These generally relate to posture, way of doing things, choice of activity, response to pain or psychological stress, and in the balance achieved between rest, recreation, work, and exercise. In other words, osteopathy is a holistic treatment, involving the whole body and as such resembles other branches of alternative medicine, notably acupuncture.

How did this approach develop, and why, during the first century of its existence, was it so at odds with orthodox medicine? The answer lies in the theoretical basis of osteopathy and how it arose.

The community uses the osteopath's abilities most for problems of the spine and disabilities directly related to it, and it is on the success with these that the osteopath is mostly judged. However, it should be remembered that osteopathy has claimed a wider application than this. With further acceptance, perhaps leading to involvement in Britain's NHS, it is hoped that the ongoing evaluation of osteopathic methods will include its effectiveness in maladies other than those that involve the musculoskeletal system.

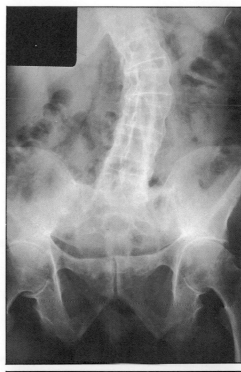

An X-ray of Ankylosing Spondylitis (*left*). The cartilages of the spine gradually fuse together until the backbone is rigid.

PRINCIPLES BEHIND OSTEOPATHY

The fundamental principle of osteopathy is that much of the pain and disability that we suffer stems from mechanical faults in the body's structure, rather than 'pathology' occurring in it. These mechanical faults, originally called 'osteopathic lesions' are now more commonly known as 'dysfunctions'. The terms — pathology and dysfunction — need to be clearly understood.

Pathology
Pathology describes changes taking place in the structures of the body, not just the fluctuations which take place during normal activity, but alterations which involve the body's processes of healing, immunity, etc, to return to normal. These are changes

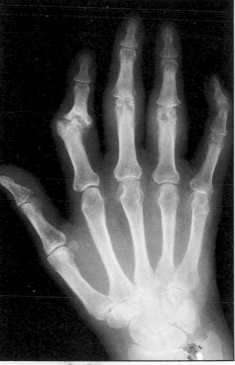

An example of rheumatoid arthritis (*left*), showing the collapse of a joint of the index finger and the fusion of the joints of the little finger.

which can be seen by the surgeon at operation, the pathologist at an autopsy, or they may require an X-ray machine or a microscope to be visible. To the layman, the most familiar examples of pathology are the inflammation and swelling around a boil as the body fights invading bacteria, the distortion of organs by the growth of cancer, and the breakdown of worn and badly nourished parts of the body in old age.

Dysfunction

In contrast to pathology, no visible changes in body structures accompany dysfunction; bones, joints, ligaments, muscles, tendons, and all the various internal organs may appear quite normal, even under the microscope or X-ray. Yet the part of the body concerned does not function normally. There might be excessive contractions of muscles, reduced movement of joints, and increased stresses on bones and ligaments, so that pain is produced. This signals that all is not well.

Orthodox doctors are used to seeing such abnormalities as tight muscles, restricted joints, and tenderness, around areas like a fractured bone, inflamed joint, abscess, or cancer. Therefore, whenever these abnormalities are found, it is not surprising that the orthodox doctor *presumes* there is some pathological cause. Even when, as is often the case, there is no evidence of a pathological cause, it is still presumed that that *is* the cause. In similar circumstances, the osteopath will always consider the possibility of pathology but, when no evidence for it can be found, the osteopath will diagnose only the dysfunction observed. The osteopath will then look for causes in the various stresses to which that part of the body is subject. It could be said that the medical profession is making false assumptions about the causes of many, if not most, of the painful situations arising in the locomotor system. This is likely for two reasons.

Over the last century, orthodox medicine has made enormous progress in understanding the ways that pathological processes can effect the body, and developing drugs and techniques to modify these processes. The repeated, often 'dazzling' successes have led doctors and laymen alike to believe that eventually *all* ills would have found an identifiable pathological cause, and subse-quently, a 'cure' could be devised. Over the last decade or two, however, many people, both within medicine and without, have begun to think that the search for pathological explanations for illness is yielding less and less that is useful. There is also the fact that more and more resources are being expended, and that the risks from the wide range of drugs now being used for pathological illnesses are increasing.

The second reason why there are false assumptions about disorders in the musculoskeletal system is that, in orthodox medical opinion, there is no acceptable explanation for the prolonged pain experienced by many patients with musculoskeletal problems. Researchers in neurophysiology accept that there could be non-pathological causes for such pain, but the education of practising doctors obviously lags behind the thinking of the research trail-blazers. In diagnosis, the infinite variety of ways in which people can appear ill are classified into one of a range of 'labels'. All practitioners, whether orthdox or unorthodox, find it difficult to recognize the situation when they need a new label; there is always a tendency to stick on one of those already in the repertoire, even if the similarity is tenuous, and the practitioner is forced to say, 'That's a very unusual case of....'

WHY IS THE EXISTENCE OF DYSFUNCTION IMPORTANT?

It might be thought that the important facts about an illness are whether it will get better or not, and whether this will require treatment — arguments about causes can be left to the professionals. This is not so; the concept of dysfunction has many implications of direct importance to anyone who suffers from it. Each pathological illness has, what doctors call, a natural history. This describes the situations when that disease occurs, and its time scale of healing or resolution. On their knowledge of this natural history is based the doctors' prognoses, their assessments of future prospects. When the diagnosis of a pathology is made in the locomotor system, most prognoses fall into one of two sorts: 'Give it time and it'll heal up' or 'The damage that has occurred is permanent so any symptoms which we are ascribing to it are also likely to be permanent.'

Neither of these would be helpful to a sufferer from dysfunction who had been wrongly diagnosed as having a pathological disorder. The first suggests that there is some process in operation which will largely resolve the problem, irrespective of what the patient does. In fact in the case of dysfunction, the sufferer's decisions and actions are very important. When incorrect, a disability may be greatly prolonged, even to the extent of permanence. When a disability is prolonged, the second prognosis may be given as the diagnosis shifts to one of irreparable damage. Again, it may be suggested that the sufferer is powerless, in this case to 'set the clock back' and must 'learn to live with it'. However, an osteopath, diagnosing dysfunction, will often regard permanent changes in musculoskeletal structures as irrelevant to the symptoms suffered. If the stresses imposed on those structures are changed, then pain and disability even of months' or years' duration can be alleviated and in some cases disappear. In short, the individual must learn to live *without* his or her pain. To an important extent, therefore, the impacts of the two types of diagnoses, pathological or dysfunctional, are different.

The existence of a pathological disorder would suggest helplessness and could encourage passivity in an individual, whereas the presence of dysfunction calls for insight into the cause, and appropriate action by the sufferer himself. Not surprisingly, most people prefer the latter interpretation, and this is probably a factor in the increasing demand for osteopathic treatment. But what reasons are there for considering this approach more than just a good sales ploy to attract orthodoxy's failures? What do osteopaths really believe is happening in the bodies of those who suffer, and whom they treat? While there are plenty of differences of opinion among osteopaths, there is general agreement about the basic causes and persistence of most musculoskeletal pain. Confirmation of these ideas by research workers has made great strides, but there are many pieces of the jigsaw still to be fitted. The osteopathic explanation for pain should not be thought of as in any conflict with orthodox medical opinion. Indeed, the major orthodox authorities in this field freely state that in, for example, back pain they do not know the cause of the majority of their patients' disorders.

DYSFUNCTION

There are many ways in which the body structures may be misused, so that some parts are subject to abnormal levels of stress. These stresses, whether they are caused by excessive pressure on, or tension in the structure, may produce pain. This is not in dispute, but where there is controversy is in the explanation for persistent pain after the stress is removed. Orthodoxy holds that only an actual injury can explain this persistence; osteopathic thinking is that there is pain and disability because some muscles are overactive, and are contracting for longer periods and to a greater extent than is normal. This abnormal muscle activity is thought to have a dual effect; firstly, pain may be generated from the muscle directly (rather akin, perhaps, to the pain of cramp) or from the structures to which its increased tension is passed on, such as tendons and joints; secondly, the pain signals produced by muscle overactivity may eventually become a cause for further overactivity in the same muscles that produced them.

The mechanism for this second effect is that pain signals pass up the nerves to the spinal cord where they are fed into its myriad interconnecting nerve fibres. Some of these signals, passing as tiny electrical currents along the nerve fibres, are known to be relayed to the terminals of the nerve cells which control muscles. The pathway therefore exists for a so-called *closed loop* — the term 'vicious circle' would be most apt for this suggested reaction in which, as muscle spasm produces pain, part of that pain response is the production of further muscle spasm which produces further pain, and so on, *ad infinitum*, if the feedback around the loop is sufficient. The theory of muscle overactivity explains many of the features of dysfunction, the central notion of osteopathy, and it has received considerable support. What hard evidence is there for its actual existence and what range of maladies can it hope to treat?

RESULTS OF RESEARCH

Working in the 1940s, Professor Irvin Korr, a physiologist, cooperated with osteopaths to investigate abnormal function in the spine. He used electrical measurements from within muscles to record their increased activity and to show that some of the slight changes which osteopaths think important were real, and capable of objective measurement. Because they take long practice to recognize, these changes (the so-called osteopathic lesions) had often been ascribed by orthodox doctors to the realm of osteopathic imagination. Korr and his colleagues developed further methods of demonstrating these lesions (or somatic dysfunctions as they are also called) and showed that they could be produced in normal, healthy volunteers by subjecting them to quite subtle stresses, such as raising the heel of one shoe by as little as half-an-inch for a day. The fact that they could demonstrate the persistence of these changes for hours, and even days, after removal of the source of the stress, seemed to confirm that dysfunction could be induced and persist in situations where the most sceptical critic would find it difficult to offer a pathological explanation.

The loop may be broken by the structures involved being temporarily prevented from relaying any nerve impulses by means of injections with local anesthetic. The effect of these injections, as a trip to the dentist will confirm, is at most an hour or two, usually less, and yet, in many situations of prolonged pain, relief has been much longer than this, and has often been permanent. Many instances of this phenomenon are recorded in the medical literature. A report by Dr Jeremy Fairbank in 1981 showed that when local anesthetic was injected into the spinal joints of people who had suffered back pain for several months, about half of them were relieved of pain.

The relief of pain usually extended well after the effects of the anaesthesia should have worn off, and in almost half the relief was permanent. In other reports, the precise site of injection differs but frequent permanent 'cure' is by no means a rarity. To many orthodox researchers, this effect is unexpected and inexplicable. If persisting pain occurs in damaged or otherwise pathological

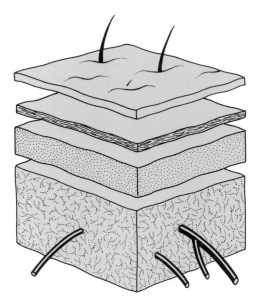

Dysfunction can be indicated by the electrical conductivity of skin tissue (*above*) which the osteopath detects by touch.

Manipulating a lumbar invertebral joint (*right*), and an invertebral joint in the upper spine (*below right*).

structures, how can temporary anesthesia relieve the pain for long periods when orthodox treatments require days or weeks to take effect? For osteopaths, these findings are quite explicable and a welcome justification from an unexpected source.

HOW MANIPULATION WORKS

Despite its use since prehistory, the precise way manipulation works is still unknown. At first sight, it seems simple: if something is jammed, whether it be a drawer in a chest of drawers or a joint in the human body, a well-applied push in the right direction might be expected to work wonders; or if something is stiff, whether it be a hinge or a joint in the human body, then to take hold of it and firmly move it through its usual free range would seem an obvious thing to do. Certainly, there are some osteopaths, and not a few doctors who manipulate, who do think that they are freeing 'jammed' or 'seized' joints. Also, there are some joints which do feel as though they are 'stuck' and become free after manipulation. However, in the majority of situations where an

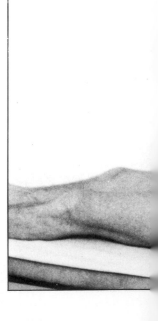

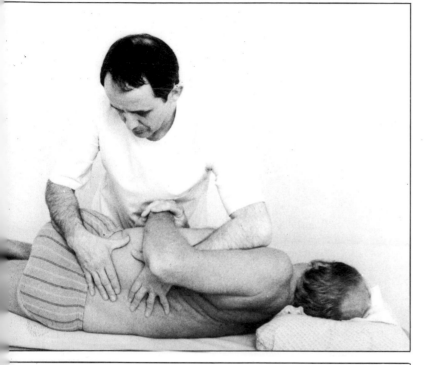

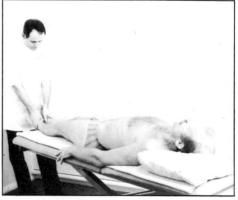

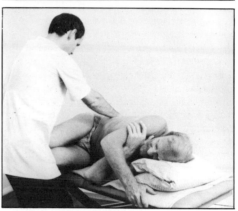

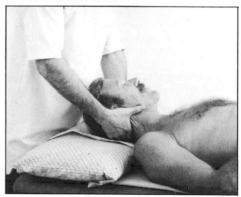

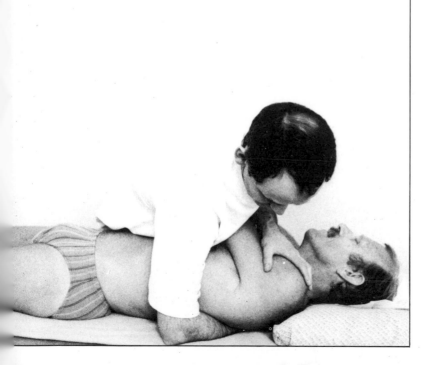

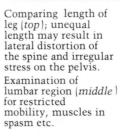

Comparing length of leg (*top*); unequal length may result in lateral distortion of the spine and irregular stress on the pelvis.

Examination of lumbar region (*middle*) for restricted mobility, muscles in spasm etc.

Examination of cranium and upper neck (*bottom*), — a very vulnerable part of the spine.

osteopath uses manipulation, the restriction of joint movement is probably caused by the overactivity of some of the muscles which move that joint; for every movement, some muscles must relax and lengthen as others tighten and shorten — if dysfunction prevents some muscles from relaxing normally, then restriction of joint movement is the result.

If a purely mechanical explanation for the effects of manipulation is rejected by most practising osteopaths, what do they think is happening? Some believe that the *gate theory* (see page 145) comes into operation. It is thought that as the affected part is massaged and manipulated, the sensory signals reporting pressure and movement actually 'close the gate' on pain signals reaching the spinal cord. If the pain signals are prevented from reaching their target, then the closed loop, which can perpetuate dysfunction and pain, may be broken.

This is one of several theories currently being considered, but theories, although fascinating to the protagonists, are of little importance to those who use or receive manipulative treatment. A treatment should only be established and survive on the sole criterion that it is effective — that its benefits can be shown to outweigh any harm it does. Indeed, how many orthodox treatments work is also unknown, even when the theory behind their original use is disproved, the treatments continue to be used simply because they work.

Manipulation in practice
Osteopaths use their hands to treat patients, but there is no set osteopathic treatment for each condition. Manipulation is based on the principles of engineering such as the use of leverage, measured thrust and balanced counterforce, calculated positioning, clearing and localized traction and expansion, and osteopaths vary their techniques according to the needs of each individual patient.

It is commonly believed that for manipulation to be effective it needs to be vigorous, even rough and painful. This is not so, even with the high velocity thrust techniques (which produce the 'click'). These techniques restore the mobility and function of a joint and are generally painless, or only momentarily painful. In fact, a good

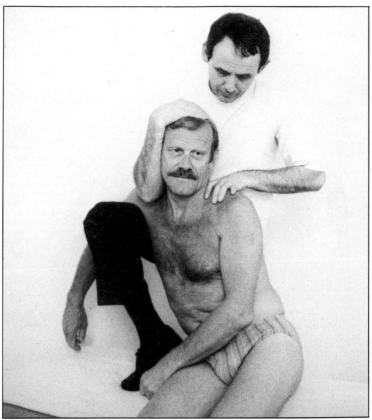

A manipulation for joints at the nape of the neck (*above*).

Assessing movement of joints in the lumbar spine (*right*).

Assessing movement of spinal joints in the thoracic area (*above right*).

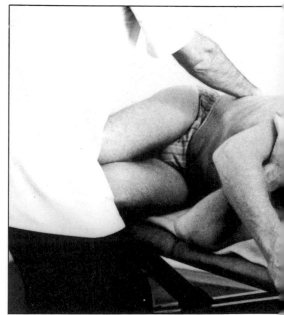

132

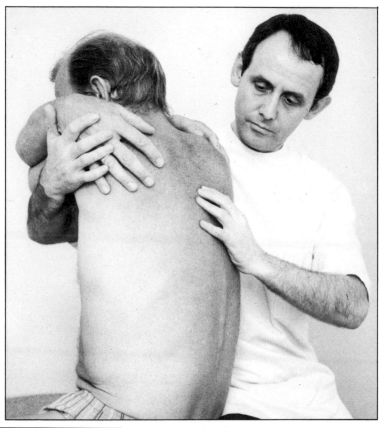

and torn muscle, should really only be used for quite specific conditions, but are often used very loosely by doctors not versed in very precise musculoskeletal diagnosis. Accordingly when osteopaths say such cases are suitable for their treatments, they are not claiming that the condition can be cured, only that patients with that diagnosis given to them would be appropriate for osteopathic assessment.

Many osteopaths treat patients for a variety of other problems, such as breathing difficulties, mild blood pressure, digestive and gynaecological upsets. This is in keeping with Still's original concept of osteopathy as a complete system of medicine. Nowadays practitioners feel that, for patients to get the best care, osteopathic treatment and orthodox medicine should cooperate. The extent to which manipulation can affect the conditions mentioned above is as yet unknown, but the safety of that treatment in the osteopath's hands makes its use a sensible adjunct or alternative, especially where othordox remedies are not effective or carry unacceptable risks.

ASSESSMENT OF A PATIENT

In his or her assessment of each individual, the practitioner takes account of factors which fall into five main groups. Each group overlaps with the others, but it is convenient to assess the problem in this way. The groups are *anatomy*, *body use*, *pathology*, *dysfunction*, and *psychology*.

ANATOMY

The patient will be examined for any anatomical defects which could produce pain, dysfunction, or pathology. These are usually due to the failure of growth to produce symmetry. By methods we know virtually nothing about, each half of the body's skeleton and muscles usually grow as a perfect mirror image of the other. This is important to maintain balance without undue stress. Of the many ways that the body can become out of balance by injury or unequal growth, the most commonly seen are differences in leg length. About one-twelfth of the population have one leg at least one-half inch shorter than the other; usually they are unaware of this because,

manipulator seldom causes any pain.

Among the wide range of techniques an osteopath might employ are massage-like movements to relax muscles, articulation or passive repetitive joint movement to improve the quality or range of movement of a joint, and some practitioners use gentle release techniques to ease away stress in tissues.

SUITABLE CASES FOR OSTEOPATHIC TREATMENT

The range of situations in which osteopaths believe they may be effective varies from one practitioner to another. Painful conditions of the head, neck, back, chest, and limbs, even after an apparent injury, often have origins in dysfunction and, as such, would be suitable for treatment. A variety of descriptions used in ordinary medical practice, such as fibrositis, neuralgia, neuritis, sprains, arthritis, prolapsed disc although the base of the spine tilting to one side causes the body to lean to the short-leg side, the spine adapts by curving to bring the bodyweight back over the feet. This adaptation maintains the balance of the body as a whole, but it means that some muscles alongside the spine are constantly active in standing whereas normally, the standing position is maintained with almost no effort from back muscles. This is one of the reasons why, among those who attend specialist clinics for long-term back pain, people with leg-length differences are found twice as often as would be expected by chance.

An osteopath recognizes imbalances in the body by observing how the patient stands, and by comparing the heights of hip bones, skin folds, and other visible features on each side of the body. With practice, differences down to a quarter of an inch in leg length can be recognized. The only reliable confirmation of these findings comes from X-rays taken with the patient in a standing position; measurements can then be taken from the film. Unfortunately, all routine X-rays are taken with patients lying down. The orthodox doctor, therefore, loses the opportunity to see the way the patient's spine is actually responding to supporting body-weight and adapting to any imbalances present. An osteopath who finds significant leg-length difference, will often recommend the wearing of a lift, especially in younger patients. The lift need be nothing more complicated than an extra thickness of leather or rubber under one heel.

While this anatomical assessment is important, it should be remembered that the majority of sufferers of back pain or other disability have no anatomical defects, and we must look elsewhere for causes. Moreover, many people with such defects lead comfortable lives due to successful adaptation and, perhaps, the good fortune that they have avoided some of the stresses in their lifestyle which might have uncovered their vulnerability.

BODY-USE

After assessing his patient's body structure, the osteopath will then consider the uses to which that structure is put. There is a school of thought that states that man's problems

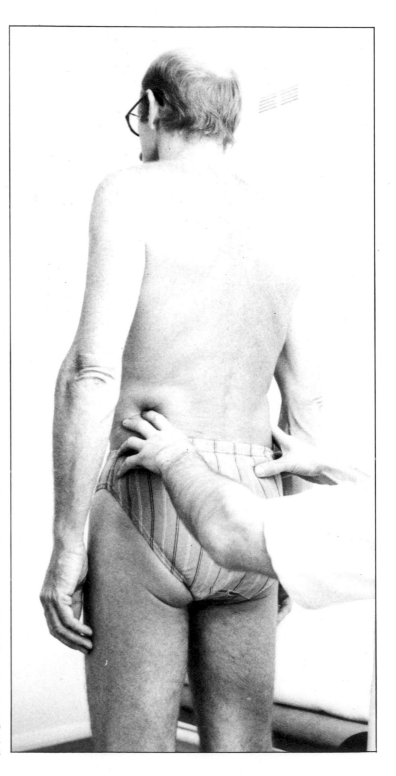

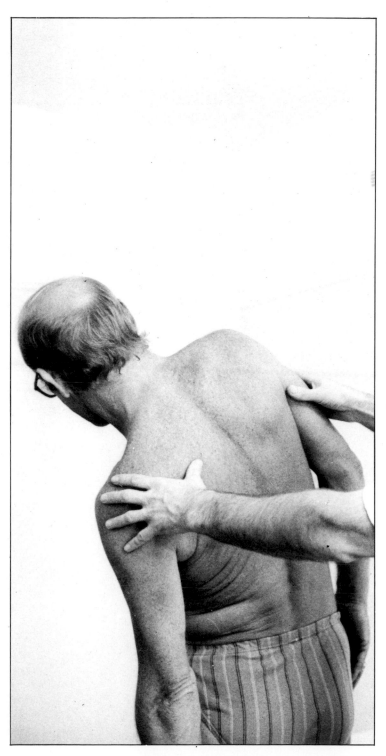

began when he started to move about on two legs, and that by so doing he subjected his spine, which had evolved to serve the needs of a four-legged creature, to stresses which it could not cope with. Most osteopaths would reject this view. Their knowledge and skill is dedicated to bringing their patients towards a comfortable and efficient use of the spine; and they believe this is an attainable goal. The idea that the skeleton is fundamentally unsuited to its purpose and that man is destined to back disability almost as his birthright is unacceptable.

It is obvious, however, that very many people suffer considerably from spinal problems and few escape them completely throughout their lives. If this is not a confirmation of the basic unsuitability of the

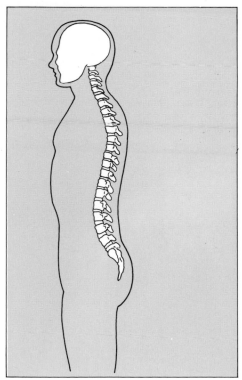

The patient is examined for tilted pelvis; one cause of this is difference in leg length.

The spine is tested for its range of sideways movement.

spine for man's use of it, what is the explanation? In attempting to understand this situation, we should perhaps consider that man's evolution has taken him beyond the predominantly instinctive control of his behavior that characterizes other animals. He has thereby adapted, learned, and developed a lifestyle so far divorced from his *hunter-gatherer* origins that one cannot be surprised if his innate patterns of body-use have undergone changes to equip him for existence in the twentieth century. The adjustment of instinctive responses is the purpose of our species' uniquely protracted learning period, each individual benefiting from his community's historical experience as he acquires information about language, abstract concepts, skills, mores, taboos and all that enables the group to function. Where change has been rapid, a community's ability to teach its young a successful lifestyle may lag behind. Adapting the human structure to the automobile, workbench, production line, office chair, heavy repetitive lifting, and a multitude of other situations has been difficult and all appear to threaten an individual's ability to function comfortably. The amount of back pain suffered in our community is, therefore, not an inevitable consequence of a faulty and inappropriate mechanism, but a monitoring signal, sending information to stimulate us to learn better how to use the body structure.

POSTURE

Posture describes the way that a person uses skeleton and muscles to support his weight. Ideally, the spine acts as a column of short cylindrical building blocks which, if they are held sufficiently straight and upright, bear most of the weight of the body above the waist. These blocks are the *bodies* of the vertebrae; between them are the gristly, shock-absorbing *discs* which provide a measure of flexibility to the column. The column of discs and vertebral bodies is very strong, having a breaking strain approaching one ton in an average man, and almost half a ton in a 84 lb person. The other structures of the spine are the muscles which generate the force for its movement, and the bony projections from the back of the vertebral bodies, which form a protective canal for the delicate spinal cord, and provide short, strong levers for the muscles to

Many day-to-day activities can involve prolonged periods with the spine curved at an awkward angle, affecting neck and shoulders in the process. Ironing, typing, washing up and the factory bench are four common examples.

Gardening (*left*) is a common cause of back strain, especially at the beginning of the gardening season, when many people are ill-prepared for heavy lifting and severe jolts to the body.

act upon. Parts of these projections are in contact and glide over each other, thus forming *facet joints* which control the direction of movement of that portion of the spine. These structures, lying behind the column of vertebral bodies, are not adapted to take compressive loads; if such a loading is imposed, the facet joints glide over each other but then have to bear the imposed load. This constantly stretches or compresses component parts in a way for which they are not adapted.

One of the most obvious examples of this misuse of the spine is in the common postural fault of *lordosis* of the lumbar spine. (Strictly speaking *lordosis* is a descriptive term for *any* concave curve of the spine when viewed from behind. Some concavity is normal in the lumbar region and the neck, but when the term is used describing posture, it is often used to imply excessive concavity.) Here the load-bearing column has 'buckled' out of line, and the structures behind it, which are designed for initiating and controlling movement, are coming under load. Maintenance of this posture as a regular feature of an individual's body-use produces pain from the compressed structures and in the longer term accelerates the effects of 'wear and tear', slowly damaging the spine so that pain, at first a reversible effect of misuse and malfunction, may become permanent.

When the practitioner recognizes excessive lordosis by the hollowed appearance of the lumbar region, he or she will try to instruct the patient to use the spine differently. This involves learning to control the position in which the pelvis is held. With the lordotic spine, the pelvis is tilted further forwards than in normal posture; when the 'foundations' of the spine are held in this position, lordosis is inevitable. Learning to control the pelvis is a knack which some people find hard to acquire, but, even if several months are involved, it is a worthwhile exercise. If a patient can alter the weight-bearing of the spine, this may be all that is required to restore comfort and well-being.

Other postural faults that often cause painful symptoms and may require correction are slumping of the spine between the waist and the nape of the neck, and hunching of the shoulders with an excessive

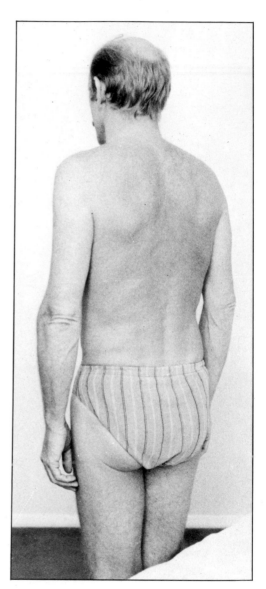

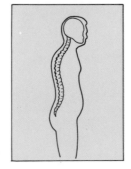

An example of curvature of the spine (*above*) where the load-bearing of the legs and pelvis is incorrectly distributed to the spine, thus causing tension to both the muscles and bones of the spinal column.

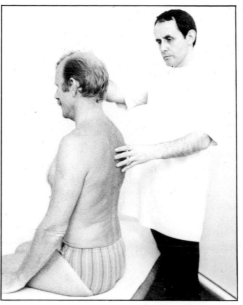

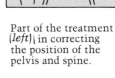

Part of the treatment (*left*)\ in correcting the position of the pelvis and spine.

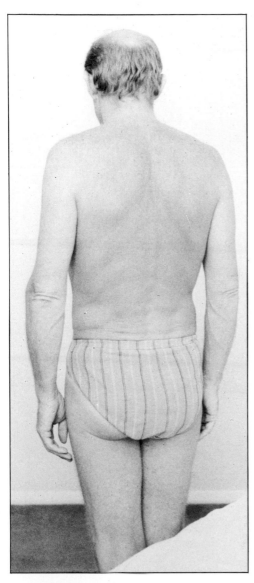

lordosis of the neck, so that the head is pulled down towards the shoulders. These faults are often found together and are frequently a consequence of excessive lumbar lordosis; it is as though all the usually gentle curves of the spine have buckled as gravity has pressed down on them.

LIFESTYLE

We now come to the considerations of lifestyle. These will be assessed by the osteopath who enquires, not only about the patient's work, but also how much traveling is involved in his or her daily routine — for many commuters, prolonged sitting in a car may be more stressful than anything done at work. Work positions, such as stooping over desks or benches which are too low, or adopting a slumped, hunched sitting posture, may all increase stresses on the structures of the spine. These can produce pain at the time, and also induce dysfunctions from which pain may be experienced long after the particular activity ceases. Housewives are subject to some of the most severe occupational stresses: lifting wriggling toddlers, carrying vacuum cleaners upstairs and using them in confined spaces, making beds, lifting and carrying boxes of groceries, preparing food at

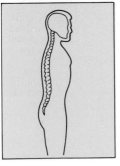

Correct spinal posture (*above*) continues load-bearing 'flow' through the whole length of the body.

counters of unsuitable height. As factories and offices have been made more comfortable, housewives have become, relatively speaking, the heavy laborers of society. Yet, with the demands and pressures on them, they often neglect the well-being of their bodies.

Rest and recreation must be considered by the osteopath: is sufficient time given to them, are there hazards involved in the particular ways chosen? To rest slumped in an easy chair may take the load off the legs, but may be the severest stress the lumbar spine has to endure during the whole day. Many sports are potentially harmful for some people; jogging, squash, karate, aerobics all have their casualties among the unwise and ill-prepared. Walking, cycling and swimming are, perhaps, the least

harmful, and one or other of these activities will often be advised for those who are insufficiently active to have built up heart and muscle strength.

Throughout the osteopath's assessment of and advice about lifestyle, the osteopath will be using the experience of pain as an indicator of stress, and trying also to get the patient to use pain as *information* — a signal from 'inner space' — whose purpose is to induce changes in body-use. Although this may seem obvious, many people feel that it is weak or cowardly to 'give in' to pain and will persist in painful activities, even taking pride in their stoicism. Osteopathic theory and experience suggests that this merely prolongs the dysfunctions, so that pain is often suffered beyond the period when the body structure is overstressed. This can even

Correct posture is as important in sleep as it is when awake (*below*). More and more people are realizing how necessary a firm mattress is to support the full length and weight of the body.

cause constant, long-standing distress.

PATHOLOGY

Symptoms produced directly by a pathological complaint such as the pain of swollen, tender, and inflamed joints afflicted by gout or rheumatoid arthritis, will not be improved by manipulative treatments. On the other hand, dysfunction can occur alongside pathology, often as a secondary defect. In these cases, although the pathology sets up dysfunction, other stresses may aggravate and increase the dysfunction to such an extent that most symptoms are caused by it. If the dysfunction can be treated, the patient will benefit considerably, even if the original complaint persists.

A hard game of squash (*above*) may do more harm than good to the physically unprepared; and sitting in a favorite armchair (*right*), while it may take the weight off the legs may throw great strain onto the spine and lumbar muscles.

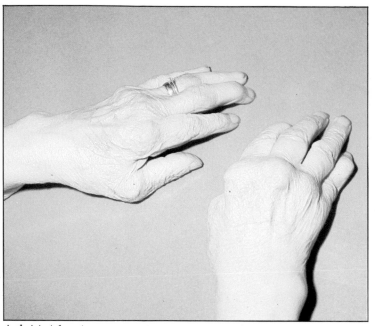

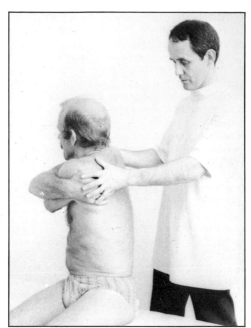

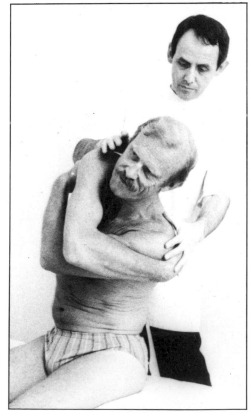

Arthritis (*above*), a common pathological disorder causing swollen and painful joints, can be eased by manipulative treatment.

An awareness and understanding of the effects of pathology is, therefore, necessary for practising osteopathy. The osteopath can often recognize that a patient is not suffering from dysfunction and will, therefore, suggest that it could be more useful to look for a pathological cause for the patient's illness. In this latter case, the osteopath will refer the patient back to the GP, offering to reassess the patient if a pathology is not found. Over the last decade, this sort of cooperation between GPs and osteopaths has increased so that it is now a frequent occurrence.

DYSFUNCTION

During an examination for dysfunction, the osteopath will decide which joints are limited in either their *active* movement, as when the patient moves that part, or in their *passive* range of movement which is assessed by the practitioner moving the parts involved with the patient relaxed. The examination will also determine which muscle groups are under increased tension, and which other structures in the body show signs of abnormalities due to increased sympathetic nervous activity, usually seen as abnormal sweating, temperature or circulation.

Although briefly stated, this part of the assessment uses the bulk of the osteopath's particular skills. Repeated careful examination of normal and abnormal body structures are required before the differences between them can be recognized; and for this reason from 500 to 800 hours of supervized 'hands on' experience will be part of the training of either a doctor or a layman who uses these methods.

PSYCHOLOGY

It is considered important to determine what the patient's pain *means* to him, and what he expects to happen in the future. Searching questions often uncover fears that 'my back is falling apart' or is weak. Patients may believe they have arthritis or degeneration of the joints which can never get better, and that pain or disability will be with them to the grave. These beliefs, which have often, regrettably, resulted from medical diagnoses, are usually faulty, cause distress, and may even delay recovery. Pessimism about the future can result in depression or anxiety; both these emotions can have some effect

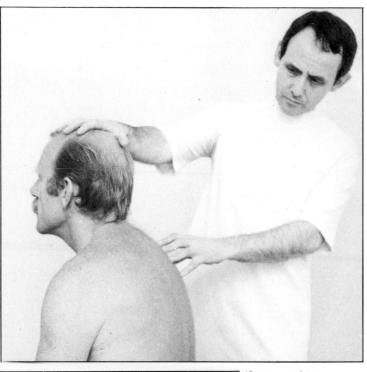

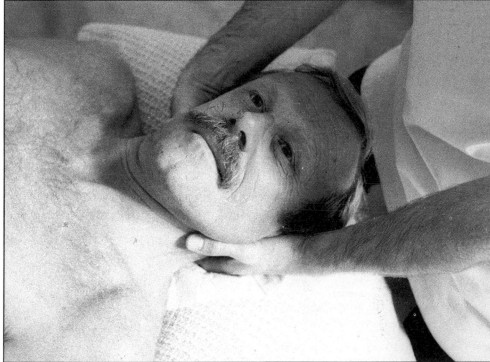

Shown on this page and opposite are tests the osteopath does for dysfunction in the patient. The osteopath is assessing the patient's range of movements, both active and passive, in the upper spine and neck.

States of mind such as aggression (*right*) or depression, can critically affect posture if sustained over long periods.

on the musculoskeletal system and so can cause more pain.

Anxiety increases muscle tension generally and, as Professor Korr was able to demonstrate, this happens to a much greater extent in areas which are already dysfunctioning. In the upper spine and neck, this general tension is particularly marked; in response to pain or a sense of being under threat, there is an instinctive reaction which involves hunching up the shoulders and pulling the head down by tightening the neck muscles. Probably this has the purpose of protecting the otherwise vulnerable neck.

However, for many with pain originating in the neck, hunching aggravates the pain, and another type of vicious circle is formed: pain produces hunching, hunching increases pain, which increases hunching, and so on. If a person is given insight into this mechanism of response, both the pain and the anxiety about its cause, this may help him to get rid of this harmful pattern. Also, by relieving anxiety, muscle tension may be reduced generally.

As students of body language know, depression is expressed in certain unconscious body movements. Asked to im-

Facial expressions (*left*) have always reflected a person's state of mind, and could well play a part in helping the osteopath form his diagnosis.

itate someone feeling despondent, most of us would adopt a sagging or slumping posture. These postures stretch the elastic supporting structures of the spine and become painful after a matter of hours. If these are maintained for weeks or months, the ability to return to comfortable efficient postures may be affected.

For these reasons, improving the patient's morale has not just a psychological effect but also alters the physical condition of the patient. Another psychological factor which can affect the patient involves the gate theory of pain perception, which sug-

gests that a person's state of mind may actually be capable of preventing or reducing the relay of pain signals upwards in the spinal cord to the brain.

The effect of the patient's personality on his or her response to pain must also be considered. When an activity brings on pain, some people will give in and stop, others will continue the activity in increasing pain. Why a person reacts in one or other of these ways needs to be examined, if advice is to be appropriate. For many, there is the moral stigma attached to 'giving in' and a belief that by struggling against pain they will earn the approval of others or of some supreme being. Phrases such as 'a cross to bear', and 'a martyr to back pain' give an inkling of such an attitude. If, because of this attitude, a patient is unable to recognize that an activity is physically harmful, then some form of counselling is necessary to prevent the possibility of long-term, self-induced pain and disability.

ARRANGEMENTS FOR OSTEOPATHIC TREATMENT

While osteopathic treatment will not hinder natural recovery, it would be a waste of time to seek treatment when such a recovery is probable. How long a person waits before treatment is sought will usually depend on the patient's resources, but even when money is no object, treatment too soon after symptoms appear distracts the sufferer from the all-important actions that should be taken to minimize stress on the affected part — not only to hasten recovery, but in order to reduce future vulnerability.

Mostly, when back and neck pain occur suddenly, recovery is well in hand within one week and complete within a fortnight. It is when the pain is more protracted that osteopathic intervention will be most useful; therefore, those who have not begun to recover after the first week are likely to suffer for a longer period than the average person, and could arrange for a consultation without being accused of not allowing their natural powers of recovery to work. This decision will always be a personal one; actors, dancers, sportsmen and others with a strong reason to continue full activity will often consider treatment within hours of painful symptoms appearing.

How to find an osteopath

Many people expect that their general practitioner would not wish them to seek help in the alternative field, but generally they would be wrong. Most doctors are now interested in osteopathy; many are active supporters and seek such treatments themselves.

Your GP's advice, when you arrange osteopathic treatment, could be helpful in several ways. There may be reasons why osteopathy is not suitable for you; although most osteopaths would recognize these and

not treat you, your doctor holds the only comprehensive record of your health care, so his advice is important. Further, your doctor will usually know which trained osteopaths practise in your area and may be able to help you choose whom to consult.

If your doctor has recommended conventional treatments, such as pain-relieving or inflammation-reducing drugs, these can be taken while you are receiving osteopathic treatment, although your osteopath's ambition will be to make them unnecessary by relieving your symptoms. It is because the two approaches are not in conflict and can be used side by side that increasingly the term *alternative* medicine is being replaced by *complementary* medicine.

The consultation

Osteopathic practice varies considerably; some practitioners make very rapid diagnoses which they follow with equally rapid treatments, and often appear to achieve results which are satisfactory to their patients. Little time is spent on talking to the patient, either to enquire about his or her response to the symptoms, or to explain the reasons for the problem, or to give advice for the future. The patient has been a passive recipient of treatment which has used a narrow range of skills. Some people prefer this approach; they lend their bodies to the therapist for a short time, and are not asked to be involved in or responsible for the cure. Interference in their lives is limited and temporary.

If this approach results in relief of symptoms without too rapid a recurrence, then for the patient it is perhaps adequate. But methods of this sort are against the tide of change in osteopathy, which would consider it essential to involve the patient in understanding the origins of whatever complaint, and securing cooperation in dealing with it. This might well include an initial course of manipulative treatment, but would extend beyond that to seek out the causes, both physical and mental, and attempt to change the conditions producing it.

A typical consultation with a practitioner using the latter approach would take the following course: five to ten minutes' discussion of the symptoms, a similar period of physical examination, then 10 to 15 minutes' treatment would follow with the session concluded by explanations and advice. Subsequent appointments would vary according to results; rapid recovery would allow more time to be spent on information about prevention of further episodes; a slow response would mean detailed re-examination at each session, so that a precise diagnosis could be made and treatment decided upon.

Duration of treatment

Few patients or therapists would persist with treatment when pain has ceased, but, when symptoms persist, there is debate about how many sessions should be carried out before treatment is abandoned. For those who experience benefit after osteopathic manipulation, their improvement is usually quite rapid. While only a few patients arise from the couch proclaiming themselves cured, a definite improvement within 24 hours of the first treatment is experienced by most. If there is not improvement after the second treatment, it is possible that the condition will not respond at all to that practitioner's methods, and the value to the patient of further sessions is doubtful. While many osteopaths would view this requirement — effectiveness after only two sessions — as somewhat harsh, many patients are often treated weekly for months, with no reduction in symptoms or disability. This practice does no good to the reputation of osteopathy, and to continue treatment distracts the patient from the possibility that his lifestyle needs changing rather than continuing passive treatments.

Provided pain is reduced or the patient can perform more activities comfortably, then treatments should continue until there is no noticeable improvement over the previous two sessions. This 'rule of thumb' will not apply if there is a change of activity or sudden stress, and a relapse occurs, or if there is too great an interval between treatments — most practitioners would con-

The British School of Osteopathy (*below*), in Suffolk Street, London.

sider more than a week's interval too long. Using this rule, the great majority of patients will receive between two and five sessions.

CHIROPRACTIC

The practice of chiropractic is said to have originated with Hippocrates and the term, derived from the Greek, means 'treatment by manipulation'. Chiropractic was founded in 1895 by David Daniel Palmer (1845-1913) of Iowa. It was his belief that displacement of a part of the skeletal frame could press against nerves 'which are the channels of communication' and interfere with their 'carrying capacity'. Palmer believed that this resulted in one or more of a wide range of symptoms including backache, headache, indigestion and psoriasis. The chiropractor's aim is to deal with the cause of the disorder — displacements of the spinal vertebrae — rather than the symptoms.

The main differences between chiropractic and osteopathy are chiefly historical, though chiropractors use X-rays far more fre-quently than osteopaths and put more emphasis on neurological and phyiscal examination of their patients. The method of manipulation used by chiropractors and osteopaths varies too, chiropractors using less leverage and treating the individual vertebrae more directly.

Consultation with the chiropractor
The chiropractor will first take a detailed medical history and then make orthpedic tests followed by a neurological and physical examination of the patient. This will generally be supported by an X-ray and, in some cases, by tests on blood and urine samples. The manipulative treatment is based on a high-velocity thrust directly on the vertebra to achieve an 'adjustment' of the joint.

There are many kinds of chiropractic couch, ranging from a simple bench to the model illustrated here, that can change angle and raise or lower particular areas of the body.

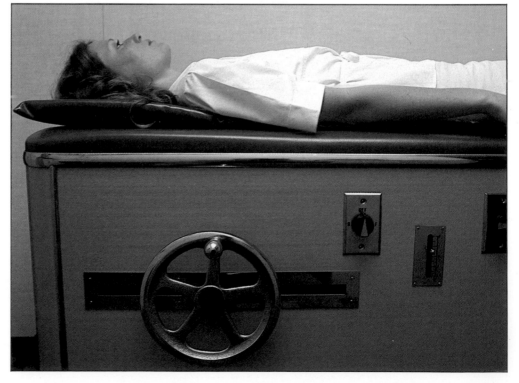

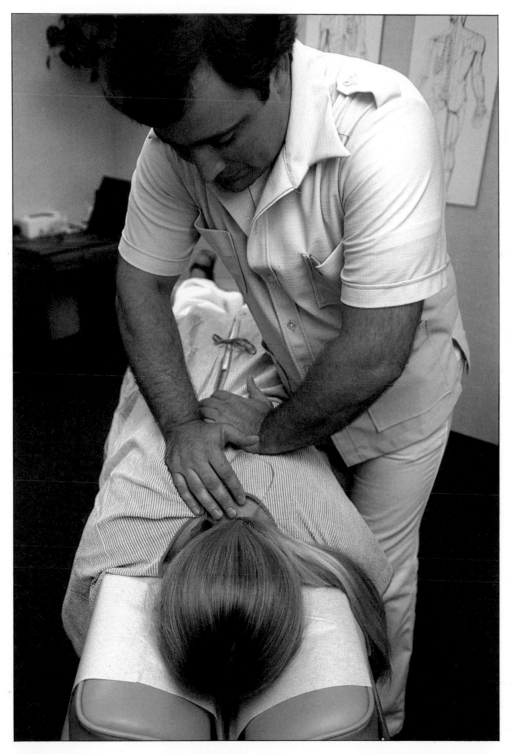

Chiropractic treatment (*left*) differs from osteopathy in that X-rays are frequently used as part of the diagnosis. Chiropractic, which focuses on mechanical disorders of the spine, uses less leverage, but closer contact and thrust on the vertebra needing treatment. But the difference is dwindling as chiropractitioners and osteopaths absorb more and more of each other's manipulative techniques. Research in the USA and Australia has shown that chiropractic is particularly effective in treating back pain and migraine. The therapy is State recognized in many countries — not, however, in Britain — making it one of the most widely recognized alternative therapies in the world.

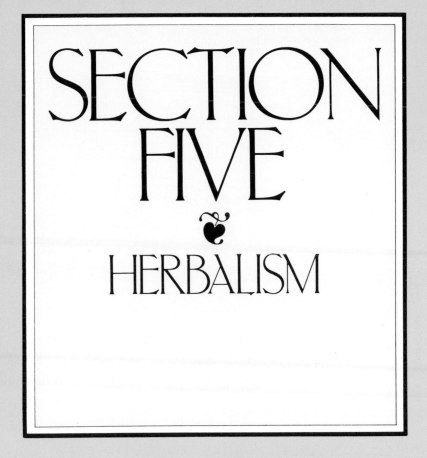

SECTION FIVE

& HERBALISM

HERBALISM, which has been in existence fo thousands of years, is a method of medicine which seeks to use remedies from plants for the prevention and cure of diseases.

The botanist describes a herb as a plant with a soft stem with no woody fibers, which dies beneath the ground after flowering. But generally a herb is viewed as any part of a plant which can be used as a medicine, food, seasoning, dye, scent or cosmetic.

From earliest times man has been discovering the healing properties of certain plants. The Chinese kept meticulous records of their herbal remedies in the compendia called Pen-ts'ao — a combination of pharmacology and pharmacopoeia — which was compiled over 5,000 years ago by Emperor Wen Shen-nung and was the first authoritative chronicle of its kind in Chinese history.

The ancient Egyptians, too, had remarkable insight into the use of herbs, and the famous Papyrus Ebers (about 1,500 BC) names over 700 herbal medicines. When the Pharaoh Tutankhamun was buried, the contents of his tomb included a bottle of perfumed oil which was still found to be potent some 3,000 years later. In the Middle East of 3,000 BC, records show that the Persians firmly believed in the powers of plants, and give mistletoe as a remedy for epilepsy. The extensive library belonging to the Assyrian King Ashurbanipal (668-627 BC), housed at his palace at Nineveh, contained clay tablets, at least some of which mention the medicinal use of herbs. Today these tablets can still be seen at the British Museum in London. The Greek physician Hippocrates (460-377 BC), named the Father of Medicine, refers to 300 medicinal plants in his writings, and the Roman author Pliny, known for his *Historia Naturalis* (Natural History) dedicated seven out of thirty-seven volumes of his celebrated work to medical botany. Other medical authorities of the classical world, such as Theophrastus and Dioscorides and Galen described the use of herbal remedies in lengthy discourses on medical botany which were still being studied by doctors in the seventeenth century AD.

With the advent of printing during the Renaissance, the herbal remedies of antiquity became more accessible in the form of printed textbooks. The English printer and translator, William Caxton (1422-1491), printed scores of medical manuals. The dawn of scientific medicine in the seventeenth century led to the beginnings of a split between the 'new philosophy' of reason and experiment and a previous tradition of 'science', which bundled together ancient doctrines with elements of magic and astrology. A late adherent of this semi-occult tradition was the astrologer and physician Nicholas Culpeper (1616-54), who, in the mid-seventeenth century, produced a monumental treatise on herbal medicine in the English language: *The English Physician and Complete Herbal* (1653). By translating the physician's pharmacopoeia from Latin into English, Culpeper drew strong opposition from the medical establishment of the time, which was jealous of its professional mysteries, now revealed to the public gaze.

At the same time, the herbalists' ancient authority was being undermined by the emergence of inorganic remedies. This had begun with Paracelsus (1493-1541), a famous Swiss alchemist and mystic, who with his followers did much to indoctrinate the use of chemistry in medicine. During his lifetime, Paracelsus made many crucial breakthroughs and was the first to apply laudanum and antimony in pharmacy. As scientific interest in plants became more botanical than medical, herbal remedies became almost obsolete as inorganic mixtures took precedence.

It was not until the eighteenth and nineteenth centuries that a revival in herbalism began to develop in North America. A variety of herbal remedies which blended traditional lore from the American Indians with the folk medicine of rural communities became the basis of patient medicines peddled by traveling 'medicine men', 'snake doctors' and quacks of every description. The majority of herbalists were laymen with little or no medical background. Samuel Thomson, a self-taught herbalist and a New Hampshire farmer won a more lasting reputation with his own herbal treatments which were later patented as a whole range of remedies.

By 1838 over one-sixth of the American population were disciples of Thomson. Nevertheless, as a boom in the herbal

The Greek physician
Hippocrates (468-377
BC), regarded as the
father of modern
medicine, knew the
properties of 300
medicinal herbs.

Bay tree (*left*). The
leaves are used for
rheumatism and fever,
and an oil extract for
bruises and sprains.

Angelica

Camomile

Valerian

Angelica (*above*) — a tonic that also treats coughs, fever and flatulence.

Top — left to right: Camomile — a soothing, aromatic stimulant that aids digestion and sleep. Also a diuretic. Comfrey — for stomach complaints, and an astringent for bruises, bites and skin inflammation. Basil — stimulates appetite, relieves flatulence and constipation.

Bottom — left to right: Valerian — a tranquilizer that treats insomnia and nervous headache. Sorrel — a laxative, and used for treating mouth and throat ulcers and heavy menstrual flow. Borage — treates hysteria and depression, stimulates the kidneys.

154

Comfry

Basil

Common Sorrel

Borage

Evening primrose, long used in herbal medicine, is now the subject of orthodox medical experiment. Research shows that it may be effective in treating premenstrual tension, preventing heart disease and in treating multiple sclerosis, diabetes and rheumatoid arthritis, among other diseases.

industry continued, so did the sales of weird and wonderful plant extracts and patent medicines reputed to work wonders on the human mind and body. Once again, the herbalists found their efforts tainted with a reputation for superstition and quackery — while the rapid advances of medical science presided over by Pasteur, Koch and Virchow, among others, pushed herbal practices into obscurity once more.

HERBALISM TODAY

The 1960s saw a widespread dissatisfaction with orthodox medicine. Despite the miraculous achievements in the conquest of disease, medical science seemed impersonal. Scandals such as the thalidomide tragedy and the widespread use of drugs to treat psychological states seemed to suggest a science that was cold and remote, unresponsive to individual needs. However ill-founded, this impression grew, and many people turned to so-called 'natural' therapies. In this climate, the renewal of interest in herbalism grew apace, until today herbal health shops are commonplace.

Meanwhile, herbalism itself has found increasing acceptance in the medical world, which, having inherited a vast legacy herbal treatments, is still sorting out their valuable attributes from the purely imaginary or magical. Worldwide research on the evening primrose plant, *Onenothera biennis*, the seeds of which contain the only available natural source of gammalinolenic acid (a vital fatty acid needed by the body) is being carried out in many areas. Initial investigation has suggested that it may be effective in treating multiple sclerosis, diabetes, rheumatoid arthritis, cardio-vascular disease, schizophrenia and breast disease. Recently a number of tests have produced some convincing figures on the plant's value. St Thomas's Hospital, London, conducted a double-blind study with primrose treatment (Efamol) on women suffering from premenstrual tension and showed an 85 percent success rate. Bristol Infirmary, Bristol, have also had positive results with it for bringing eczema under control, and a hospital in Inverness, Scotland, claims its usefulness in the treatment of alcoholism. The Feverfew plant,

Tanacetum parthenium, was tested on migraine sufferers, and, compared to conventional treatment, the Feverfew remedy had a higher recovery level. In the Far East, scientists at the National Taiwan University Center, Taipei, have been conducting experiments on seaweed since 1978 and have indicated that certain 'new' kinds of seaweed could contain antiseptic and anti-cancer properties.

As scientists continue to probe into medicinal plants on a worldwide scale, the number of herbalists is growing. In Britain, anyone can set themselves up as herbalists, as the law allows people to buy and sell medical herbs. The Medicine Act of 1968 nevertheless prevents anyone other than a physician or pharmacist selling dangerous herbs, although there is nothing to stop anyone from growing them.

THEORIES OF HERBAL MEDICINE

Herbal medicine has left its mark through many civilizations, recording man's fascination and acceptance of nature's curative powers. It went through many phases of waxing and waning popularity, but in the seventeenth century a whole realm of ideas became linked to herbs. The Doctrine of Signatures gave more weight to the popular Christian belief that certain medical plants symbolized parts of the human body, which the corresponding herbs could effectively treat. For instance, the leaves of Birthwort (*Aristolochia clematis*) were similar in shape to a woman's womb and therefore helpful during labor. The blood-like liquid from Woundwort (*Stachys sylvatica*) was an aid to wounds. Another theory was that the position of the stars governed when and how herbs were to be gathered.

MODERN THEORIES

Today, as the biochemics in plant life are scientifically analyzed, we are made more aware that the traditional herbal theories were not entirely without foundation. A plant goes through many transitions during its lifespan, and at certain periods the balance of its active substances may vary within its different sections — one reason why the timing of harvesting herbs is so

The modern drug, atropine, is derived from belladonna (deadly nightshade), a poisonous herb which was commonly used in the past as a beauty aid. Applied as drops, it caused the pupils of the eyes to dilate, thereby making them more attractive.

herbal medicine and what pharmaceutical companies put on the market today, there may in the future be a closer parallel between the two as many more plants are examined for their chemical constituents.

Indeed, there are many examples of modern drugs which are still closely related to their herbal origins: for instance, *dixogin* (foxglove) and *atropine* (*Belladonna* — Deadly Nightshade). Antibiotics, too, are in a sense herbal, since they are based mostly on substances produced by fungi. In spite of a growing demand on the drug industry to produce new and effective products, herbal drugs are often too expensive to be produced on a commercial scale. Herbalists disagree with the commercial process of isolating the active property of a herb from which to recreate a synthetic drug in the laboratory; they hold that other substances in the plant are there for a purpose. A frequently quoted example is that of *Rauwolfia*, an Indian herb that was introduced as a treatment for high blood pressure about 20 years ago. Although it worked quite well for this, unfortunately it also caused depression in some patients. According to herbalists, this was because Western doctors used the 'active principle' (reserpine) instead of the complex extract. The idea is that whole extracts usually contain not one but many substances, some of which counteract each others' effects so as to promote a cure that is safer and more gradual.

Since herbal medicine is designed mostly for the individual, and drug companies produce for the mass, there is a basic difference in approach. The soil, and the harvesting and storing of herbs affect their medical potency — factors which modern mass pharmacology, which needs to know how a drug works, and therefore needs drugs of a consistent standard and quality, may not allow for.

The ancients might not have been so well equipped as twentieth-century scientists, but their herbal medicine has lasted for thousands of years. It seems certain that new drugs will continue to emerge from the plant world.

There are undoubtedly thousands of valuable substances waiting to be discovered — the destruction of the tropical rain forests of South America is a disaster in this respect.

The early nineteenth century brought us

crucial. Locating a part of the plant when it is at its most active is a challenge to modern science, yet centuries ago herbalists knew they had to pick the roots of the dandelion in the autumn months when its active ingredients reached potency. The roots were used for liver complaints, and today scientists have discovered it has two alkaloids and is a hepatic stimulant.

As in the animal kingdom, our forefathers were intuitively drawn to certain plants when they felt something was wrong with bodily functions. The bark of the cinchona tree was chewed by South American aborigines for relieving malaria, but it was not until centuries later that scientists isolated quinine as the active property. Although there is a vast difference between

our painkillers, the twentieth century our synthetic drugs, bad eating habits, a cavalier disregard for the planet's ecology and the stresses and diseases of a technological age. Herbalism is an attempt, in the medical field, to redress this imbalance.

IN PRACTICE

Although herbalists today are qualified in their particular practice, few have an orthodox medical background.

The herbalist normally gives the patient a thorough examination and gets details of his medical history and dietary habits. He will probably want to know of any allergies, genetic defects, whether or not the patient was breast fed or bottle fed (some diseases have been associated with bottle feeding) and general environmental conditions. In some cases he may take blood and urine samples, and may check blood pressure and use X-rays to support his analysis. Regularity of treatment, which can last from weeks to months, is important. The herbalist is treating the body as a whole, and the treatment he gives is tailored to the needs of the individual. Herbal medication is designed to help the body as a whole and to stimulate certain responses to cure a disease. Nearly every malfunction of the body can be treated herbally. Either one or many herbs are administered to the patient in a low dosage in the form of pills, juices, powders, ointments or infusion tinctures.

Ginseng, used for thousands of years in China as a general tonic and curative, is now a popular medicinal herb in the West. It is available in a variety of forms, including granules, tablets and teas.

159

Many herbal teas make not only refreshing drinks but also have certain medicinal values. For example, camomile tea, one of the most popular herbal teas, is a good aid to digestion and upset stomachs, while an infusion of borage leaves is said to be a pick-me-up after a hard day.

PREPARING HERBAL REMEDIES

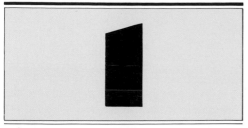

Infusion
This is a tea produced from a herb. A teaspoon of the leaves, flowers and stems is covered with a cup of boiling water and left in a container with a tight lid to steep for approximately ten minutes. Strain before drinking. Often honey is added to improve the flavor. Usually the infusion is drunk while warm, but in the case of colds or coughs, it should be taken hot. Herbal teas are mainly taken in regular small doses, and a daily intake can be between one and four cups.

Decoction
With this method the roots, twigs, berries, seeds and bark are used. They are put into an enamel pan (one ounce of material to a cup of water) with cold water, brought to the boil and simmered for 20-30 minutes to extract the plant's ingredients. Strain before using, and take the same dosage as for infusions.

Cold compress
Dip a cloth into a lukewarm infusion or decoction and apply to the skin.

Juice
To extract juice from plants, either cut them into tiny pieces, or crush them.

Ointment
Boil the plant parts until its properties are extracted. Strain and add some olive or vegetable oil. Return to heat and simmer until water has been absorbed into the mixture; beeswax can be added to make the desired consistency.

Poultice
Apply either hot or cold directly to the skin. The plant is crushed into a pulp and then placed on the affected area. It can also be wrapped in a piece of cloth or gauze. If applied hot, the pulp is heated, or, alternatively, put onto a wet, warm cloth, or made as an infusion/decoction by adding more herbs and then dipping a clean cloth into the mixture. A dried or powdered herb can be applied by adding hot water, or it can be sprinkled on the skin and held in place with a piece of cloth or gauze. Poultices are an ideal treatment for inflammation, bruises, wounds and abscesses.

COMMON HERBS AND USES

NOTE: These herbal uses are for a general guidance only where the whole or part of the plant has been used in either an infusion, decoction, tincture, tisane, or poultice form.

Borage (*Borago officinalis*)

Angelica (*Angelica archangelica*)

Angelica	Stimulant, tonic, carminative, coughs, rheumatic pains, expectorant, flatulence, fever, nervousness, pleurisy, delayed menstruation.
Basil	Carminative, antispasmodic, appetizer, tonic, aromatic, insect bites, delayed menstruation, vomiting, constipation, nervous complaints.
Bay	Aromatic, appetizer, rheumatism and fever, oil of bay — for bruises and sprains.
Borage	Tonic, pectoral, febrifuge fever, stimulates kidneys, helps milk flow in nursing mothers, hysteria, depression.
Camomile	Aromatic, antispasmodic, antiseptic, stimulant, stomachic, fever, nervous conditions, swelling, sores. Camomile oil for stomach cramps, relieves menstrual spasms, induces sleep, helps kidney and bladder complaints, fatigue.
Comfrey	Astringent, refrigerant, emollient, anodyne, expectorant, demulcent, dysentry, diarrhoea, stomach ulcers, bleeding gums, heavy menstrual flow, bruises, bites, sores, lung problems, whooping coughs, inflammation, mouthwash.
Elder	Diuretic, laxative, purgative, measles, bronchial conditions, scarlet fever, colds, induces perspiration, skin complaints, wounds.
Marjoram	Calmative, tonic, stomachic, carminative, **diarrhea**, flatulence, colic, menstrual cramps, coughs, rheumatism, sprains, inflammation, bruises, sore throats.
Mint (peppermint)	Carminative, refrigerant, antispasmodic, stomachic, tonic, headaches, painful menstruation, insomnia, nervousness, coughs, migraine, aids digestion, flatulence, abdominal aches.
Parsley	Diuretic, carminative, antispasmodic, expectorant, rheumatism, menstrual problems, coughs, cystitis, dropsy, insect

Rosemary (*Rosmarinus*)

French thyme (*Thymus vulgaris*)

Sage (*Salvia coccinea*)

	bites, stings, asthma, gallstones, eye inflammation (eyelids), urinary ailments.
Rosemary	Stomachic, stimulant, antispasmodic, tonic. Helps malfunction of liver, gall bladder, stomach complaints, bruises.
Sage	A digestive, antispasmodic, astringent. Aids upset stomachs, (nervous **diarrhea**, gastritis), gargle for throat problems, hair conditioner, hair dye (grey hair), induces perspiration, nervousness.
Sorrel	Diuretic, astringent, laxative, helps digestion, heavy menstrual flow, ulcerated mouth and throat, fever, **hemorrhages**.
Thyme	Antiseptic, carminative, expectorant, antispasmodic, coughs and colds, sore throat, phlegm, whooping cough, headaches, **diarrhea**, baths useful for rheumatism, circulation, bruises.
Valerian	Tranquilizer, flatulence, nervous headache, insomnia, overstrain.

BOTANICAL NAMES OF HERBS

Agrimony	*Agrimonia eupatoria*
Alfalfa	*Alder (alnus spp.)*
Aloes	*Aloe vera*
Angelica	*Angelica archangelica*
Aniseed	*Pimpinella anisum*
Arnica	*Arnica montana*
Asafetida	*Ferula assa-foetida*
Asparagus	*Asparagus officinalis*
Avens or Herb Bennet	*Geum urbanum*
Balm or Lemon balm	*Melissa officinalis*
Balm of Gilead	*Populus gileadensis*
Balsam of Peru	*Myroxolon perierae*
Barley	*Hordeum vulgare*
Basil	*Ocimum basilicum*
Bayberry	*Myrica cerifera*
Bearberry	*Arctostaphylos uva-ursi*
Belladonna (deadly nightshade)	*Atropa belladonna*
Benzoin	*Styrax benzoin*
Bilberry or blueberry	*Vaccinium myrtillus*
Birch	*Betula alba*
Blackberry	*Rubus villosus*
Black cohosh	*Cimicifuga racemosa*
Bladderwrack	*Fucus vesiculosus*
Blue flag	*Iris versicolor*
Bogbean or Buckbean	*Menyanthes trifoliata*
Boneset	*Eupatorium perfoliatum*
Borage	*Borago officinalis*
Buchu	*Agathosma betulina*
Buckwheat	*Fagopyrum esculentum*
Burdock	*Arctium lappa*
Cajuput	*Malaleuca leucadendron*
Camphor	*Cinnamomum camphora*
Caraway	*Carum carvi*
Cardamom	*Cardamom*
Cascara	*Rhamnus purshianus*
Catechu	*Acacia catechu*
Catnip or Catmint	*Nepeta cataria*
Cayenne	*Capsicum minimum*
Celandine	*Chelidonium majus*
Celery	*Apium graveolens*
Centaury	*Centaurium erythraea*
Camomile (German)	*Matricaria recutita*
Camomile (Roman)	*Chamaemelum nobile*
Chervil	*Anthriscus cerefolium*
Chickweed	*Stellaria media*
Chicory	
Chives	
Cinnamon	*Cinnamonum zeyaricum*
Cinchona	*Cinchona spp.*

Cleavers	*Calium aparine*
Cloves	*Eugenia caryophyllus*
Comfrey	*Symphytum officinale*
Coriander	*Coriandrum sativum*
Corn Silk	*Zea mays*
Cowslip	*Primula veris*
Cramp Bark	*Viburnum opulus*
Cubebs	*Piper cubeba*
Cucumber	*Cucumis sativus*
Dandelion	*Taraxacum officinale*
Devil's claw	*Harpagophytum procumbens*
Dill	*Anethum graveolens*
Elder flower	*Sambucus nigra*
Elecampane	*Inula helenium*
Elm	*Ulmus campestris*
Evening primrose	*Oenothera bienis*
False unicorn root	*Chamaelirium luteum*
Fennel	*Foeniculum vulgare*
Fenugreek	*Trigonella foenum-graecum*
Feverfew	*Chrysanthemum parthenium*
Foxglove	*Digitalis purpurea*
Fig	*Ficus carica*
Fumitory, common	*Fumaria officinalis*
Garlic	*Allium sativum*
Gentian	*Gentiana lutea*
Geranium	*Geranium maculatum*
Ginger	*Zingiber officinale*
Ginseng	*Panax ginseng*
Goldenseal	*Hydrastis canadensis*
Hawthorn (maytree)	*Crataesus oxyacantha*
Hops	*Humulus lupulus*
Horseradish	*Armoracia lapathifolia*
Horehound	*Marrubium vulgare*
Houseleek (or hens and chickens)	*Sempervivum tectorum*
Hyssop	*Hyssopus officinalis*
Iceland moss	*Cetraria islandica*
Indian snakeroot	*Rauwolfa serpentina*
Jamaica dogswood	*Piscidia erythrina*
Jimson weed	*Datura stramonium*
Juniper ·	*Juniperus communis*

Kava	*Piper methysticum*	Raspberry	*Rubus idaeus*
Kola	*Cola spp.*	Red clover	*Trifolium pratense*
Krameria	*Krameria triandra*	Rhubarb	*Rheum palmatum*
		Rosemary	*Rosmarinus officinalis*
Lady's slipper	*Cypripedium pubescens*		
Laurel	*Laurus nobilis*	Saffron (Autumn crocus)	*Crocus sativus*
Lavender	*Lavandula officinalis*	Sage	*Salvia officinalis*
Lemon	*Citrus limonia*	St John's wort	*Hypericum perforatum*
Licorice	*Glycyrrhiza glabra*	Sarsaparilla	*Smilax spp.*
Lime (linden)	*Tilia platyphyllos*	Sassafras	*Sassafras albidum*
Linseed	*Linum usitatissimum*	Senna	*Cassisa senna*
Lobelia	*Lobelia inflata*	Shepherd's purse	*Capsella bursa-pastoris*
Lungwort	*Lobaria pulmonaria*	Skullcap	*Scutellaria spp.*
Lemon verbena	*Lippia citroidora*	Skunk cabbage	*Symplocarpus foetidus*
		Snake root	*Polygala senega*
Ma-huang	*Ephedra vulgaris*	Solomon's seal	*Polygonatum multiflorum*
Mayapple	*Dodophyllum peltatum*		
Marigold	*Calendula officinalis*	Sorrel	*Rumex acetosa*
Marjoram	*Origanum majorana*	Southernwood	*Artemisia abrotanum*
Marshmallow	*Althaea officinalis*	Spinach	*Spinacea oleracea*
Meadowsweet	*Filipendula ulmaria*	Squaw weed	*Senecio aureus*
Motherwort	*Leonurus cardiaca*	Squill	*Urginea maritima*
Mugwort	*Artemisia vulagaris*	Stinging nettle	*Urtica dioica*
Mullein	*Verbascum thapsus*	Stone root	*Collinosonia canadensis*
Mustard	*Brassica nigra*	Sunflower	*Helianthus annuus*
Myrrh	*Commiphora molmol*		
		Tansy	*Tanacetum vulgare*
Nettle	*Urtica dioica*	Tarragon	*Artemisia dracunculus*
Nutmeg	*Myristica fragrans*	Turnip	*Brassica rapa*
Oak	*Quercus robur*	Valerian	*Valeriana officinalis*
Oat	*Avena sativa*	Vervain	*Verbena officinalis*
Olive	*Olea europaea*		
Onion	*Allium cepa*	Walnut (Black walnut)	*Juglans nigra*
		Walnut (Lemon walnut)	*Juglans cinerea*
Parsley	*Petroselinum crispum*	Walnut (English walnut)	*Juglans regia*
Passion flower	*Passiflora incarnata*	Watercress	*Nasturtium officinale*
Peach	*Prunus persica*	White horehound	*Marrubium vulgare*
Pennyroyal	*Mentha pulegium*	White poplar	*Populus tremuloides*
Periwinkle	*Vinca rosea*	White willow	*Salix alba*
Peppermint	*Mentha piperita*	Wild cherry	*Prunus serotina*
Pilewort or lesser		Wild lettuce	*Lactuca virosa*
celandine	*Ranunculus ficaria*	Wind flower	*Anemone pulsatilla*
Pine	*Pinus strobus*	Wintergreen	*Caultheria procumbens*
Plantain	*Plantago major*	Witch hazel	*Hamamelis virginiana*
Pleurisy root	*Asclepias tuberosa*	Woodruff	*Asperula odorata*
Prickly ash	*Xanthoxylum spp.*	Wormwood	*Artemisia absinthium*
Poke root	*Phytolacca americana*		
Poppy (opium)	*Papaver somniferum*	Yam	*Genus dioscorae*
Pumpkin	*Cucurbita pepo*	Yarrow	*Archillaea mullefolium*
		Yellow dock	*Rumex cripus*
Quassia	*Picrasma excelsa*		
Queen's delight	*Stillingia sylvatica*		

AILMENTS AND GENERAL HERBAL REMEDIES

Elder (*Sambucus purpurea*)

Comfrey (*Symphytum*)

Chamomile (*Matricaria chamomilla*)

Abrasions	Infusion of fresh flowers of St John's wort in olive oil; lovage.
Asthma	Fennel, eucalyptus, horehound, elder **flower, hyssop infusion, aniseed, licorice** root, pleurisy root, chamomile.
Athlete's foot	Red clover blossoms (boiled), dried comfrey leaves and water, goldenseal root tea, infusion of fresh or dried thyme leaves.
Bleeding (gums) (nose)	Sage (mouthwash). Nettles.
Boils	Teas made from burdock, echinacea, goldenseal, barberry, yellow dock, comfrey, figs.
Bruises	Compress of comfrey, witch hazel.
Burns	Chamomile tea (cold), raw onions and potatoes, compress of comfrey.
Colds	Hot elderberry wine (add sugar or honey), onions and garlic, chamomile, sage, rosemary, peppermint.
Constipation	**Dandelion, figs, olive oil, nettles, licorice,** alder, blackthorn, fennel, molasses, prunes, slippery elm, spinach.
Coughs	Elder blossom, sage, calamint, sunflower seed oil.
Dandruff	Apple cider vinegar, rosemary, sage.
Diarrhea	Infusion of blackberry root, meadowsweet, cinnamon, comfrey root, eldeberry, peppermint, raspberry leaf.
Dyspepsia	Dandelion, caraway.
Earache	Mullein oil, plantain.
Fatigue	Peppermint, rose hips, marjoram, agrimony.
Fever	Elder, cayenne, boneset, yarrow, vervain, catnip, tincture of aconite, peppermint tea, yarrow tea.

Gums (sore)	Sage.
Hayfever	Wood betony, mullein tea.
Headache	Hops, mistletoe, rosemary, wood betony, chamomile, mint, poppy, lavender (compress), peppermint tea.
Inflammation	Comfrey, plantain, witch hazel (externally), parsley poultice.
Insomnia	Hops (pillow), lady's slipper root, aniseed, valerian, passionflower, skullcap, chamomile, geranium (sniffing), linden.
Menopause	Lady's slipper, mistletoe.
Menstrual complaints	Nettle tea, mistletoe, lady's mantle tea, cranberry, parsley, rose hips, mints, tansy (with caution), evening primrose oil, red raspberry leaf tea.
Migraine	Mistletoe, rosemary, lime flower tea, peppermint tea, feverfew.
Nervousness	Celery, mistletoe, rosemary, damiana, lady's slipper, olive oil, valerian, marjoram.
Oedema (fluid retention)	Juniper berries, parsley, celery, cornsilk, fennel.
Piles	Lesser celandine, pilewort.
Rheumatism	Dandelion, celery, rosemary, parsley, cuckoopint (externally), ground elder, hyssop, mugwort, chamomile, nettles.
Sore throat	Red sage tea (gargle), stinging nettle (gargle), garlic, thyme (gargle).
Sprains	Comfrey oil, arnica.
Stings and bites	Plantain, oil of eucalyptus, grated onion, horseradish (externally), crushed basil leaves.
Toothache	Oil of capsicum, oil of cloves, elder (held in mouth).
Vomiting	Spearmint, chamomile, peppermint.

Marjoram (*Origanum onites*)

Peppermint (*Mentha piperita*)

Parsley (*Petroselinum crispum*)

DANGEROUS HERBS

Left to right: Deadly nightshade, poison ivy, foxglove.

Adonis	Colchicm	Foxglove	Mistletoe	Santonica
Areca	Conium			Savin
Aconite	Convallaria	Gelsemium	Nux vomica	Scopolia
Arnica	Crotalaria			Squill
	Croton oil	Henbane		Spurge
Belladonna	Croton seed	Hellbore	Poison hemlock	Stavesacre seeds
Bittersweet	*Cucurbita maxima*	Hollarrhena	Poison ivy	Stropanthus
			Poison oak	Slippery Elm bark
Calabar bean	Daffodil	Ignatius bean	Pomegranate bark	
Camphor (internally)	Duboisia			Tonka beans
Celandine (externally)	Elaterium	Jaborandi	Quebracho	Tobacco (internally)
Cathaedulis	Embelia	Jimsonweed		
Cenopodium ambrosiodes	Ephedra		Ragwort	Veratrum
Cinchona	Ergot	Lobelia	Rauwolfia	Wormwood
Cocculus indicus	*Erysimum canescens*	Mandrake	Sabadilla	Yohimbe bark

COMMON DRUGS BASED ON PLANT EXTRACTS

Coca (*Erythroxylum coca*)	Cocaine.
Deadly nightshade (*Atropa belladonna*), Henbane (*Hyoscyamus niger*), Thorn-apple (*Datura stramonium*)	They all contain chemically associated alkaloids — hyoscyamine, atropine, hyoscine.
Ergot (*Claviceps purpurea*)	Contains such alkaloids as: lysergic acid, the base for LSD (diethylamide 25), bromocriptine, ergometrine, ergotamine.
Fenugreek (*Trigonella foenum-graecum*)	Diosgenin.
Foxglove (*Digitalis purpurea*)	Contains glycosides: digitoxin and digoxin.
Madagascan periwinkle (*Virica rosea*)	Two alkaloids: vincristine, vinblastine.
Ma-huang (*Ephedra vulgaris*)	Ephedrine.
May apple (*Podophyllum peltatum*)	Contains toxin used in cancer treatments.
Opium poppy (*Papaver somniferum*)	Contains papaveretum, diamorphine (heroin), morphine, papaveline, noscapine.
Yam (*Gemus dioscoreae*)	(Source of hormones for contraceptive pill) contains: corticosteroids, saponin, diosgenin.

GLOSSARY OF HERBALISTS' TERMS

Alternative	Agent that produces a gradual change towards good health.	Mucilaginous	Emits soothing quality to swollen areas.
Anesthetic	Causes absence of sensation.	Nephritic	A medicine which acts on nervous system to calm the nerves.
Anodyne	Relieves pain.		
Anticoagulant	Prevents clotting.	Pectoral	Relief for chest and lungs ailments.
Antiemetic	Relieves vomiting.	Purgative	An agent that causes bowel relief.
Antiseptic	Destroys or inhibits bacteria.		
Antispasmodic	Relieves or checks spasms.	Refrigerant Sedative	Reduces excess body heat. An agent which has a direct effect on a particular disease.
Analgesic	Relieves or stops pain.		
Aperient	Causes bowel movement.	Diaphoretic	An agent that produces perspiration.
Aphrodisiac	Arouses sexual desire.	Digestive	Helps digestion.
Astringent	Makes organic tissue contract.	Diuretic	An agent that increases the flow of urine.
Balsam	Healing or soothing agent.		
Bitter	Bitter properties which promote movement of saliva and gastric juice to increase appetite and aid digestion.	Emetic	Causing vomiting.
		Emollient	Agent used externally for a softening and soothing effect.
Calmative	Agent that has calming or tranquilizing effect.	Expectorant	Promotes the release of mucus from lungs and air passages.
Cardiac	Agents that affect the heart.	Febrifuge	Reduces or stops fever.
Carminative	Relieves gas from intestines.	Hemostatic	Halts bleeding.
Cataplasm	Poultice.	Hepatic	A drug which works on the liver.
Coagulant	Causes clotting.		
Counter-irritant	Agent to produce an irritation to counteract irritation elsewhere.	Stimulant	An agent that excites or quickens functional activity.
		Stomachic	An agent that stimulates, strengthens and tones the stomach.
Depressant	Agent which reduces nervous activity.		
Depurative	Agent that purifies — particularly the blood.	Tonic	Strengthens and stimulates the system.
Laxative	Causes bowel movement.	Vermifuge	Destroys worm.

SECTION SIX

NUTRITION AND NATUROPATHY

WE ARE WHAT WE EAT' is the principle underlying a number of therapies which define or restrict the type or amount of food we eat in order to promote good health, prevent disease and in some cases actually cure disease. Health food regimes, high-fiber and weight-reducing diets and vegetarianism are examples of diet management aimed at the prevention of disease and the promotion of good health. Naturopathy, based on the belief that we have the complete resources within our bodies not only to maintain good health but also to combat disease, is a holistic therapy using various forms of hydrotherapy, breathing exercises and yoga as well as diet and fasting; it also claims to cure certain types of disease. Veganism and macrobiotics, for example, are diets and lifestyles based on philosophical principles, while others such as natural foods and high-fiber diets are based on simple nutritional rules.

Nutrition is a relatively new science. It is only during this century that experts have been able to define accurately the contents of foodstuffs and tell us how our bodies use them. Nutritionists now agree that the average Western diet, with its emphasis on refined, fatty, sugar-laden foods, is a major cause of disease in most civilized societies. While orthodox doctors are increasingly aware of this and urge their patients to eat sensibly in order to prevent obesity and heart disease, it is the alternative therapies with their more precise guidelines and rules that have offered many people more practical help over the last few decades. One of the most popular diets is the one centred around health foods or 'natural foods'.

Health food stores, selling wholemeal grains and pulses as well as organically grown vegetables, have been well established in the USA for years and are now common in many countries. Their success exemplifies the trend away from canned and refined food containing preservatives and other chemical additives to more natural products.

NUTRITION AND DIETS

Since the 1960s, there has been a growing interest in 'natural foods'. This interest goes hand in hand with the increasing popularity of various forms of alternative medicine, and although natural foods are not, strictly speaking, medicines, they are, of course, related to health. And they do, perhaps, qualify as an 'alternative' type of therapy because they are foods which are free from chemical additives, are unrefined and are, as far as possible, organically grown.

Green leafy vegetables such as cabbage provide vitamins A, B, C, E and K as well as iron, iodine and other valuable minerals.

Most fruits, particularly citrus fruits, are rich in vitamin C and the sugars in fruits are an instant and natural source of energy.

Colorful vegetables, such as carrots, are an important source of vitamin A. Carrots also contain vitamin E.

Wholemeal grains provide roughage, essential for the digestive system and are a valuable source of vitamins B, E and K, as well as minerals.

Most vegetable oils are polyunsaturated fats, unlike animal fats which increase cholesterol — linked to heart disease — in the body.

Honey is a natural source of sugar and is rich in minerals such as calcium and magnesium.

Eggs, although high in cholesterol, are very rich in protein and contain vitamins and minerals in good quantities.

Fish is a particularly important source of protein and contains a wide range of essential vitamins and minerals.

Pulses such as lentils, dried peas, soya beans, chick peas and haricot beans provide vegetable protein and are also a source of vitamin B and of iron and other minerals.

The body's alimentary canal, a passage which runs from the mouth to the anus, processes all food and liquids taken into the body. By a series of complex processes, it extracts essential nutrients to nourish cells, organs and bones and eliminates the rest as waste.

Saliva glands start digestion process

Oesophagus pushes food to stomach

Stomach mixes food with gastric juice

Liver breaks down fats

Gall bladder stores bile

Duodenum produces hormones to stimulate pancreas

Pancreas controls glucose in blood

Colon absorbs water

Small intestine is main site of digestion and absorption

Rectum expels faeces through anus

Generally, they will not be found among the prepackaged, plastic-wrapped or deep-frozen sections of a typical supermarket, nor will they be found in the kitchen of the average family.

It is difficult to pinpoint precisely when this trend began, but some of its origins can be seen in the 1950s in the 'health food' crusades of the American dietician Gayelord Hauser and others who urged the consumption of wheat germ, blackstrap molasses, yeast and other 'unrefined' foods. Further support was provided by books such as Adelle Davis's rather over-exuberant *Let's Eat Right to Keep Fit*, and Rachel Carson's *Silent Spring*, which dramatically exposed the effects of pesticides on food and environment alike. Gradually, a great many people became aware that the foods bought in grocery stores and markets were likely to be contaminated by chemicals, rendered flavoursome by additives, or depleted by refinement of all their natural goodness.

What are natural foods?
Natural foods are whole foods (grown naturally and unchanged in any way), or foods derived from whole foods, containing all or almost all of their original nutrients; they are unprocessed or unrefined; and they contain no additives or preservatives. Such foods include organically grown fresh fruit and vegetables, grains, nuts, pulses and some vegetable oils. Meat, fish and poultry provide a problem since it is often difficult to find fresh meat and poultry that has not come from animals fed or injected with growth hormones; and fish, although not usually treated with such chemicals, can absorb toxins from polluted waters. Eggs, also, unless they are genuinely free-range, are not a natural food.

There is no firm evidence that plants grown organically — that is, in soil enriched with natural manure in the form of animal droppings or composted vegetables — are nutritionally better than those grown with chemical fertilizers. Yet common sense suggests that, if certain pesticides kill insects and birds that feed on some of our food plants, then the same chemicals can be passed on to humans. The cumulative effect of even small amounts of pesticides or other chemicals on the human body could be pro-

A SENSIBLE DIET

	Energy (cals)	Protein (g)	Fat (g)	Starch (g)	Sugar (g)	Fibre (g)	Cholesterol (mg)	Calcium (mg)	Magnesium (mg)	Iron (mg)	Zinc (mg)	Vitamin B1 (mg)	Vitamin B2 (mg)	Vitamin C (mg)	Vitamin A (mg)
Breakfast															
Wheatflakes 35gm (1.4oz)	121	4.0	1.2	23.3	2.1	4.4		11	42	2.6	0.7	0.09	0.02		
Sugar 5gm (0.2oz)	15				5.0										
5 slices wholemeal bread[1]	452	18.4	5.7	83.3	4.4	17.8		48	195	5.2	4.2	0.55	0.13		
Thinly spread butter, or polyunsaturated margarine, for 5 slices	145	0.1	16.4				46[2]	3							166
Marmalade 20gm (0.8oz)	52				14.4	0.1		7			0.1			2	2
Milk, for cereal and drinks during the day, 450gm (0.75 pint)	290	14.8	17.1				63	540	54	0.2	1.6	0.18	0.86	7	173
Lunch															
1 small slice of chicken 30gm (1.2oz)	42	7.4	1.6				22	3	7	0.2	0.5	0.02	0.06		
1 small slice of cheese 30gm (1.2oz)	119	7.8	10.0				21	240	75	0.1	1.2	0.01	0.15		103
Lettuce, tomato 100gm (4oz)	14	0.9			2.8	1.5		13	11	0.4	0.2	0.06	0.04	20	
Small piece fruit cake 40gm (1.6oz)	143	2.0	5.2	6.0	17.2	1.2	16	24	10	0.6	0.2	0.04	0.02		
Fresh orange 120gm (4.8oz)	42	1.0			10.2	1.8		49	16	0.4	0.2	0.08	0.02	46	7
Dinner															
Lentil soup, no fat, 200gm (8oz)	93	7.1	0.3	15.3	0.7	3.5		12	23	2.3	0.9	0.15	0.06		3
2 thin pork escalopes, 50gm (2oz)	111	16.1	5.3				55	4	15	0.6	1.7	0.44	0.13		
Mushroom sauce 100gm (4oz)	52	1.1	3.6	0.8	3.1			30	4	0.3	0.3		0.05		
Large jacket potato, 250gm (10oz)	204	3.5	0.2	61.0	1.5	6.0		6	37	0.7	0.5	0.25	0.10	15	
Peas (2oz)	21	2.5	0.2	0.5	1.7	2.5		15	11	0.7	0.3	0.12	0.03	7	50
Carrots 100gm (4oz)	19	0.6	0.1		4.2	3.1		37	6	0.4	0.3	0.05	0.04	4	2000
Stewed apple 150gm (6oz)	90	0.4			23.4	2.4		21	30	0.3	0.1	0.03	0.03	16	4
Natural yoghurt 100gm (4oz)	52	5.0	1.0		6.2		7	180	18	0.1	0.6	0.05	0.26		6
Nut topping 10gm (0.4oz)	52	1.1	5.2	0.2	0.3	0.5		6	13	0.2	0.3	0.03	0.01		
Total (rounded up)	**2129**	**94**	**73**	**190**	**114**	**45**	**230**	**1249**	**566**	**15**	**14**	**2**	**2**	**117**	**2624**

[1] These values are given under breakfast for convenience, but the slices of wholemeal bread may be eaten at other times of the day. Butter or margarine should be thinly spread — only 20gm (0.8oz) is allowed per day.
[2] This value is for butter only.

found. Research is continuing in this field, and only time will tell precisely how damaging such toxins are, not only to the soil, but also to ourselves.

Ideally, one should grow one's own fruit and vegetables and rear one's own animals, but this is, of course, impractical for city-dwellers. Natural foods are now produced commercially and a great deal of profit has been made from them. They are relatively expensive and genuine products can be found in specialized health food shops and market gardens. Make sure, however, that you are buying the real thing. 'Farm' eggs, for example, are not necessarily free-range eggs.

The case for fiber
Orthodox nutritionists now believe what naturopaths and other health enthusiasts have preached for decades. Fiber (or roughage) is essential to good health; it is also a component missing from white flour, white rice and all refined sugars since, in these instances, it is removed in the manufacturing process. Fiber is a paradox, Although it is indigestible and has no nutritive value, it is now believed that roughage, by helping to prevent constipation, reduces the incidence of major diseases of the colon and rectum. It may also help to remove excess cholesterol from the bloodstream and so help to reduce the possibility of heart disease.

Fiber is the structural part of a plant, the connective tissue that supports the cells. It is found in raw fresh fruit and vegetables and, in a more concentrated form, in cereals such as coarse bran or whole grain. Wholemeal flour, brown rice and brown spaghetti, all containing the source of roughage — the grain husks themselves — are now widely available. Bran or wheat germ sprinkled on food is another way of taking in fiber.

Cholesterol and polyunsaturated fats
Cholesterol is a substance found in human and other animal systems and found only in food of animal origin — meat, cheese, eggs, milk, cream and animal fats in general. It is an essential body substance which forms the basis of several hormones, but if present in excess can cause blockage in the arteries, which can lead to heart disease. It has also

Exercise and movement therapies such as aikido (*above*), a Japanese martial art form, help to loosen stiff joints and muscles and improve circulation. The fitness and body-awareness that come from such therapies help to maintain a healthier physical state generally.

DESIRABLE WEIGHTS FOR ADULTS	HEIGHT Feet Ins	Metres	WEIGHT Stones lbs	Kilograms	HEIGHT Feet Ins	Metres	WEIGHT Stones lbs	Kilograms

WOMEN   SMALL FRAME   (Aged 25 and over)

	Feet Ins	Metres	Stones lbs	Kilograms	Feet Ins	Metres	Stones lbs	Kilograms
	4 10	(1.47)	6.6 - 7.4	(43-46)	5 5	(1.65)	8.4 - 9	(53-58)
	4 11	(1.49)	7.1 - 7.6	(45-49)	5 6	(1.67)	8.7 - 9.3	(55-59)
	5 0	(1.52)	7.2 - 7.8	(46.50)	5 7	(1.70)	9 - 9.6	(57-61)
	5 1	(1.55)	7.5 - 8	(47-51)	5 8	(1.73)	9.2 - 10	(59-63)
	5 2	(1.58)	7.7 - 8.3	(49-53)	5 9	(1.75)	9.5 - 10.2	(61-65)
	5 3	(1.60)	7.9 - 8.5	(50-54)	5 10	(1.78)	9.8 - 10.5	(63-67)
	5 4	(1.63)	8.1 - 8.8	(52-56)				

WOMEN   MEDIUM FRAME   (Aged 25 and over)

	Feet Ins	Metres	Stones lbs	Kilograms	Feet Ins	Metres	Stones lbs	Kilograms
	4 10	(1.47)	7.2 - 8.	(46-51)	5 5	(1.65)	8.8 - 9.9	(56-63)
	4 11	(1.49)	7.4 - 8.2	(47-53)	5 6	(1.67)	9.1-10.2	(58-65)
	5 0	(1.52)	7.6 - 8.5	(48-54)	5 7	(1.70)	9.4-10.5	(60-67)
	5 1	(1.55)	7.8 - 8.7	(50-55)	5 8	(1.73)	9.7-10.7	(62-68)
	5 2	(1.58)	8 - 9	(51-57)	5 9	(1.75)	10 - 11	(63-70)
	5 3	(1.60)	8.2 - 9.3	(53-59)	5 10	(1.78)	10.2-11.3	(65-72)
	5 4	(1.63)	8.5 - 9.6	(54-61)				

WOMEN   LARGE FRAME   (Aged 25 and over)

	Feet Ins	Metres	Stones lbs	Kilograms	Feet Ins	Metres	Stones lbs	Kilograms
	4 10	(1.47)	7.9 - 8.9	(49-57)	5 5	(1.65)	9.5-10.7	(60-68)
	4 11	(1.49)	8 - 9.1	(51-58)	5 6	(1.67)	9.7-11	(62-70)
	5 0	(1.52)	8.2 - 9.3	(52-59)	5 7	(1.70)	10 -11.2	(64-72)
	5 1	(1.55)	8.4 - 9.5	(53-61)	5 8	(1.73)	10.3-11.6	(66-74)
	5 2	(1.58)	8.6 - 9.8	(55-63)	5 9	(1.75)	10.6-12	(67-76)
	5 3	(1.60)	8.9-10.1	(57-64)	5 10	(1.78)	10.9-12.3	(69-78)
	5 4	(1.63)	9.2-10.4	(58-66)				

MEN   SMALL FRAME   (Aged 25 and over)

	Feet Ins	Metres	Stones lbs	Kilograms	Feet Ins	Metres	Stones lbs	Kilograms
	5 1	(1.55)	7.9 - 8.4	(51-54)	5 9	(1.75)	9.8-10.7	(63-68)
	5 2	(1.58)	8.1 - 8.4	(52-55)	5 10	(1.78)	10.2-11	(65-70)
	5 3	(1.60)	8.5 - 8.9	(53-57)	5 11	(1.80)	10.6-11.2	(67-72)
	5 4	(1.63)	8.6 - 9.1	(55-58)	6 0	(1.83)	10.9-11.6	(69-74)
	5 5	(1.65)	8.8 - 9.5	(56-60)	6 1	(1.85)	11.1-12.1	(71-77)
	5 6	(1.67)	9.1 - 9.7	(58-62)	6 2	(1.91)	11.6-12.6	(73-79)
	5 7	(1.70)	9.5-10.1	(60-64)	6 3	(1.93)	11.11-12.11	(75-81)
	5 8	(1.73)	9.7-10.4	(62-66)				

MEN   MEDIUM FRAME   (Aged 25 and over)

	Feet Ins	Metres	Stones lbs	Kilograms	Feet Ins	Metres	Stones lbs	Kilograms
	5 1	(1.55)	8.6 - 9.3	(54-59)	5 9	(1.75)	10.6-11.6	(66-73)
	5 2	(1.58)	8.9 - 9.3	(55-60)	5 10	(1.78)	10.10-11.11	(68-75)
	5 3	(1.60)	8.12- 9.10	(56-62)	5 11	(1.80)	11 -12.2	(70-77)
	5 4	(1.63)	9.1 -9.13	(58-63)	6 0	(1.83)	11.4 -12.7	(72-79)
	5 5	(1.65)	9.4 -10.3	(59-65)	6 1	(1.85)	11.8 -12.12	(74-82)
	5 6	(1.67)	9.8 -10.7	(61-67)	6 2	(1.91)	11.13-13.3	(76-84)
	5 7	(1.70)	9.12-10.12	(63-69)	6 3	(1.93)	12.4 -13.8	(78-86)
	5 8	(1.73)	10.2-11.2	(64-71)				

MEN   LARGE FRAME   (Aged 25 and over)

	Feet Ins	Metres	Stones lbs	Kilograms	Feet Ins	Metres	Stones lbs	Kilograms
	5 1	(1.55)	9.1-10.2	(58-65)	5 9	(1.75)	11 -12.6	(70-79)
	5 2	(1.58)	9.3-10.4	(59-66)	5 10	(1.78)	11.3 -11.5	(72-81)
	5 3	(1.60)	9.5-10.7	(60-68)	5 11	(1.80)	11.6 -12.10	(74-83)
	5 4	(1.63)	9.7-10.9	(62-69)	6 0	(1.83)	11.13-13.1	(76-85)
	5 5	(1.65)	9.8-11.1	(63-71)	6 1	(1.85)	12.4 -13.11	(78-88)
	5 6	(1.67)	10.2-11.6	(65-73)	6 2	(1.91)	12.5 -14.1	(80-90)
	5 7	(1.70)	10.6-11.11	(67-75)	6 3	(1.93)	12.9 -14.5	(82-92)
	5 8	(1.73)	10.7-12.1	(68-77)				

VITAMINS

Vitamins	Function	Source	Daily Requirement
A	Good for night vision.	Liver, kidneys, carrots, spinach, apricots, parsley, beans, broccoli, cod-liver oil.	5000 IU *
B1 Thiamine	Functioning of nervous system, heart and liver.	Liver, beef, lamb, pork, asparagus, brewer's yeast, wholemeal bread, Brazil nuts, peanuts, bran, brown rice.	1.5mg
B2 Riboflavin	Good vision, clear eyes.	Liver, kidneys, meat and yeast extract, avocados, beans, mushrooms, peas, spinach, wheat germ, yoghurt.	2mg
B3 Niacin	Breaks down fats, protein and carbohydrates. Important for mental health.	Liver, kidneys, meat, chicken, tuna, sardines, salmon, mackerel, peanuts, wheat germ, wholemeal bread.	15mg *
B5 Pantothenic	For functioning of adrenal gland.	Liver, kidneys, mushrooms, peanuts, brewer's yeast, bran.	
B6 Pyridoxine	Aids metabolism, forms antibodies and red blood cells. Functioning of nervous system.	Liver, chicken, mackerel, bananas, wheat germ, Brazil nuts, walnuts, wholemeal bread.	2mg
C	Maintains the essential protein, collagen; helps healing of wounds, scars etc; preventative against viral and bacterial infections.	Liver, asparagus, broccoli, cabbage, grapefruit, oranges, lemons, blackcurrants, bananas, melons, watercress, leeks, lettuce.	50mg *
D	Helps bone building.	Sardines, herring, mackerel, cod-liver oil, apples, carrots, cabbage, parsley, leeks, tomatoes.	400 IU *
E	Helps circulation system, and ageing process; used to increase fertility.	Tuna fish, cod's roe, cod-liver oil, olive oil, apples, carrots, cabbage, parsley, leeks, tomatoes.	20 IU
K	Prevent hemorrhaging.	Broccoli, brussels sprouts, cabbage, cauliflower, potatoes, strawberries, wheat germ.	rarely supplemented

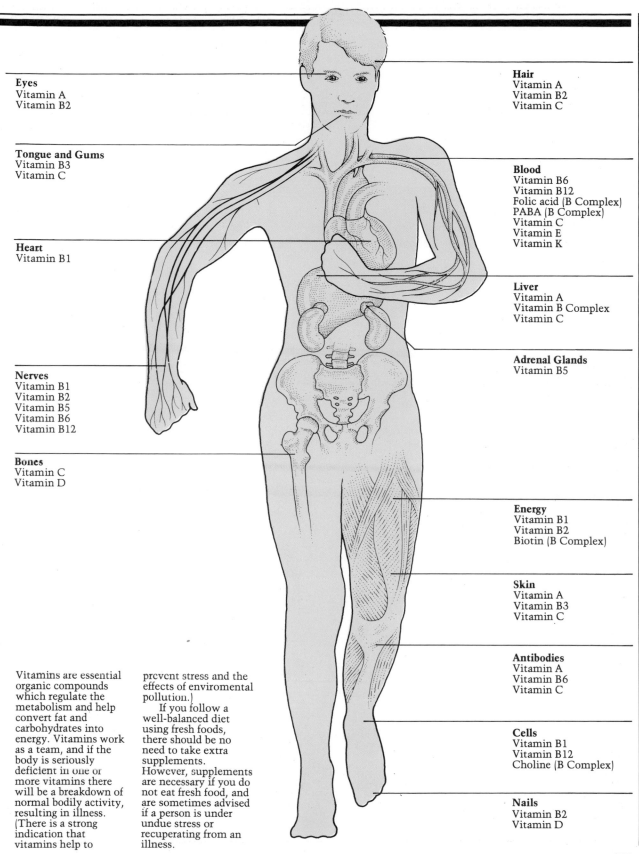

Eyes
Vitamin A
Vitamin B2

Tongue and Gums
Vitamin B3
Vitamin C

Heart
Vitamin B1

Nerves
Vitamin B1
Vitamin B2
Vitamin B5
Vitamin B6
Vitamin B12

Bones
Vitamin C
Vitamin D

Hair
Vitamin A
Vitamin B2
Vitamin C

Blood
Vitamin B6
Vitamin B12
Folic acid (B Complex)
PABA (B Complex)
Vitamin C
Vitamin E
Vitamin K

Liver
Vitamin A
Vitamin B Complex
Vitamin C

Adrenal Glands
Vitamin B5

Energy
Vitamin B1
Vitamin B2
Biotin (B Complex)

Skin
Vitamin A
Vitamin B3
Vitamin C

Antibodies
Vitamin A
Vitamin B6
Vitamin C

Cells
Vitamin B1
Vitamin B12
Choline (B Complex)

Nails
Vitamin B2
Vitamin D

Vitamins are essential organic compounds which regulate the metabolism and help convert fat and carbohydrates into energy. Vitamins work as a team, and if the body is seriously deficient in one or more vitamins there will be a breakdown of normal bodily activity, resulting in illness. (There is a strong indication that vitamins help to prevent stress and the effects of enviromental pollution.)

If you follow a well-balanced diet using fresh foods, there should be no need to take extra supplements. However, supplements are necessary if you do not eat fresh food, and are sometimes advised if a person is under undue stress or recuperating from an illness.

181

MINERALS

Mineral	Function	Sources	Daily intake
Calcium	Builds and maintains bones and teeth	pilchards, sardines, clams, mussels, parsley, spinach, broccoli, haricot beans, molasses, bran, almonds, Brazil nuts, yoghurt	600mg
Chlorine	Helps cell metabolism	fish, meat, carrots, celery, lettuce, tomatoes, watercress, salt, milk	see *sodium*
Chromium	Regulates blood-sugar levels	shellfish, chicken, green vegetables, fruit, bran, honey, nuts, brewer's yeast	a trace
Cobalt	Aids vitamin B12 functioning and red blood cells	meat, green vegetables, fruit, wholegrain cereals	a trace
Copper	Helps enzymes and in formation of red blood cells	liver, shellfish, bran, wheatgerm, wholegrain cereals, Brazil nuts	2.5mg *
Fluorine	Strengthens bones, prevents tooth decay	seafood, fluorinated water	1mg
Iodine	Necessary for thyroid hormone	seafood, shellfish, spinach, lettuce, sea salt	a trace *
Iron	Helps carry oxygen to cells and to form hemoglobin	liver, kidneys, meat, sardines, molasses, shellfish, parsley, spinach, watercress, sunflower seeds, nuts, eggs, red wine	15mg
Magnesium	Necessary for nerve and muscle function, cell metabolism; agent in utilizing other vitamins and minerals	seafood, meat, avocados, haricot beans, Brazil nuts, muesli, wheatgerm	300mg
Manganese	Helps blood sugar levels, activates enzymes; helps reproductive processes	kidneys, lentils, parsley, watercress, apricots, bran, almonds, walnuts	a trace
Phosphorus	Helps growth and repair of cells; passes on genetic hereditary patterns	liver, fish, meat, wheatgerm, brewer's yeast, cheese, eggs	1g
Potassium	Helps muscle control and water balance	dried beans, lentils, potatoes, spinach, soya beans, dried apricots, almonds, Brazil nuts	4g *
Selenium	Anti-oxidant; related to Vitamin E; may prevent some cancers	kidneys, liver, nuts, seafood, wholegrain cereals	a trace
Sodium	Cellular metabolism, prevents excess fluid loss; balances acid-alkali levels	chicken, green vegetables, carrots, lentils, peas, pulses, bran, salt, water	2-5g *
Sulphur	Helps formation of body tissues; detoxant	chicken, fish, haricot beans, soya beans, nuts, cheese, eggs, milk	available in protein *
Zinc	Helps enzymes and proteins; digestion	liver, shellfish, sunflower seeds, bran, wholemeal flour, eggs	a trace

TOTAL BODY CONTENT OF MINERALS FOR AN AVERAGE MAN

Phosphorus	1,000 g
Sulphur	780 g
Potassium	140 g
Sodium	140 g
Chlorine	95 g
Magnesium	19 g
Iron	4.2 g

Generally, a person's intake of the major minerals is far greater than the body actually requires and only in exceptional circumstances is it necessary to take mineral supplements. Normally, the amount of minerals absorbed by the body balances the amount lost in sweat and urine.

been found to play some role in cancer of the colon, stomach and breast.

Foods high in animal (saturated) fats cause normal cholesterol production to increase, or at least cause the body to retain more cholesterol. Vegetable (polyunsaturated) fats have been shown to be cholesterol-lowering in humans and animals. Foods rich in cholesterol and saturated fats include all but the leanest meats, butter, most cheeses, yoghurt, ice cream, egg yolks, shellfish and avocados (especially high in saturated fat). Polyunsaturated fats are the main fats found in plant foods such as nuts, seeds, pulses, grains and vegetables. Some fish is also high in polyunsaturates.

The average Western diet is far too high in saturated fats, and it makes obvious sense to eat as few animal fats as possible. It is important to emphasize that the nutrients contained in high-cholesterol foods can be readily obtained from other sources. There is no need to stuff our bodies — and our children's — with high-protein, high-cholesterol foods, in the belief that they are essential 'body-building' foods.

The ideal healthy diet

The ideal diet is a simple one. Essentially it should contain proteins, fats, carbohydrates, vitamins and minerals.

The average adult human needs about 10oz (280g) of protein a week; babies, growing children and pregnant mothers need rather more. An adult needs only about 1oz (28g) of fat a week for the body to manufacture its essential fatty acids. It is therefore unlikely that anyone will suffer a fat deficiency. Carbohydrates come in three forms — sugars, starches and cellulose. Sugars and starch provide energy, but excess not used as energy is stored in the body as fat. Cellulose has no energy value but provides the necessary fiber we need to aid digedstion and elimination. The average weekly intake of carbohydrate should be about 16oz (450g). For intake of minerals see chart on page 182. Some general principles to follow are:

1 Eat more fresh fruit and vegetables. They contain protein as well as fiber.

2 Eat more *raw* fruit and vegetables. If they are cooked, boil or steam for only a short time so as not to lose vitamins and minerals.

3 Eat more fiber in the form of wholegrain bread, pasta or pastry.

4 Reduce the intake of refined carbohydrates like white bread, flour etc.

5 Reduce the intake of high-fat animal foods such as meat, milk, butter and cheese.

6 Eat or drink as little refined sugar as possible. Fruit can supply all the sugar you need.

7 Reduce the intake of salt. There is some evidence that this may reduce high blood-pressure.

8 Drink plenty of water; it helps to flush out waste matter from the body — tap water is perfectly adequate.

9 Avoid canned and processed foods, too many condiments such as bottled sauces and pickles, and too much frozen food. They all contain chemical additives.

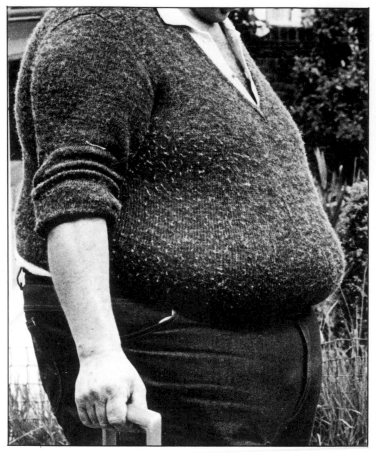

Obesity is a major health problem in the West, and one which can only be approached through an informed attitude to diet and nutrition. The metabolism of the girl on the right can cope with junk food, but in a slower metabolism an onslaught of highly caloric foods is more likely to produce the profile on the left.

The problem of obesity

Along with poor nutritional habits goes obesity, one of the major problems in Western society. It affects literally millions of people, and hundreds of diets have been worked out to make weight reducing as quick and as easy as possible — most of them rely on a dramatic reduction of calorie intake and are efficient only in the short-term. There is, in fact, no easy answer to weight control. To lose weight, you must reduce your intake of food. Crash diets certainly do this, but they fail to treat nutritional practices as part of the individual's total pattern of living. Unless the overweight person can alter his or her eating habits over a period of time — by cutting down on high-calorie but nutritionally-low foods — then all efforts will be in vain. Even more, crash dieting can seriously impair an individual's health sometimes irreparably.

Everybody has a 'natural' weight at which they feel comfortable and, naturally, it varies from individual to individual depending on height, body type, bones and so on. The aim of dieting should be to find that natural weight and stick to it. Excessive dieting to become thin, perhaps because fashion so dictates, can be extremely dangerous. In women, it can lead to that extremely serious disorder, *anorexia nervosa* — a psychiatric illness usually caused by compulsive dieting and resulting in metabolic disorder.

There are many nutritionally-sound diets that an obese person can follow. One of the best is that recommended by Weight Watchers. It does perhaps contain too high a protein intake but its advantage is that it aims to change a person's lifestyle. As a rule of thumb, the overweight person should lose no more than 1lb-2lb (½-1kg) per week after the first couple of weeks of dieting. Dieting should always go hand in hand with exercise. This not only burns up calories but also tones up the body and helps to redistribute weight.

Most important of all in tackling obesity is the person's mental attitude. If dieting is viewed as mortification of the flesh it will never succeed. A positive approach to the benefits of healthy food and the cultivation of a genuine pleasure in eating it are essential to long-term weight stability.

MORE RADICAL NUTRITIONAL PROGRAMS

There are, of course, more radical nutritional programs undertaken by many people who lead alternative lifestyles. Some embrace basically sound ideas and have positive benefits; others are more extreme and unless followed with particular care can be dangerous for some people.

Vegetarianism

By far the largest group of vegetarians are those who eat eggs, milk and milk products as well as all plant food, but do not eat flesh foods such as meat, fish and poultry. A vegetarian diet can be as healthy as any other — indeed, some would argue healthier — as long as it is well-balanced. Eggs, cheese, and milk as well as pulses and nuts are excellent sources of protein. Vegetables and fruit contain all the necessary minerals and vitamins. The vegetarian will generally consume less calories than his meat-eating counterpart, so obesity is rarely a problem. There are very few fat vegetarians! There may be the need, with very slender or particularly active vegetarians, to increase calorie intake with such foods as nuts. Overall, the vegetarian diet, with its emphasis on fresh fruit and vegetables is extremely healthy as long as enough protein and fiber are included in it.

Vegans

The strict vegan will not eat any animal product at all, including milk, eggs or honey. Moreover, many vegans have strong philosophical convictions that prohibit the use of any products made of leather, fur or animal parts of any kind. It is a rather difficult creed to live by, since animal by-products are so extensively used in the Western world; rubber used for car tires, for example, contains animal fat. Nutritionally, veganism has certain disadvantages. The diet is deficient in vitamin B12, since this vitamin is found almost entirely in animal products. Lack of this vitamin can cause very serious anemia and degeneration of the spinal cord, leading to nervous disorders. The vegan diet also contains little vitamin D which is important for the development and growth of strong bones in children. The vitamin is produced by sunlight but in Northern countries or in rainy or smoggy areas this can be a problem. On the whole, veganism should be embraced only with very careful thought.

Macrobiotics

Macrobiotics is a philosophically-based system which promotes health through the use of certain nutritional principles. Developed in Japan about 70 years ago by Dr Sagen Isiduka, the therapy was popularized in the West through the teachings and books of Isiduka's successor, Dr Georges Ohsawa. The macrobiotic diet claims to produce 'wholeness' by creating a balance between the two forces of nature — yin (passive, centripetal, feminine) and yang (positive, centrifugal, masculine). Foods fall into one or other of these categories with vegetables classified as yin, and meat, fish and poultry as yang. According to Ohsawa, health results when a proper balance of these forces is maintained; disease is the result of an imbalance. The proportion for a normal healthy person is usually 5 of yin to 1 of yang, although apparently the yin-yang balance varies from individual to individual and also from time to time depending on a person's state of health. The macrobiotic diet is centered on cooked grains, cooked vegetables and miso soup. Miso is a black paste made from fermented soya beans, sea salt and a grain, such as brown rice. Miso is high in enzymes believed to be valuable to the digestive system and it is considered to be a source of vitamin B12. Only small amounts of raw salad and fruit are eaten and little if any meat. There are various stages in macrobiotics, each one leading to a more grain-centered. Ohsawa claims that there is one food, brown rice, which is perfectly balanced between yin and yang. The celebrated total brown-rice diet is suggested as a

COMPOSITION OF FOOD

Beefsteak

Water: 64%	
Protein: 18%	
Fibre: 0	
Carbohydrate: 0	

Liver

Water: 64%	
Protein: 19%	
Fibre: 0	
Carbohydrate: 0	

Pork

Water: 64%	
Protein: 17%	
Fibre: 0	
Carbohydrate: 0	

Mackerel

Water: 68%	
Protein: 17.5%	
Fibre: 0	
Carbohydrate: 0	

Butter

Water: 16%	
Protein: 0.5%	
Fibre: 0	
Carbohydrate: 0.5%	

Cheese

Water: 4.2¼%	
Protein: 25%	
Fibre: 0	
Carbohydrate: 2%	

Lamb

Water: 64%	
Protein: 18%	
Fibre: 0	
Carbohydrate: 0	

Chicken

Water: 63%	
Protein: 20%	
Fibre: 0	
Carbohydrate: 0	

Cod

Water: 81%	
Protein: 17.5%	
Fibre: 0	
Carbohydrate: 0	

Bread

Water: 36%	
Protein: 7.8%	
Fibre: 0%	
Carbohydrate: 50%	

Eggs

Water: 74%	
Protein: 12%	
Fibre: 0	
Carbohydrate: 1%	

Milk

Water: 87%	
Protein: 3.5%	
Fibre: 0	
Carbohydrate: 4.5%	

COMPOSITION OF FOOD

Cabbage	
Water: 90%	
Protein: 3.5%	
Fibre: 1%	
Carbohydrate: 5%	

Carrots	
Water: 89%	
Protein: 1.5%	
Fibre: 1%	
Carbohydrate: 8%	

Mushrooms	
Water: 92%	
Protein: 2%	
Fibre: 5.5%	
Carbohydrate: 0	

Peas	
Water: 81%	
Protein: 6%	
Fibre: 1.5%	
Carbohydrate: 11%	

Grapefruit	
Water: 88%	
Protein: 1%	
Fibre: 0.5%	
Carbohydrate: 10	

Apples	
Water: 84%	
Protein: 0.5%	
Fibre: 2%	
Carbohydrate: 13%	

Kidney beans

Water:	12%
Protein:	24%
Fibre:	4.5%
Carbohydrate:	55%

Lettuce

Water:	94%
Protein:	1.5%
Fibre:	1%
Carbohydrate:	3%

Potatoes

Water:	80%
Protein:	2%
Fibre:	0.5%
Carbohydrate:	17%

Tomatoes

Water:	95%
Protein:	0.5%
Fibre:	1%
Carbohydrate:	3%

Peanuts

Water:	5%
Protein:	16%
Fibre:	2%
Carbohydrate:	16%

Rice

Water:	12%
Protein:	7%
Fibre:	1%
Carbohydrate:	77%

10-day diet to cleanse the body. Each mouthful of brown rice must be chewed 30 times for thorough mastication and liquid intake should be limited to preferably one-and-a-half cups per day. If followed for longer periods, it can, of course, lead to serious deficiencies. The other disadvantage of the macrobiotic diet is that it seems to be low in certain nutrients, particularly vitamins A and C. The high salt content of miso is another cause for concern. Like veganism, macrobiotics is a difficult lifestyle to follow properly and should only be undertaken with genuine conviction.

NATUROPATHY

Naturopathy is a holistic therapy and encompasses not only diet — although this is central to the naturopathic philosophy — but also various forms of hydrotherapy, massage and exercise. The naturopathic belief is that we have within our own bodies complete resources and means for achieving health, maintaining health and combatting disease. The rule is 'Let nature heal'. Never interfere. You must encourage nature by such means as fasting, special diets, water therapy and massage but more than this could be interference and could confuse the body in its simple struggle for health.

The laws of hygiene and health maintenance
The naturopath's laws of hygiene or the laws of how to maintain health and prevent disease are, in essence, extraordinarily straightforward and pure commonsense. Few would dispute them. The naturopathic laws of health are as follows:

1 Be responsible for your own health, and aware of your own body needs.

2 Be aware that body, mind and spirit form a unity that must be regarded as such in all efforts to achieve total health.

3 Eat moderately and healthily. The diet must be vegetarian (or contain very little meat) and rich in fresh fruit and raw vegetables, derived from pure sources. Processed, refined foods and foods with any chemical additive are banned.

4 Drink healthily and avoid alcohol and coffee stimulants.

5 Take exercise and breathe healthily. Yoga is encouraged, as is walking or out-of-doors exercise.

6 Avoid stress and resolve stress problems in the environment. Relaxation and, in some quarters, meditation are encouraged.

7 Ensure proper sleep and rest.

As the Greeks would say, moderation in all things. As a prescription for health, many of us would not quibble with this formula for a long life. Putting it into practice is perhaps a little more difficult.

The cause of disease
Naturopaths believe that if the body and mind are healthy, then disease will not strike. This might be so for psychosomatic diseases and degenerative diseases. These diseases can arise from imbalances that most would agree upon, such as bad eating habits or stress. However, the naturopath goes further and states that germ and virus infections only affect and cause diseases in unhealthy bodies.

To summarize, naturopathy holds that most of the diseases that affect us can be prevented by our attention to our total body-mind needs and our means of attaining this balance. We must in our own sphere become aware of these needs. This unattainable ideal is made more difficult by the universal pollution of the world today. Not only do we have to cope with food and water pollution, but now air pollution (lead, sulphur residues). Such unknowable factors as radioactivity threaten everyone's health universally and there is little that the individual can do about such factors.

Naturopathic diet
Much attention is paid by the naturopath to food. Food is one of the most important factors affecting health, and it is a factor one can easily manipulate. There is no doubt that food affects health though to what extent it does so is, however, disputed by the various schools of orthodoxy and unorthodoxy. A vast number of today's diseases can be shown to be the result of bad nutrition. The diet of the Westerner can be sum-

med up as too sweet (too much sugar), too rich (too much animal fat) and too soft (too little fiber. The diet in the last 100 years has become increasingly divorced from its natural sources. Meat, even lean meat, is fatty due to intensive stock rearing. Milk and cheese are chemically treated and artificially heated. Bread is refined. Sugar, a highly refined extract, is dangerous in excess. Many foods contain a vast number of chemicals to emulsify, flavour, color and preserve. But worse than all this is the lack of balance in diets generally. The intake is weighted unhealthily in favor of rich food, sweet food and cooked food.

The naturopath, on the contrary, makes sure there is a large amount of raw vegetable salad and raw fruit in his or her diet and that if carbohydrates are eaten, they are unrefined. Nuts, seeds and pulses in the diet make sure there is good protein of vegetable origin and far less of animal origin. Protein of animal origin, as has been mentioned, is high in saturated fats. That of vegetable origin is rich in unsaturated fats. The latter are healthy, the former unhealthy. Animal fats contribute to heart disease, hardening of the arteries, strokes and blood pressure. They contribute to the increase in breast cancer and gall bladder disease. Vegetable fats have certain fatty acids in their make up, which are essential for good liver function and health. The riches of the Western way of life in the last 100 years have in fact led to a decline in the quality of general food intake and overall nutrition which is quite dramatic. Once the pattern has been set it is difficult to change it. But naturopathy attempts to do just this.

The naturopathic diet is high in vegetable matter, half of which is taken raw. The emphasis is on vegetable protein. This type of protein, if taken from varied sources, as is easy to do, is rich and perfectly adequate as a source of amino acids. The diet is high in fiber, very low in animal fats (cheese is the only example) and has no added sugar. Decaffeinated coffee is taken rather than the normal type, which in naturopathy is regarded as a poison.

Finally, the food, where possible, should be grown on organically fertilized soil. This is not always possible but is a goal to strive for. Food and especially vegetables grown on artificially fertilized soil and sprayed with

THE NATUROPATHIC DIET

Breakfast: Muesli, bran and milk or yoghurt. Wholemeal toast, or porridge made from coarse oatmeal. Decaffeinated coffee.
Lunch: A good mixed raw vegetable salad. Ingredients such as raw carrot, cabbage, radish, celery, beetroot, spring onion, cucumber, spring greens or raw spinach, etc. Nuts, seeds, sprouted seeds for protein and also goat cheese, cottage cheese, baked potato as source of protein. The layer just within the outer skin of the baked potato is little known as a good source of protein. Fish and chicken is allowed if vegetarianism is declined. Fruit, if necessary, to follow.
Evening meal: Three (at least) cooked vegetables. Root vegetables such as parsnip and rutabaga are nutritious. Soya, cheese, nuts and seeds can provide protein. Lentils and chick peas too provide excellent protein. Vegetable soup and wholemeal bread. Yoghurt and fruit to follow, or baked apple.
Snacks: nuts, raisins and fruit.

chemicals is regarded in Naturopathy as second best. The dangers are the chemical contamination and, in the case of vegetables, the high nitrate content.

TOXEMIA

The naturopathic concept is that to maintain health the body-mind unit must be in harmony with the environment. If harmful influences are allowed to invade or influence the body-mind unit, then breakdown occurs and disease manifests.

The term 'toxemia' has been coined in naturopathy to explain the deterioration in health that is seen in the body when the basic rules of health and hygiene are ignored. One could explain toxemic man very simply by stating that the body has too much food of inferior quality to cope with and too little exercise and oxygenation to aid in the combustion of the food. The result is that the system clogs up. Our bodies eliminate waste products through the lungs (breathing out carbon dioxide and water), the skin (sweat and waste products), kidneys (salts, nitrogenous waste and water through the urine) and lastly, but not least, the bowels (fecal matter). If the system overloads, then there is blockage of the channels involved. The liver, which sifts all food and decontaminates all chemicals as they enter the body, becomes fatty and congested. The lymphatic system becomes sluggish. The lymph ducts drain all tissues in the body and take away waste material from the cells themselves to drain it into the venous system. The skin becomes oily or out of condition, similarly the hair and scalp. The mucous surfaces of the lungs, nose and throat become congested and catarrhal. The colon becomes constipated. In a constipated colon, toxic matter from the fecal mass is reabsorbed back into the circulation, hence the headache and the feeling of sickness associated with constipation and colon dysfunction.

Within the naturopathic concept, where the disease forms and what organs it affects are governed by inbuilt or inherited weaknesses, or by the mental attitudes of the person. It is stressed by many these days that the mind is behind all phenomena experienced by the patient.

The psychosomatic element is certainly influential in many diseases. Even the common cold can come as a result of stress, plus congestion. Among the diseases that are thought to have a psychosomatic element are ulcerative colitis, asthma, spastic colon, duodenal ulcer, dyspepsia, rheumatoid arthritis, eczema, psoriasis, coronary heart disease, cancer and arthritis. One cannot escape the influence of the mind. Logically, therefore, true healing or holistic healing as it is now called, should involve the retraining or therapy of the mind. Such techniques as yoga, relaxation and visualization are important from this point of view. For the naturopath, the patient's own insight into his or her condition is part and parcel of the healing process and a *sine qua non* of true healing.

Once disease has crystallized into certain definable patterns, then naturopathic techniques are brought to bear on the body and mind to release the healing force within the patient's own being. The naturopath would hold that you can aid and hasten the healing process in disease by such means as fasting and rest.

The techniques vary in their emphasis as to whether the condition is acute or chronic, or where the disease is in the body. But combinations of these same therapies are used as a basic therapy for all disease. Some of the health hydros and spa centers of the last 50 years have kept their therapy focused on these simple approaches and achieved a great deal. However, interest is now centered on alternative medicine in all its aspects, and herbal medicine, homoeopathic medicine and acupuncture are used, often alongside naturopathic techniques. The pure naturopath scorns such aids and would aim to keep his approach as simple as possible. These disagreements tend to be philosophically based. There is an argument that if one concentrates one's energies on a medicine, even though it is a natural product, then the true principles of naturopathy, such as fasting and diet therapy, tend to be overlooked.

FASTING

Fasting in naturopathy generally implies fasting on fruit or vegetable juice. Rarely does one carry out a pure water fast. The reason for this is that the body loses potassium on a prolonged fast and potassium (rich in fruit and vegetables) is a very important mineral to the body. A naturopath might prescribe a fruit-juice fast for anything from three to 20 days, but a three- to seven-day fast on fruit or vegetable juices can be carried out at home, and a short three-day fast can be a beneficial thing for most people.

Why is a fast therapeutic? It is said that it rests the digestive processes of the body so the body can set about healing itself. It is supposed to take the strain off the liver and digestive processes, and frees the body to carry out repair work and eliminative work to get rid of unwanted toxic matter from the body.

It is interesting that in the first two days of any fast one experiences withdrawal symptoms from food, drink and stimulants. Symptoms such as headache, feeling cold, nausea, fatigue and depression are quite common in the first two days of a fast. These generally clear, and one can have a distinct sense of well-being later. After the fast is finished and the therapist judges that sufficient elimination has been achieved, the fast is gently broken by introduction of a raw fruit and vegetable diet. During the fasting process, other measures are brought to bear on the patient to encourage elimination. These include hot and cold water therapy, massage and friction brushing to the skin, and colonic irrigation. The latter is a technique whereby water is passed in and out of the colon through a long enema tube for about half an hour to thoroughly wash the bowel out.

RAW FRUIT AND VEGETABLE DIETS

For the naturopath, a diet consisting of raw fruits and vegetable salads is the next step in the stimulation of the body by dietetic means. There are certain elements in raw food which are lost in cooking and processing. These include minerals, vitamins and enzymes, very essential for the healing process. A raw diet also low in fat, protein and cereal carbohydrate still places very little load on the liver and digestive mechanisms and the process of toxin elimination, and healing can still go on unimpeded. In a word, this sort of diet can provide calories for energy, vitamins and minerals for healing, but still not clog up the works.

Both fasting and raw fruit and vegetable diets can be carried out by the individual as self-help techniques. However, extreme caution must be exercised. Neither should be carried out for any length of time except under medical supervision. Moreover, naturopaths believe that they are part of a whole health program and that their benefits will be limited if practised in isolation and without the mental commitment to the naturopathic way of health.

SHORT FASTS AND SPECIAL DIETS

The Schroth cure
The Schroth cure was devised by Johann Schroth who was born in Czechoslovakia in 1798. The treatment can be carried out for a week and up to three weeks. It consists of alternating 'dry' and 'wet' days. A dry day

A typical naturopathic diet, which is sustaining enough for anyone to continue it for a long period of time, might consist of the following:

Breakfast: Muesli (soaked overnight in water), mixed with lemon juice, honey and grated apple.
Lunch: A good and varied mixed salad. Raw and grated carrots, grated beetroot, celery, cress, spring onion, cucumber, raw cabbage, sprouted seeds, baked potato, goat cheese. Oil and cider vinegar dressing. Nuts and raisins.
Evening meal: Same. Fruit as dessert.

consists of nothing but dry toast with a wet body pack applied in the evening, and on a wet day one is allowed toast, cooked oats and apple sauce, and a pint of wine, tea or fruit juice. The diet is designed to dry out the body and provoke elimination of uric acid wastes and other metabolic by-products. A full week on the Schroth cure is taken in a special clinic where the cold wet packs are given by a nurse and the diet carefully regulated. Many people claim to have benefited from such treatments.

The Grape cure
Various diets have been devised where only one fruit is taken over a number of days to provoke elimination. The Grape Cure has been made famous by two or three books written on the cure by those who have put it to the test and found benefit. It is not advisable to undertake such extreme diets except under professional supervision. In the Grape Cure, 1½ to 3lbs (0.5 to 1.3kg) of fresh grapes are taken daily. One eats nothing but grapes in fact, but one can eat as many of these as one wishes. It is best to prepare for such a severe régime by a semi-fast first, two or three days on raw fruit and vegetables. The Grape Cure is said to be good for rheumatic complaints and arthritis, due to the high content of acids and organic mineral matter the grape contains. It must be pointed out, however, that it is dangerous to carry out this diet as a self-help measure for more than a few days.

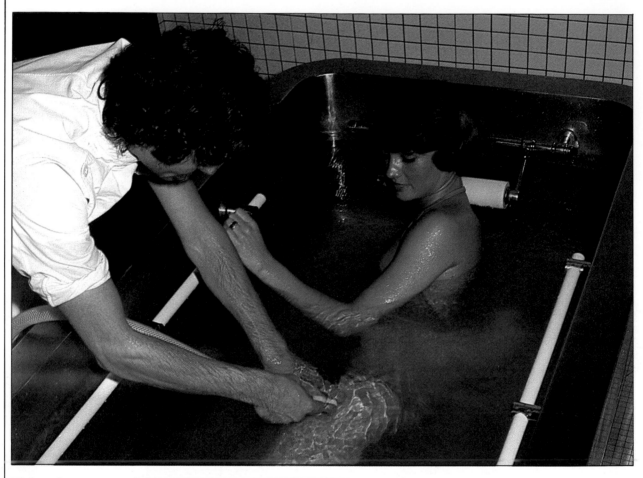

Thalassotherapy (*above*) is a salt-water treatment currently gaining great popularity in France.

HYDROTHERAPY

Water and especially cold water on the skin is used extensively in naturopathy. The skin is regarded as a sensitive organ of elimination and temperature regulation. Cold compresses, for instance, are applied from head to foot in cases of fever, and the same compress is used to stimulate elimination in illnesses of chronic congestion. The skin is richly supplied with blood vessels and sweat glands and both these are worked upon by such techniques as compressing or douching.

The cold compress
The cold compress involves wrapping a wet sheet around the patient who is then wrapped in a wool blanket. Sweating is induced

by the compress and this is one of its purposes, so aiding elimination.

Baths
Many types of bath are advocated in nature cure. These include arm baths, foot baths, hot baths followed by saunas, and the water jet which is used to focus on particular areas of the body. All treatments are designed to encourage movement of blood and lymph, to stimulate deep organs and organs of elimination such as the liver and kidney, and to prevent congestion. The cold sitz bath is said to be of great benefit in pelvic disorders such as chronic salpingitis, fibroids and menorrhagia, constipation and piles. For this purpose, a baby bath can be commandeered or one can use the ordinary bath. In either receptacle, enough water is run in to cover the pelvis when sitting in the bath. One first

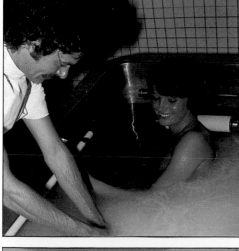
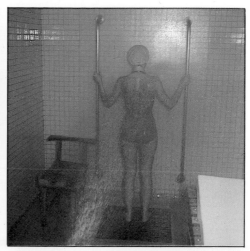

During thalassotherapy a patient receives a sea-water bubble bath (*far left*) after which she is hosed down with a powerful jet of sea-water (*left*).

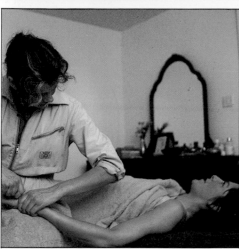
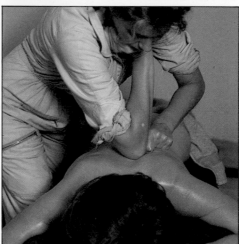

Masseuses use a wide variety of techniques involving rubbing, kneading, slapping with cupped hands, and 'hacking' with the sides of the hands.

Shown here are treatments to the fingers, the upper spine and the lower back.

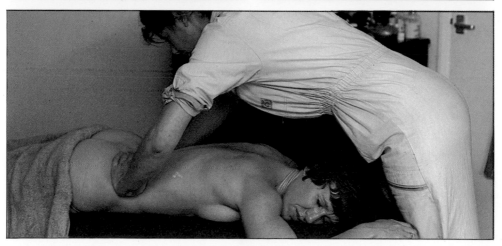

uses hot water and sits in this for two minutes and then switches to cold and sits in this for two minutes. During immersion it is best to massage the abdomen and back to aid the process of stimulation. This is also said to be a way of reducing inflamed piles.

MASSAGE

After bath treatment, massage is often given to assist the healing and regenerative process. Massage, properly performed, will promote the supply of blood to various areas treated, and assist in venous drainage and lymphatic circulation. It also relaxes the patient and allows for tension and congestion to disseminate and clear. There are various forms and schools of massage which have arisen over the years, but the most important prerequisite is that the masseur should be in tune properly with the needs of the patient. A sympathetic and individual touch is needed at all stages.

BREATHING AND YOGA

The naturopath holds we must exercise our lungs to enable them to come alive, as often as we can. Yoga techniques, with the emphasis on deep breathing, are excellent. The more strenuous postures, such as head-stand or the shoulder-stand, are not recommended, if the physique is not used to this. But the breathing and stretching exercises generally are excellent, together with deep relaxation. Rhythm is an important part of all breathing and yoga enables rhythm to be sensitively incorporated into its techniques.

Exercise, such as swimming and walking, is highly recommended by naturopaths as a means of keeping fit. In these days of sedentary life, it becomes more important than ever that we use our bodies for exercise where possible. The naturopath also believes that it is a way of becoming conscious of our total health needs.

Regular exercise can combat depression by increasing the flow of oxygen to the brain. The breathing exercise shown here relaxes the neck muscles and expands the chest.
1 Stand with your feet apart, arms by your sides. Breathe in.
2 Breathe out then raise your shoulders and bring your arms forward. **3,4** Breathe in and take your shoulders back as far as you can. relax.

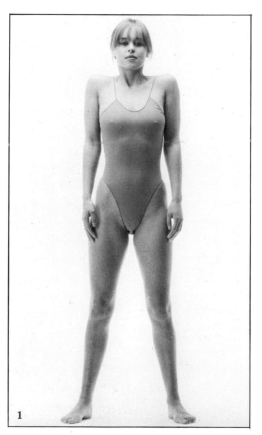

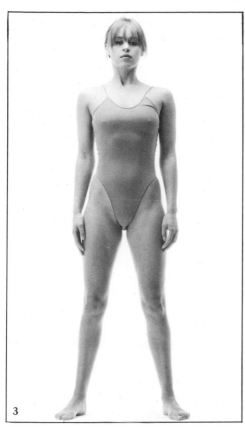

3

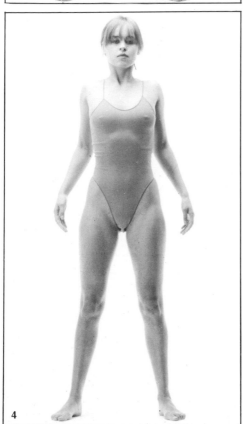

4

5

This exercise tones your muscles and limbers you up. Stretch your arms straight out in front with palms touching, then bring your arms around behind your back and clasp your hands together. Slowly bend backwards, looking up, and lean back as far as you can (5). Then bend forwards, unclasping your hands, and bring your arms up over your back. Hold for 10 seconds and relax.

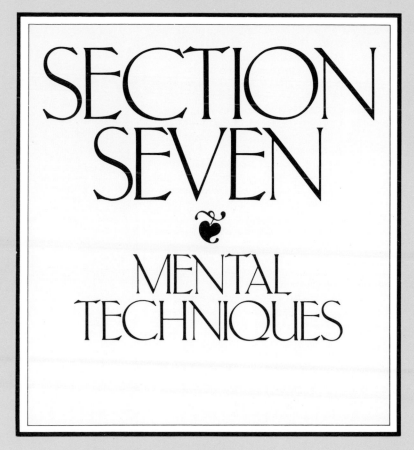

SECTION SEVEN

MENTAL TECHNIQUES

THERE IS A SENSE in which all the treatments described in this book are 'mental techniques', in that they all, to a greater or lesser extent, rely on enlisting the patient's mental attitude and feelings to assist recovery. The treatments described in this chapter, however, are characterized by the fact that they place the mind at the center of the stage and use a psychological or psychophysical approach as the primary means of influencing the symptoms.

The range of alternative therapies that employ a psychological approach is extraordinarily wide. Indeed, these days, many orthodox psychiatrists regard psychotherapy itself as something of a 'fringe' activity, for clinical trials have usually shown little or no benefit from psychotherapy, compared with placebo treatments. Certainly, the more elaborate and time-consuming forms of psychotherapy, such as Freudian psychoanalysis (from which most other forms of psychotherapy ultimately derive), are viewed with a good deal of scepticism by most orthodox psychiatrists. Whatever the truth of this, psychotherapy — being primarily a treatment for psychological symptoms — is altogether too large a subject to tackle in a single chapter. The treatments described here are, however, used for physical as well as psychological symptoms, and are also (with the possible exception of hypnosis) firmly within the realm of alternative therapies.

SOME BASIC ASSUMPTIONS

In spite of all the differences in method that separate them, the alternative mental techniques all share certain basic assumptions about the nature of the problems with which they deal. These are worth looking at in some detail, because they explain a good deal about the ways the various therapies are applied.

Body and mind are intimately related
Unlike the great civilizations of India and China, the West has always been rather uncomfortable with the question of the body-mind relationship. From the seventeenth century onwards, there was an increasing tendency to emphasize a mechanical view of the body. As time went by, this was extended to the mind as well, until mental activity

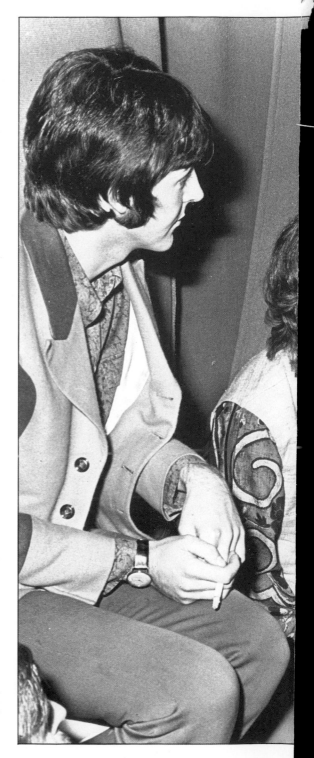

Meditation has always been a part of religious practice, but it was not until the 1960s, when the Beatles embraced the transcendental meditation of their guru, the Maharishi Mahesh Yogi (*right*), that it became a cult among the young inspiring the 'counter-culture of the hippie movement.

was seen as a mere by-product of physical activity in the brain. For a time, this way of thinking led doctors to regard physical disease as the only 'real' form of disease; anything else was somehow not quite respectable.

In the twentieth century, however, it has been recognized that some diseases at least are 'psychosomatic', in that they are either caused, or made worse, by psychological factors. This does not involve any change in the prevailing materialistic view that body and mind are one. Rather the contrary, in fact, for advances in knowledge about how the brain controls the 'unconscious' processes of the body, via the glandular and autonomic (involuntary) nervous system, provide a perfectly respectable physiological explanation for such effects. For this reason, the term 'psychosomatic' has recently fallen into disrepute, for it implies that body and mind are two separate things rather than different aspects of the same thing, as the materialists maintain.

Much argument has gone on among orthodox doctors about how important mental factors in disease really are. Some 10 or 15 years ago, such factors were increasingly regarded as important, but today the pendulum appears to be swinging back the other way, and it is less fashionable to attribute physical disease to psychological causes. Indeed, there is a growing tendency to look for physical causes, even of mental disorders.

Practitioners of alternative medicine, in contrast, nearly always emphasize the role of mental attitudes and emotions in the causation of physical disease and, naturally, this is particularly true in the case of the alternative mental therapies.

The role of stress

'Stress' is a word that is used a great deal in alternative medical circles. It is, in fact, used so widely that it has become a nebulous concept, almost impossible to define with any exactness. One sometimes feels that it is a word that can mean anything the user wants it to.

One interpretation of 'stress' focuses on the 'flight or fight' reaction. The idea is that the human body and nervous system evolved at time when it was appropriate to cope with emergencies by some form of physical response — flight or fight. If you are faced by a sudden physical emergency, you prepare for it by increasing your heart rate, breathing rate, and blood pressure, together with a whole range of other changes affecting the intestines, muscles, eyes, skin, and so on. This is fine for a confrontation with a tiger, but less suitable for an interview with your boss or bank manager. Many common situations in everyday life elicit reactions of this kind; a typical example is driving in heavy traffic. Studies have shown that many motorists react to even minor emergencies on the road with startlingly large increases in heart rate and blood pressure.

A number of cardiologists have suggested that some forms of disease, especially high blood pressure and heart attacks, result from frequent exposure to the situations that cause inappropriate flight or fight responses. If repeated often enough, these doctors believe, stresses of this type may cause permanent changes.

Many practitioners of alternative medicine would go much further, and would invoke 'stress' in a much wider sense as a cause — sometimes as *the* cause — of almost every kind of disease. For example, one school of thought regards cancer as a partly stress-induced disease. More precisely, it is not so much the stress itself that causes the illness, but rather the patient's inability to cope adequately with the stress.

The problem with this theory is that it is difficult to define what is meant by 'stress'. Researchers — including doctors — who have looked into this question have used a large number of life events as causes of stress. One such study lists 43, ranging from death of a spouse, as the most severe kind of stress, down to the Christmas season and minor violation of the law, at the other end of the scale. The various stresses are ranked in order of importance and are assigned numerical values according to their position on the scale. It is interesting that not all the events are unhappy ones — marriage, pregnancy, and outstanding personal achievement are also included. Using this scale, the researchers, who were doctors at the University of Washington School of Medicine, were able to predict the likelihood of illness in a given individual with reasonable accuracy.

All the same, we should be cautious about accepting the stress theory of disease at face

Increased heart rate, breathing rate and blood pressure plus changes affecting the intestines, muscles, eyes and skin — the symptoms of the 'flight or fight' reaction to an emergency. The motorist often produces the symptoms without being able to either fight or flee.

All sorts of situations produce stress, from the acute distress of the old lady with housing problems (*right*) and the physical stress of the couple rushing to catch a train (*below*), to the innumerable demands a mother faces in looking after her family (*bottom center and right*).

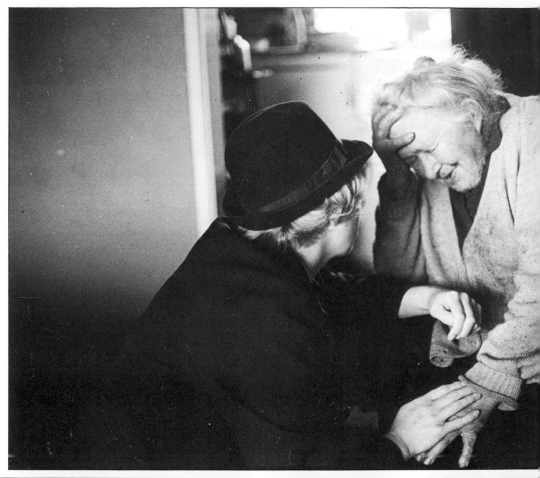

value. Stressful events, in the widest sense, are so much part of life that almost everyone can recall experiencing at least one such episode in the year or 18 months preceding a major illness. The point was neatly made by the late Richard Asher, a British doctor and writer, who quoted a passage from an eminent physician, written in 1871. This was an eloquent description of how the stress of modern life caused disease in businessmen. It recommended as an antidote the practice of relaxation: 'commune with your own heart in your chamber, and be still.' In presenting this passage, Asher mischievously pretended that the eminent Victorian had been talking about peptic ulcer which, of course, everyone now 'knows' is caused by stress; he then revealed that the disease in question was not peptic ulcer, but general paresis — that is, syphilitic disease of the brain! As he pointed out, it is easy, but fallacious, to reason that because the pace of modern life is increasing and the incidence of a disease such as peptic ulcer is also increasing, the two must be connected.

The whole question of the relationship between stress and disease is, thus, a very complex one. It seems certain that stress, however defined, plays a part in causing or worsening many diseases, but it is difficult to know how big this part is, and it probably varies considerably from one person to another. Each case has to be judged on its merits, and very often the best guide will be the patient's own common sense. If you yourself believe that stress of some kind is at the root of your problem, you may well be right; but if there is any room for doubt, it is essential that you obtain a proper medical diagnosis before assuming that the cause is stress and nothing else.

SOME TECHNIQUES FOR COPING WITH STRESS

Almost everyone develops his or her own techniques for dealing with the stresses of everyday life. These include going for a walk or a run, gardening, pursuing a hobby, or simply sitting down in front of the television with a drink. Sometimes these are not enough, in which case the answer may be systematic relaxation.

This involves relaxing the muscles in a

progressive routine. Some people advocate beginning with the feet and working upwards to the face, while others begin with the face and work downwards. It probably does not matter much which method you adopt, provided you are systematic about it; in either case, the muscles of the face, neck and shoulders are the most important groups to attend to.

Relaxation can be done sitting in a chair (either an upright one or an armchair, whichever you prefer) or lying flat on your back on the floor or a bed. You then work progressively through all the main muscle groups in the body — face, neck, shoulders, arms, chest, abdomen, thighs, and legs — making sure they are relaxed. This sounds — and is — almost childishly simple, yet for many people it is surprisingly difficult to achieve at first. You may be quite unaware that you habitually hold certain muscles, especially those of the shoulders and face, in a state of chronic tension. This causes fatigue and sometimes pain. A good way of relaxing the muscles is first to tense them up as much as possible and then to let go; in this way, you build up an awareness of what tension and relaxation actually feel like. This is important, because lack of awareness of sensations in the body is a major cause of accumulation of tension; many of us are simply out of touch with our own bodies, which then have to send increasingly strident signals to our brains in an attempt to attract attention. If you practise simple relaxation for a time, you become increasingly able to pick up subtle sensations in different parts of the body, and these may then correct themselves merely by being brought into awareness.

A simple relaxation routine of this kind is easy for most people to learn, and can be fitted into a busy routine without difficulty; from two to five minutes daily is all that is required. Other relaxation techniques can be found in the many books on the subject and people can, of course, attend classes. Your local newspaper can provide information on the latter.

People who can relax easily and deeply often find that they tend to drift off into a pleasant dreamy kind of mental state, which is neither waking nor sleeping, but something in between the two. This appears to be a particularly valuable form of rest and 'recreation', and it leads to a sense of physical and mental wellbeing. It is very similar to the kind of state that is brought about by meditation, which can, at least in its simplest form, be regarded as a profound form of relaxation. Meditation, in other words, takes over where simple relaxation leaves off.

MEDITATION

Various forms of meditation have been with us for a long time, usually in association with religious or philosophical systems, for which reason they have usually been a minority interest. In the 1960s, however, the position changed dramatically when an Indian teacher, Maharishi Mahesh Yogi, brought his system of Transcendental Meditation to the West. Although Maharishi was an Indian monk and his meditation derived from the Indian tradition, he presented it in secular terms as a method of relieving stress, and he did not emphasize, at least in public, the underlying metaphysical beliefs. Largely for this reason, and also because it was easily learned and effective, Transcendental Meditation spread quickly in most countries of the world and is now popular with hundreds of thousands of people. Since then, numerous other forms of meditation have been advocated. Some are traditional ones that came into prominence because of the popular interest, some are clearly plagiarized versions of Transcendental Meditation, and still others are secular forms devised by Western doctors and psychologists and lack any kind of philosophy or metaphysics.

The range is so wide that it is difficult to generalize, but common to most of them is the need to develop a particular kind of awareness. One Western scientist has described meditation as 'a family of techniques that have in common a conscious attempt to focus attention in a non-analytical way, and an attempt not to dwell on discursive ruminating thought'. Maharishi defined the state achieved in meditation as 'restful alertness': the meditator is awake, but is not thinking *about* anything — ideally, in fact, is not thinking at all. This state is unfamiliar to most Western psychologists, but is extensively described and discussed in ancient Indian texts.

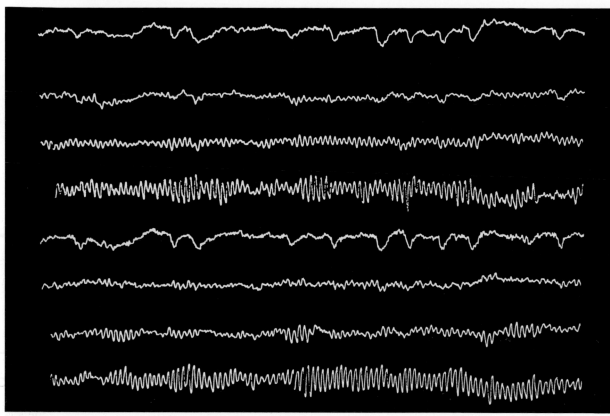

Yet attaining this state of restful alertness, although pleasant in itself, is not the final aim of meditation. What really matters is that the deep rest provided by meditation supposedly undoes the harmful effects of stress and, thus, leaves the meditator better able to cope with the demands of everyday life. Meditation, therefore, is meant to be a thoroughly practical activity, even though it also has, in many cases, profound metaphysical implications.

These are impressive claims. Are they justified? Because of the widespread attention that it attracted in the 1960s, meditation has been studied more fully by scientists. The results have been interesting and go a long way towards supporting some of the claims made on behalf of meditation.

During meditation there are decreases in breathing rate, heart rate, blood pressure, muscle tone, and the ability of the skin to conduct electricity. (Skin conductance is a physiological indication of the amount of stress that a person is experiencing; in-creased skin resistance indicates relaxation of tension.) There are also changes in the pattern of the electrical activity of the brain, as detected by the electroencephalogram (EEG), that suggest that meditators are hovering on the borderline between sleeping and waking.

These findings agree with what meditators claim is happening, although they are not unique to meditation. Relaxation and hypnosis produce similar changes. It is fair to point out, however, that most published studies have been made on people who have not been meditating for very long, and the findings for more experienced meditators may be different.

There is also some evidence that meditation brings about long-term beneficial changes. People seem to become less anxious and neurotic after learning to meditate, and they respond differently to stress: their heart rate and blood pressure rise and fall more quickly, which suggests that the effects of stress are 'damped out'

A normal read-out from an Electroencephalogram (EEG), a machine used to monitor the electrical activity of the brain. In tests made on people in meditation, EEG readings suggest that the subject is in a state between sleep and consciousness.

more quickly in meditators. Meditation has also been effective as a treatment for alcoholism, insomnia, and mildy raised blood pressure, although it is uncertain whether it works better than more orthodox treatments for these disorders.

If meditation works, are there any dangers? They are usually not serious, but they do exist. Even relatively stable people find that meditation causes sudden release of emotion in the form of laughter, tears, or sudden changes of mood. This experience is usually beneficial, and it is probably an indication that meditation is working. However, less stable people may find it distressing, and emotional release is particularly likely if meditation is too prolonged. Fifteen to twenty minutes is enough to begin with; longer periods of meditation should only be undertaken in a group with an experienced leader, who knows what may occur and how to deal with it. There are some groups of patients for whom meditation is not advisable: they include sufferers from psychoses such as schizophrenia, even if they are currently well; there is some evidence that patients who are still receiving drug treatment for schizophrenia may relapse on starting meditation. Epilepsy may also be made worse by meditation.

It is possible to learn some forms of meditation from tapes or books, but many people prefer to learn with a group, at least to start with. To some extent, the choice of method must be a personal one; some people may feel happier with a physical method (hatha yoga) and others with a mental technique, such as mantra meditation. Whatever the choice, it is important to choose a well-established organization, for there are, unfortunately, some bogus gurus about. The Transcendental Meditation method is particularly easy to learn, and has the advantage that all its teachers have undergone a standardized and rigorous training that equips them to instruct people properly, and to supervise their progress responsibly. Although this method does have a philosophical background, it is not essential to become involved with this in order to practise the technique. Transcendental Meditation is commonly taught in four-day courses and information about centers in your area can be found in local newspapers or magazines.

APPLIED MEDITATION

Although many people take up meditation as a means of coping with stress, this is not the real purpose of meditation. Those who

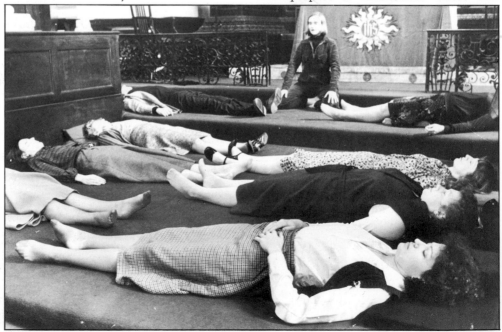

A lunch-time group meditation session in London. As we learn more about eastern techniques of relaxation, so more and more people are taking advantage of a systematic approach to dealing with the stresses of everyday life.

continue the practice sooner or later come to consider it as much more than a method of relaxation, and see it as a means of achieving self-integration. The physical and psychological benefits, although real enough, are a by-product, rather than an end. There are, however, a number of therapies that are intended to help people to cope with particular problems, and which are related to meditation — that is, they involve the experience of states of consciousness similar, if not identical, to those produced by meditation. They could, therefore, be called 'applied meditation' on the analogy of 'applied science'. They include autogenic training, biofeedback, and hypnosis. Probably not all practitioners of these disciplines would accept the link with meditation, but it seems justified because they all tend to bring about what have been called altered states of consciousness.

AUTOGENIC TRAINING

This technique was devised by a German neurologist, Johannes Schultz, in the early years of this century, and is in many ways a Western form of yoga; indeed, it is likely that Schultz was influenced by yoga. It consists of a graded series of exercises, starting with acquiring the ability to feel one arm first as

Hatha yoga combines meditation, posture and breathing in exercises that aim to bring mind and body into harmony with each other. Certain exercises are especially beneficial to pregnant women (*above*), and the technique is well suited to group sessions (*left*).

Taking one's own pulse or temperature is a form of biofeedback, which has been extended to include the monitoring of all kinds of bodily activity. Here, the Swami Prakashanand Saraswati is taking part in an experiment that attempts to monitor the effects of meditation sessions.

heavy, and later as warm. Progressively more ambitious exercises follow, but the aim is not so much to achieve particular physical effects, as to accustom the pupil to experience a mental state of 'passive concentration'. The resemblance to 'restful alertness' is evident. Like meditation, autogenic training can release pent-up emotions in a powerful or even distressing way. It has been found to be beneficial in the same kinds of problems as has meditation — anxiety, insomnia, and mild hypertension. These improve 'non-specifically', simply as a result of the experience of 'passive concentration', but at a more advanced stage pupils can learn specific techniques for particular problems. This brings autogenic training closer to self-hypnosis, with which it has a good deal in common. Although extremely popular in France and Germany, autogenic training is not yet readily available in all parts of the USA.

BIOFEEDBACK

This is a grandiose name for a quite simple idea. All it really means is providing the subject with information about what is going on in his body. For example, simply taking your own pulse is a form of biofeedback; to some extent, you can monitor your own state of tension or relaxation from your pulse. All biofeedback techniques are elaborations of this basic principle. It is possible to monitor the temperature or electrical resistance of the skin, or the pattern of the electrical activity in the brain, and to convey this information to the subject in various ways. For example, the skin temperature can be indicated on a dial, like a car speedometer; the electrical activity of the brain may be displayed visually, by a pattern of lights, or it may be used to sound a buzzer whenever a particular pattern appears.

For many years, there had been reports that Indian yogis could achieve remarkable control over their heart rate, and other supposedly unconscious processes. It was then found that this mysterious ability was not confined to strange mystics, but was almost universal. If ordinary Westerners are provided with knowledge of how their bodies are behaving by means of

instruments, they too can learn to control these processes. Sometimes they do so by concentrating on particular kinds of thoughts, or visualizing particular scenes, and sometimes they are not sure themselves how they do it. In most cases, however, it is necessary to attain a particular kind of relaxed attentiveness; in other words, something like a meditative state. This can occur while trying to achieve control over some peripheral part of the body, such as the temperature of a finger, but some researchers have deliberately got their subjects to try to induce the kind of EEG changes that typically occur during meditation. This has led to claims that biofeedback can bring about a meditative state quickly and efficiently, although this has been disputed.

The biofeedback principle has been applied to therapy in various ways. It has been used as an adjunct to other treatments, such as autogenic training; pupils find it quicker and easier to achieve warmth in a limb, if they are supplied with information about small changes in temperature as they occur. It has also been used as a treatment for

headaches, by monitoring the tension in the neck and shoulder muscles. By helping people to relax, biofeedback can sometimes reduce blood pressure, and assist with other stress-related disorders.

As with many new discoveries, when biofeedback was first described it was greeted with wild over-enthusiasm. It was claimed to be the royal road to the control of all automatic processes in the body, and the Western answer to the occult mysteries of the East. Subsequent experience has tempered this enthusiasm, but it remains an interesting technique and a useful tool for people interested in experimenting with the interface between body and mind. Like autogenic training, biofeedback is not readily available in all parts of the USA. Although there are several kinds of biofeedback machines on the market, the technique needs to be taught before it can be used for self-help.

HYPNOSIS

Although hypnosis seems to have been known in most cultures throughout the

Jean-Martin Charcot (*above* with patient) was an enlightened French neurologist who did much to improve the conditions in the insane asylums of late nineteenth-century Paris. He was a firm believer in faith healing and the power of suggestion to cure disease — ideas that were too advanced for his time.

Mario Bellini uses hypnosis to aid learning. He induces sleep in his students and then plays a recording of whatever he wants them to learn. It applies the same principle of hypnosis — relaxing the subject and thereby increasing receptivity.

world, the first clear instance of its use in the West is due to Franz Mesmer, whence the term 'mesmerism'. Mesmer, an Austrian physician who achieved great renown in Paris in the late eighteenth century, used an elaborate ritual of considerable impressiveness. He had a circular tub filled with magnetized filings; handles projected from it, and up to 30 patients at a time could receive treatment by holding onto them. A French government committee concluded that Mesmer did achieve cures, but that these were due to the patients' imagination rather than to 'animal magnetism', as Mesmer claimed. Rather unfairly, this led to Mesmer's being discredited and he had to give up his practice.

Hypnosis never really recovered from this bad beginning, even though it was taken up extensively by certain eminent French doctors. One reason for this, no doubt, is its

unfortunate association with occultism and quackery; another is the fact that no one, including hypnotists themselves, has been able to agree on what hypnosis really is. The theories that have been proposed include the view that it is hysteria, or sleep, or role-playing; the one most commonly accepted is that it is hyper-suggestibility, but this is not very satisfactory either. Hypnosis, in fact, remains very much a mystery. It is probable that more than one kind of altered state of consciousness may come under the description of hypnosis, and some of these states, at least, appear to have something in common with those experienced by meditators and others.

However this may be, hypnosis has been used for many years as a form of treatment, both by doctors and lay therapists. This is done in various ways. For example, hypnosis may be used to obtain information that is not available to the patient in his normal state. Freud, at one time, used hypnosis in psychoanalysis, though he later abandoned it. Hypnosis is also occasionally used to suppress pain, especially by dentists. This seems to work particularly well for children, and usually it does not involve the induction of a 'trance', but simply consists in leading the child into an imaginative scenario that includes, as if incidentally, the fact that no pain is felt.

Most hypnotherapy, however, is concerned with the attempt to relieve specific symptoms. Sometimes, this may be part of a more general psychotherapeutic process, in which the symptom or symptoms are treated incidentally, and sometimes the specific symptom is attacked directly. At times, the mere induction of a hypnotic trance seems to have a beneficial effect by itself. A great variety of disorders have been treated successfully at one time or another; they include those one might expect, such as headaches, insomnia, and anxiety. Skin disorders also seem to do particularly well.

The question is often asked whether removing symptoms by hypnosis is safe. There can be no generally valid answer to this; it all depends on the individual case. Sometimes a symptom can be removed hypnotically without any problems, and never return. In other instances, new symptoms may appear in place of the old one, or loss of the symptom may precipitate intolerable anxiety, and even lead to suicide. What decides the outcome is whether the symptom does, or does not, stem from some deeper underlying problem that may be revealed if the symptom is removed. This is never an easy question to decide but, because it is so important, it points to the need to be very careful in selecting a hypnotherapist. This is one form of alternative medicine in which there are appreciable risks as well as benefits. The best way to find a reputable hypnotherapist is through your family doctor.

VISUALIZATION

These methods have attracted a lot of attention in recent years, mainly though not exclusively as a treatment for cancer. They could be thought of as a form of guided visual meditation, in which the patient seeks to acquire control of the defence mechanisms within the body and to direct them to deal with the problem. This is, of course, an oversimplified description; the visualization method is not intended to be practised in isolation, but forms part of a comprehensive program involving psychological adjustments, together with modifications of diet and way of life.

The visualization process itself, as described by the American doctors, Carl and Stephanie Simonton, two of its principal advocates, begins with systematic relaxation, which helps to put the patient in an altered state of consciousness. Next, the patient is taught to picture the cancer, either realistically or symbolically, and to see it being attacked by the treatment that has been given, and by his or her own defense systems. Patients may extend and amplify this visualization by making drawings and in other ways. The Simontons believe that the most vital part of the visualization is that related to the white cells in the blood, because these are supposed to represent the essential part of the defense system; patients are encouraged to see their white cells as outfighting the cancer cells.

Whether this technique actually works is very difficult to answer. However, the Simontons quote figures that show their patients to have a considerably better survival time, on average, than would be expected, and their quality of life seems to be better. It has to be remembered, however, that these patients are 'self-selected'; that is, they chose to embark on this demanding form of treatment, which means that they are exceptionally determined to recover. There is evidence from other sources that patients with a strong will to live do better than those who lack this quality, and it may be, therefore, that the Simonton patients did well because they were the kind of people who would have done well anyway.

The question whether visualization really works may thus be very difficult, even impossible, to resolve. What can be said, however, is that some patients find such an approach helpful. It provides hope and this, in itself, appears to be sufficient justification for its existence. The technique is only available in Great Britain at one or two cancer clinics.

Glossary

ACUPRESSURE — See SHIATSU

ACUPUNCTURE
Acupuncture is an ancient Chinese therapy in which the tips of needles are inserted into the skin at specific points. Acupuncturists believe that these acupuncture points are thus stimulated to affect other parts of the body.

AGGRAVATION
Aggravation is a term used by Samuel Hahnemann to denote the slight deterioration in a patient's condition before improving, when given the correct homoeopathic remedy.

ALEXANDER TECHNIQUE
The Alexander technique is a general medical therapy that concentrates on posture training and the harmonizing of mind and body. The method was created by F. Matthias Alexander, a Tasmanian stage performer. Its principles were set forth in Alexander's book *The Use of Self* (1932).

ALLOPATHY
Allopathy is a medical method employed to cure disease by producing effects on the body that differ from the effects of the disease. The term was introduced in 1842 by the Leipzig physician Samuel Christian Hahnemann, the founder of HOMOEOPATHY.

ANTHROPOSOPHICAL MEDICINE
Anthroposophical medicine is an extension of mainstream Western scientific medicine based on and inspired by the works and teaching of the Austrian philosopher and mystic, Rudolf Steiner (1861-1925). Anthroposophical physicians do not regard healing as merely the elimination of disease, but believe that the disease itself may be the process through which a patient may achieve freedom and wholeness.

APPLIED KINESIOLOGY
This is a method pioneered by the American chiropractor Dr George Goodheart to reveal the balance of energy in the systems of the body by a series of muscle-testing procedures.

ARICA SYSTEM
The Arica system is a synthesis of Eastern esoteric philosophy and aspects of Western psychology, described by its followers as 'scientific mysticism'. Its aim is unity, in individuals and in society. It was founded by the Bolivian Oscar Ichazo (1931-), and named after Arica, in Chile, where the system was first developed.

AROMATHERAPY
Aromatherapy is the art and practice of using essential oils derived from plants to treat skin disorders and other ailments. The oils may be massaged into the face and body, inhaled, or taken orally.

ASTROLOGICAL DIAGNOSIS
This is a method of diagnostic analysis that claims to reveal, by consulting astrological charts, the types of diseases the subject may be prone to.

AURA
The aura is a magnetic energy field allegedly surrounding the human body. Sensitives claim to be able to see the aura, usually as an oval light radiating various colors. These colors change with the mood of the individual and can be analysed for the purposes of diagnosis and prognosis. Aura analysis was pioneered by the theosophist C W Leadbeater. See also KILNER SCREEN.

AUTOGENIC TRAINING
Autogenic training is a therapeutic technique designed to aid recuperation of physical and mental functions. It was instituted in the late 1920s by the German neurologist J H Schulz, and is based on a series of six standard exercises embodying verbal formulae for the patient to concentrate on.

AUTONOMIC NERVOUS SYSTEM
This is a part of the nervous system in animals with backbones (including man) which governs actions that are normally considered to be more or less automatic, such as secretion.

AUTOSUGGESTION
The term literally means the process of self-administered suggestion in order to produce some kind of physical or psychological change. Popularly it has been associated with the Frenchman Emile Coué (hence Couéism), who transformed it into a systemized method of psychotherapy, based on thinly disguised hypnosis.

AYURVEDA
Ayurveda is an ancient system of sacred medicine originating and mainly practiced in India. The term means 'science of life'. The system combines religious, metaphysical, and physical practices and rejects any separation between the spiritual, mental and physical aspects of the whole man.

BACH FLOWER REMEDIES
This is a healing system based on 38 floral remedies. Dr Edward Bach (1886-1936) abandoned orthodox medicine and a flourishing Harley Street practice to collect 38 different species of flowers which he felt had healing powers. He transferred these therapeutic powers into water and administered doses of the water to his patients in order to dispel the psychosomatic causes of physical ailments.

BATES METHOD
The Bates Method of eyesight training teaches people to use their eyes in a natural and relaxed way by eliminating strain and tension. Its adherents claim that it eliminates tiredness and headaches and improves vision. The method was developed by an American ophthalmologist, Dr W H Bates.

BATH, SITZ
The sitz bath is used in HYDROTHERAPY mainly to improve the circulation of

the blood in the legs. It consists of a small hip bath in which the patient sits with his legs outside the bath. Sitz baths are usually placed in pairs, side by side, one filled with hot water and one with cold. While the patient sits in the hot bath he dangles his feet in a basin of cold water. When he transfers to the cold bath his feet are plunged into hot water.

BATHS, TURKISH
Turkish baths consist of a number of heated rooms in which the bather spends varying periods of time in order to cleanse his skin pores. The first room has a dry temperature of up to 71°C. The next room is heated by wet steam to about 53°C. The bather perspires and dirt is loosened from his skin. He then washes himself with soap and water and dries off with a rough towel. After a period of massage he finishes with a cold shower or plunge in a pool.

BATHS, WAX
Wax baths are used for arthritic and rheumatic conditions. Paraffin wax is melted in a thermostatically controlled tank, and the affected part is dipped into the wax several times until thoroughly coated. After about 20 minutes of immobility, wrapped in wax-proof paper and a towel, the wax is removed and the part briefly placed under running cold water.

BIOCHEMICS — See TISSUE SALTS

BIODYNAMIC PSYCHOLOGY
This is a method of studying and treating psychological processes from the standpoint of mind and body seen as one biodynamic development. The method was pioneered by Gerda Boyesen, a Norwegian physiothcrapist and psychologist.

BIOENERGETICS
Bioenergetics is the branch of biology that deals with the study of energy relationships in living organisms. The study of bioenergy stemmed largely from the pioneer work of Dr Wilhelm Reich, a pupil of Freud, who claimed to have discovered a continuum of energy called ORGONE. An associate of Reich's, Alexander Lowen, transformed some of Reich's ideas into a therapeutic approach which he

named Bioenergetics. The method aims to integrate mind and body into heightened self-awareness and increased energy flow.

BIOFEEDBACK
Biofeedback training has been defined as 'a procedure that allows us to tune into our bodily functions and, eventually, to control them'. The American Joe Kamiya, using complicated electrical apparatus, discovered that he could train people to increase a particular type of brain wave (alpha waves). Biofeedback is currently being used to treat an increasing number of unrelated diseases.

BIORHYTHMS
Biorhythms are three rhythms of life that are associated with variations in the physical, emotional and intellectual capacities of human beings. These rhythms were discovered jointly by two scientists working separately around the turn of the century: Dr Hermann Swoboda in Vienna and Dr Wilhelm Fliess in Berlin. The theory of biorhythms has been scientifically applied to increase efficiency and prevent accidents.

CHIROPRACTIC
The term is derived from Greek words meaning 'done by hands' and refers to a manipulative therapy that concentrates on the spinal column. Daniel David Palmer, a Canadian doctor, pioneered the modern version of this healing art. It is used principally for treating musculo-skeletal disorders and their effects on the nervous system.

CHOLESTEROL
Cholesterol is a substance that is found in human and animal systems and only in food of animal origin. Cholesterol is released when the body

needs more adrenalin. When not used up it can cause blockage in the arteries.

CHRISTIAN SCIENCE
This is a religious movement that emphasizes spiritual healing by a total reliance on God as Spirit and a concomitant denial of all material phenomena, including disease, as fundamentally unreal. The movement was founded by an American woman, Mary Baker Eddy.

CLAY AND MUD THERAPY
Antiseptic and antibiotic properties have been discovered in clay. Negative ions in the clay attract and absorb ionized toxins in the body. Clay has been used to heal sores, dysentery, and festering wounds. Mud baths have been found effective in the treatment of skin disorders.

CO-COUNSELLING
Co-counselling is a mutual aid method of personal development. It takes the form of an encounter between two individuals, called client and counselor, who have each been trained in both roles. The client works on himself, while the counselor occasionally intervenes with guidance and helpful suggestions.

COLONIC IRRIGATION
Colonic irrigation is a HYDROTHERAPY using equipment that is based on the same principles as the enema. Warm water is injected into the patient's rectum and then flows out through a two-way tube. The therapy is used in cases of constipation and other bowel disorders.

COLOR THERAPY
Color therapy is a method of using color to produce certain psychological responses. The colors used are those of the natural spectrum and are applied in three fundamental ways, using colored light, fabrics, or walls; by thought transference and aided meditation; and by metaphysical projection, regardless of distance. Color therapists make impressive claims of success in treating both acute and chronic disorders.

COPPER THERAPY
The wearing of copper rings, bracelets

and necklets to alleviate the pain from rheumatic conditions has been allocated to the realm of superstition and folklore by orthodox medical practitioners. But research has shown that copper salicylate solutions — which can be absorbed through the skin — are anti-inflammatory agents and can relieve the pain of arthritis and rheumatism.

COUÉISM — See AUTOSUGGESTION

CUPPING
This is a process of applying a vessel to the skin. Air is removed from the vessel by suction or heat to create a partial vacuum. It is used to treat congestion, asthma and swellings of all kinds.

CURATIVE EURHYTHMY
Curative eurhythmy is a therapy of movement designed to correct organic imbalances. It is based on the ideas of Rudolf Steiner and ANTHROPOSOPHICAL MEDICINE.

CYMATICS
This is the study of the relationship that exists between vibrations and matter. Vibrations from the human voice, music, heat and color have been used to treat bones, joints and muscular disorders.

DIATHERMY
Diathermy is a form of ELECTROTHERAPY. It consists of local heating of the body tissues by means of an electric current. The currents are of extremely high frequency and require special precautions to avoid burning. Muscles and joints seem to benefit most from the treatment.

DO-IN — See SHIATSU

DYNAMIZATION
Dynamization, or potency, was a term coined by Samuel Hahnemann to describe the vigorous shaking (or grinding of insoluble substances) of his medicines in order to dilute them and so make them more powerful.

ELECTROCONVULSIVE THERAPY (ECT)
ECT involves the passing of an electric current through the brain to produce convulsions or a coma in the patient. It is used in the treatment of certain psychotic conditions such as epilepsy.

ELECTROENCEPHALOGRAPH (EEG)
This is an apparatus that records the electrical activity of the brain. In order to do this, electrodes are usually attached to the patient's scalp. The instrument helps to diagnose brain damage and disease.

ELECTROTHERAPY
Electrotherapy is the branch of medicine that deals with electricity in the treatment of certain injuries and diseases. It includes DIATHERMY and microwave therapies. It also covers such therapies as ultrasonics, which uses sound pressure waves that are humanly inaudible. Pulsed high frequency therapy employs high energy radio waves with brief rest periods between each pulse to allow for the dissipation of damaging heat. Techniques involving electrotherapy are beneficial in the treatment of bone and tissue.

ENCOUNTER
Encounter is a type of group therapy in which each participant goes through a process of self-exploration. This is brought about by progressive sessions in which individuals relate to each other with expressions of emotions and analysis of attitudes.

FACET JOINTS
At the back of the vertebral bodies are certain protective bony projections. The parts of these projections that are in contact glide over each other and form what are called facet joints. These control the direction of movement of that part of the spine and may be affected by compressive loads.

FAITH HEALING
Faith healing is the practice of treating diseases of various kinds through prayer and faith in God.

FASTING
Fasting means the abstinence from eating some or all foods for varying periods of time. Most fasts under medical supervision last for a week or two and include the intake of liquids such as water or fruit juices. Fasting is not regarded as a cure but is looked on more as a physiological resting period to allow poisons to be eliminated and permit the body naturally to build up depleted defence mechanisms against disease.

FIBER, DIETARY
All plant foodstuffs contain fiber to a greater or lesser degree, but modern refining processes tend to reduce this element to negligible proportions. Fiber plays an important part in the human digestive system by aiding the efficient elimination of waste

FOMENTATIONS
Fomentations or hot compresses consist of applications of heat and moisture to various parts of the body. Lengths of hot wet linen or towelling are wrapped round the affected part.

FORMULARY
A formulary is a book that lists pharmaceutical products with their

formulas and describes how they are prepared.

FRUITARIANISM
Fruitarianism is a diet restricted entirely to fruits of various kinds, usually eaten raw.

GALVANISM
Galvanism was first used in the late 1700s and was the first of the many ELECTROTHERAPY treatments. It involves the application of direct current to the body, usually in the treatment of inflammatory conditions. Galvanism has become less popular over the years.

GESTALT THERAPY
Gestalt therapy is a psychotherapeutic learning process that was pioneered by the German psychiatrist Dr Frederick ('Fritz') Perls shortly after World War II. The German word *Gestalt* means roughly an organized, harmonized whole. Emphasis is laid on the here-and-now experience of the subject, and the happenings of the moment are often repeated and even exaggerated. Treatment aims to revitalize personal growth and enhance relationships.

GINSENG
Ginseng, used medicinally, is the root of a plant grown in China and Korea. It is a popular tonic food with aphrodisiac properties.

GRAPE CURE
The grape cure is a diet of nothing but grapes. Its advocates claim that there is no limit to the amount of this fruit one can eat. The diet is said to be beneficial in arthritic and rheumatic conditions.

HAY DIET
The Hay diet is a diet first propounded by nutritionist William Howard Hay in the 1930s. Hay's propositions, which included the knowledge and research of many of his contemporaries, concerned an understanding of the acid-alkali balance. He believed that much ill-health stemmed from acid-saturated digestions.

HEALING
Healing is a convenient portmanteau term to describe therapy brought about through interpersonal relationships. It includes such diverse bodies as faith healers, Christian Scientists, spiritual healers, and others who may use placebos and the power of positive thinking. Results range from negligible to the 'miraculous'.

HERBAL MEDICINE
Herbal medicine involves the use of plants to cure disease. Herbal remedies have been employed since ancient times. Modern herbalists tend to treat the patient rather than his specific disease, and for that reason the treatment is usually tailor-made to the patient's requirements, as the herbalist makes up his own carefully worked out prescription. In their attempt to restore the body to its natural balance and functions, herbalists will also pay attention to the patient's diet, life style and other associated factors. Orthodox physicians agree that many plants embody therapeutic properties, and extracts from these are included in some well known drugs.

HOLISTIC THERAPY
Holistic therapy is an approach to healing that treats the patient as a whole person and refuses to concentrate simply on symptoms of disease. This approach involves psychological, environmental and social factors.

HOMOEOPATHY
Homoeopathy is a form of medicine which uses agents that in healthy people produce symptoms similar to the disease being treated. Another principle of homoeopathy is that the more the remedial agent is diluted the more powerful it becomes. The system was founded by the Leipzig physician Dr Samuel Hahnemann in the early 1800s.

HOMOEOSTASIS
Homoeostasis means 'staying the same'. It refers to the way in which the body maintains its chemical and physical equilibrium within certain narrow bounds.

HYDROTHERAPY
Hydrotherapy is healing by the use of water. It includes swallowing mineral waters at spas, spraying water on the body through very fine jets, BATHS of various kinds, and underwater massage.

HYPNOSIS
Hypnosis is an artificially induced state of semi-consciousness and heightened suggestibility produced by the hypnotist on a, usually willing, subject. The art first became widely known in the West through the experiments of Franz Anton Mesmer, hence hypnosis was originally called mesmerism. Hypnosis is practised today mainly as a therapy for anesthesia and as an aid in stopping smoking.

IMPACT THERAPY
Impact therapy is a painless pressure wave treatment for the relief of pain in and the restoration of mobility to joints and muscles. Pressure is applied

to the soft tissues of a limb, which has sandbags placed above and below it. A third sandbag is then dropped on the limb from a height of a few inches to deliver a soft impact.

INHALATION THERAPY
Inhalation therapy is the practice of applying various substances in a vaporized form through the nose or mouth in order to clear the bronchial tubes and treat respiratory diseases.

IRIDILOGY
Iridology or iris diagnosis uses observation of the iris in order to diagnose disease. In order to systemize the recording and diagnosis, the iris is divided into radial and circular divisions. Modern pioneer work in this field was carried out by the Hungarian doctor, Ignatz von Peczely in the 1880s.

KILNER SCREEN
The Kilner screen is a special type of glass to permit non-psychics to detect a person's AURA. It was developed by the British scientist Walter J Kilner in the 1920s.

KIRLIAN PHOTOGRAPHY
Kirlian photography is a method of high frequency photography pioneered by Semyon Kirlian, a Soviet engineer, and his wife Valentina in the 1950s. Photographs of healthy parts of the body appear to show a radiating aura of lights, flares and sparks. Unhealthy parts appear dull and lifeless. A Kirlian photograph can show disease before it appears physically.

MACROBIOTICS
Macrobiotics is a semi-religious philosophy originating in Japan, which emphasizes a correct dietary approach in order to experience an intuitively happy, fulfilled life. It also embraces the interaction of the two principles of Yin and Yang. Yin is feminine, dark and negative; Yang is masculine, bright and positive. See also ORIENTAL MEDICINE.

MANIPULATIVE THERAPY
Manipulative therapists work on the body of a patient with their hands. They may use gentle manual traction to ease muscular tension, or they may use various massage techniques such as wringing or kneading in order to improve arterial and venous flow. See also OSTEOPATHY: ROLFING: SHIATSU.

MEGAVITAMIN THERAPY
The practice of megavitamin therapy aims to make good an alleged deficit of certain vitamins by prescribing very high doses of the missing vitamins. In this way it is hoped that diseases such as alcoholism, the common cold and mental illness may be successfully treated.

MESMERISM — see HYPNOSIS

MIASM THEORY — see PSIONIC MEDICINE

NATURAL FOODS —See WHOLEFOOD

NATUROPATHY
Naturopathy or nature cure is a method of treating disease by bringing into action the natural healing forces already in the body. The way this is achieved is by seeking out the fundamental cause of the disorder instead of dealing merely with symptoms. The cause may be psychological, mechanical or chemical. The treatment usually consists of altering the patient's life style, which may involve changes in diet, exercise, posture and outlook.

NEGATIVE ION THERAPY
This is a therapy that employs negatively charged air particles in order to improve the local atmosphere and thus alleviate pulmonary conditions. Negatively ionized air also helps noticeably in the treatment of burns and scalds. The ions are produced instrumentally by means of small generators.

NOSODE
A nosode is a homoeopathic preparation of diseased tissue or disease products that is administered in a high potency to patients who have suffered from that particular disease in the past.

ORGONE THERAPY
Practitioners of orgone therapy use a continuum of energy, which they call orgone, to treat mainly burns, wounds, scalds and cancers of the skin. The German physician, Dr Wilhelm Reich, claimed to have discovered this original life energy in the 1930s. He built a number of metal and wooden accumulators in which to trap and concentrate his orgone.

ORIENTAL MEDICINE
Oriental medicine is based on the

principle that man is an integral part of the natural environment and that health and happiness can be achieved only by living in consonance with the laws of nature. The philosophy of Taoism (the Way of Life) underlies Oriental therapy and teaches that all phenomena are activated by the movement of energy between two antagonistic yet complementary poles or extremes, known as Yin and Yang. See also MACROBIOTICS.

OSTEOPATHY

Osteopathy is a system of healing whose practitioners manipulate the structure of the body, paying particular attention to the spine. Osteopaths believe that once the structure has been remedied, the body will recover naturally to resume its normal functions. Osteopathy was founded in the late 1800s by an American physician, Dr Andrew Taylor Still.

PATTERN THERAPY

Pattern therapy embraces a group of therapies whose adherents claim that patterns or shapes not only help to cure disease but also fundamentally influence all human life. The theory maintains that whatever remedy may be administered to the patient, it is the energy patterns that accompany the remedies that actually trigger the body's natural healing processes into action.

PLACEBO

A placebo is an inactive substance administered deceptively in place of the expected drug. The fact that some 35 to 40 percent of patients receiving placebos experience what they are told to expect, points possibly to unexplored powers of the human mind.

POLARITY BALANCING

The therapy known as polarity

balancing is closely linked to various Oriental therapies, borrowing heavily from YOGA and ORGONE THERAPY. It teaches that the body's natural energy flow may become blocked, from either emotional or physical causes. This produces disease and pain. Such blockages may be removed through correct diet and exercise. The body's energy has three aspects: positive, negative and neutral. Imbalance between these poles also manifests itself in ill health.

POTENCY — See DYNAMIZATION

PRIMAL THERAPY

Primal therapy is a recent form of psychotherapy that aims to eradicate neuroses by virtually reversing them. It does this by directing consciousness back to the origins of pain and repression, which may have been suffered in childhood and have since been blocked. This 'unsmothering' technique is designed to bring out the patient's real self.

PSIONIC MEDICINE

This is a recent type of therapy, stemming in part from RADIESTHESIA, which links orthodox medicine with homoeopathy in an attempt to determine and eradicate the fundamental cause of disease. The practitioner uses a pendulum in diagnosis and prescribes radiesthetically determined homoeopathic remedies. Psionic medicine has been found especially helpful in treating chronic disease.

PSYCHIC SURGERY

This is a highly controversial practice centered on the Philippines and Brazil. The healers allegedly perform surgical operations on their patients using their bare hands only, and after removing diseased organs and tissue, heal the incision without leaving a mark.

PYRAMID ENERGY

Pyramid energy seems to be the result of a concentration of electromagnetic waves which reach their peak power when operating under a pyramidal structure. This phenomenon was discovered when it was found that small animals that had strayed into the interior of the Great Pyramid at

Giza in Egypt mummified without decomposing. Later experiments with small pyramidal replicas produced astonishing results in which blunt razor blades regained their sharpness, plant growth was stimulated and mental capacity invigorated. All this points to a new potential healing avenue.

RADIESTHESIA

Radiesthesia is the use of dowsing in diagnosing disease and prescribing the specific remedy. Diagnosis is carried out by means of a pendulum suspended over a sample of the patient's hair, saliva or blood. The choice of homoeopathic remedy is arrived at by swinging the pendulum over a list of likely cures.

RADIONICS

Radionics is a method of diagnosing disease at a distance from the patient by means of instrumented RADIESTHESIA. The instrument used, labeled by critics a 'magic box', measures electromagnetic vibration emitted by the disease and by the remedy, and the different vibrations can thus be analyzed and identified.

REFLEXOLOGY

Reflexology, formerly called zone therapy, is an ancient oriental medical practice in which the feet are deeply massaged in order to heal functional disorders in all parts of the body. It is claimed that the energy thus released travels along certain as yet unexplained channels.

RELAXATION, SYSTEMATIC

This is a progressive routine aimed at relieving the symptoms of stress. The patient relaxes the muscles systematically, starting with the face and working downwards, or vice versa. Face, neck and shoulders are the important areas.

ROLFING

Rolfing, also called structural integration, and postural release, is a body therapy involving very deep massage. The effect of this treatment is to break down abnormal connective tissue. This tissue is ordinarily brought into being because of a patient's bad posture over a period of time. Rolfing was developed as a therapy by the American biologist Dr Ida Rolf in the 1940s.

SCHROTH CURE

The Schroth cure is a special diet devised by Johann Schroth, a Czech doctor, in the 1800s. It consists of alternate 'wet' and 'dry' days. On dry days one eats only dry toast, with a wet body pack applied in the evening. On wet days one is allowed toast, apple sauce, oats, wine, tea or fruit juice. The diet aims to dry out the body and eliminate metabolic by-products.

SHIATSU

Shiatsu, or acupressure, is a Japanese body therapy combining massage and finger pressure over the ACUPUNCTURE points. The method is painless and can be used as a prophylactic either to tone up or sedate the body. As a therapy for various ailments Shiatsu also embodies the principles of a healthy diet, exercise and a balanced mental attitude.

SYMPATHETIC NERVES

The sympathetic nerves form a network in the body that virtually rings an alarm. This is evidenced in tense muscles, dry mouth, racing heart, increased sweating, etc.

TISSUE SALTS

Tissue salts is the name given to 12 essential cell nutrients whose deficiency results in diseases of various kinds. This was the theory of a 19th-century German doctor, Wilhelm H Schuessler. To counter these deficiencies, Schuessler prepared micro-doses of the missing salts for rapid assimilation.

TRANSCENDENTAL MEDITATION (TM)

Transcendental meditation is a technique for relaxing the mind and body through the silent repetition of a sacred Hindu word or syllable. As the meditator becomes lost in thought the body gradually loses all sense of stress and tension.

VEGANISM

Veganism is an extreme or more fundamental form of VEGETARIANISM. Vegetarians will eat poultry products and dairy products, but Vegans consume only plant products. Their 'milk' and 'cheese' have a soya base.

VEGETARIANISM

Vegetarianism is the practice of excluding all meat and fish from the diet. Unlike Vegans, vegetarians will eat eggs, cheese, butter, milk and cream. In order to offset possible deficiencies in the nutritional value of their non-meat diet, vegetarians and Vegans eat quantities of raw salads, fruits, grains and wholewheat bread.

VISUALIZATION TECHNIQUES

These are methods of visual meditation used mainly but not exclusively in the treatment of cancer. After systematic relaxation, patients are encouraged to picture their particular disease being attacked and overcome by the given treatment.

VOLUNTARY NERVOUS SYSTEM

This is a part of the nervous system in animals with backbones (including man) which makes all deliberate movement and action possible and controllable.

WHOLEFOOD

Wholefood is grown as nearly as possible in its natural state (uncontaminated by chemical fertilizers, pesticides and weed-killers), and is subsequently processed or refined as little as possible. Fruits, vegetables and nuts are the least affected by processing because they may be eaten raw in their natural state. But wheat, for example, has to be ground to extract the bran and make it digestible. Stone grinding removes sufficient bran while retaining the wheat germ.

YOGA

Yoga is a Hindu system of philosophy aiming at union with the Supreme Being. The word is derived from a Sanskrit term meaning 'union'. In the West, yoga has been adapted to a course of related exercises and postures designed to promote health care and spiritual development.

Index